Power and Public Relations

THE HAMPTON PRESS COMMUNCIATION SERIES

Communications and Social Organization
Gary L. Kreps, series editor

Conflict and Diversity
Claire Damken Brown, *Charlotte Snedeker*, and *Beate Sykes (eds.)*

Power and Public Relations
Jeffrey L. Courtright and *Peter M. Smudde (eds.)*

Community at Work: Creating and Celebrating Community in Organizational Life
Patricia K. Felkins

Qualitative Research: Applications in Organizational Life (2nd ed.)
Sandra L. Herndon and *Gary L. Kreps (eds.)*

Building Diverse Communities: Applications of Communication Research
Trevy A. McDonald, *Mark P. Orbe*, and *Trevellya Ford-Ahmed (eds.)*

Communication and Social Action Research
Joseph J. Pilotta

Organizational Communication and Change
Philip Salem (ed.)

Ethics and Organizational Communication
Matthew W. Seeger

Engaging Communication, Transforming Organizations: Scholarship of Engagement in Action
Jennifer Lyn Simpson and *Pamela Shockley-Zalabak (eds.)*

Communicating with Customers: Service Approaches, Ethics and Impact
Wendy S. Zabava-Ford

forthcoming

Terrorism: Communication and Rhetorical Perspectives
Dan O'Hair, *Robert Heath*, *Gerald Ledlow*, and *Kevin Ayotte (eds.)*

Power and Public Relations

160501

edited by

Jeffrey L. Courtright
Illinois State University

Peter M. Smudde
University of Wisconsin–Whitewater

GUELPH HUMBER LIBRARY
205 Humber College Blvd
Toronto, ON M9W 5L7

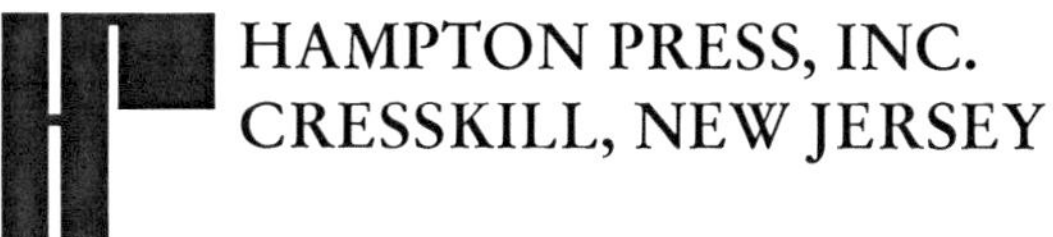
HAMPTON PRESS, INC.
CRESSKILL, NEW JERSEY

Copyright © 2007 by Hampton Press, Inc.

All rights reserved. No part of this publication may be reproduced, stored in a retrieval system, or transmitted in any form or by any means, electronic, mechanical, photocopying, microfilming, recording, or otherwise, without permission of the publisher.

Printed in the United States of America

Library of Congress Cataloging-in-Publication-Data

Power and public relations / edited by Jeffrey L. Courtright, Peter M. Smudde
p. cm. -- (The Hampton Press communication series)
Includes bibliographic references and indexes.
ISBN 1-57273-680-1 -- ISBN 1-57273-681-X
1. Public relations. 2. Power (Social sciences) I. Courtright, Jeffrey L.
II. Smudde, Peter M.

HM1221.P67 2006
659.2--dc22

2006045845

Cover art by Clinton G. Dickson

Hampton Press, Inc.
23 Broadway
Cresskill, NJ 07626

Contents

Foreword

Joe S. Epley

Too many public relations practitioner wannabes approach the profession as a communications craft that just educates or informs, seeks awards for cute creativity, or focuses more on process than results. However, the greatest value public relations practitioners bring to the table is the ability to transform applications of their communications skills with the needs of their employers into powerful persuasive outcomes.

The role of most practitioners is to provide, within the confines of uncompromising ethical considerations, communications and guidance that inspire intended audiences to behave in desired ways, whether it is to trust a company, adopt a specific philosophy, support public issue agendas, or buy a product. To do so requires that practitioners fully understand public relations as an instrument of power, and hone their skills to maximize the impact of their efforts for their employers.

Like most people of my generation, I entered the field of public relations from journalism. There were few schools or public relations reference books in the mid-to-late 1960s that concentrated on public relations. We functioned by applying our communications abilities to the realities of the society in which we operated. Unfortunately, most journalists evolving into public relations practitioners could not advance their thought processes beyond that of being a purveyor of press releases and publicity stunts. Many failed in this new profession because they could not make the adjustment demanded by public relations needs. They could only chronicle what was happening rather than influence change.

In those years when our profession moved from its adolescence into maturity, we desperately needed a body of knowledge that would make us more effective. Fortunately, through the years that body of knowledge has emerged. Power and Public Relations is an excellent addition to that body of knowledge because it provides both an academic and pragmatic analysis of excellent examples demonstrating the power of public relations.

Before changing professions, I had the good fortune to have covered politics at the state and local levels as a television reporter and editor. Politics, in is simplest terms, is pure public relations. My military career included training in psychological warfare, thus I was able to better grasp and apply the concepts and theories of influencing mass audiences.

Proof of public relations' power was established with the explosive growth of public relations consulting firms throughout smaller markets of the United States during the 1970s, 1980s, and 1990s. Had the profession stayed in the limited areas of just promotions and publicity, few practitioners would have succeeded outside the major markets and large organizations.

My personal success came first through the ability to present persuasive messages that convinced voters to approve bond referendums and use their tax dollars to back bold, innovative programs. I applied those same techniques to working with businesses on issues that involved regulatory and legislative decision makers. Public opinion influences significantly the government actions that control many business operations. In short, business survival depends on public support in many ways.

More than one potential client told me during the hiring process that I had no experience in their particular field. My stock reply was that my expertise was about influencing opinion, I could take the factors affecting their industries and the public climate in which they operated, and I could build public support for their issues. I did this by demonstrating my abilities and providing a track record that was built on getting positive results for my clients. Often this work demonstrated public relations' power to influence publics' thinking, attitudes, and action.

The various public relations disciplines are relevant across the board for most industries. One example from my past includes helping a major chemical company struggle through the embarrassing and costly throes of being among the nation's first "superfund" sites chosen by the Environmental Protection Agency. We were successful in strengthening employee loyalty and converting them to become positive messengers in the community. We were successful in alleviating the fears of neighbors and environmental groups. We also were successful in building positive understanding and support among the political leadership and news media.

Another case involved repositioning a hospital's 25-year-old image from a "charity" hospital to a most-respected teaching hospital and preferred healthcare provider, managing 17 hospitals with 23,000 employees in two states. More recently, we helped a company that makes seat belts for motor sports in protecting its reputation and product integrity after NASCAR had implied that a separated seat belt may have caused the death of racing legend Dale Earnhart.

In those and many other cases over my 37-year career in the field, we were able to demonstrate the power of public relations through a combination of talent, focused effort, multiple communications channels, and enlightened management. No one aspect worked alone. All activities were based on truth and fair play. Nothing occurred without due consideration to the impact on the end result. I firmly believe that, without that understanding of the power our profession can bring to bear, I would not have had a successful career.

How did we do this? It came through a process of learning from others as well as from our own experiences. As a self-educated practitioner and historian, I had read extensively about how our nation's political and economic strength was built on the power of persuasive arguments. In the early days, persuasive communications was demonstrated by the innate abilities of a few individuals who had the ability through oratory or printed word to sway public thought. Examples include the impact of Thomas Paine's Common Sense and Alexander Hamilton's, James Madison's, and John Jay's contributions to the Federalist Papers during the days when this nation was floundering in its struggle for survival. Others included people like William Randolph Hearst, who used his newspapers to push America into a war with Cuba in 1898. One of the most powerful examples was the passionate, nonviolent activities, and oratory of Martin Luther King, Jr., who led the nation into massive, unprecedented, and long overdue social change during the 1960s.

Demonstrations of the power of public relations are plentiful. All are learning tools. Some are global in scope, but most are local. Many come from charismatic individuals who are unwavering in their quest to bring public opinion to their way of thinking. (Two prime examples, Hillary Rodham Clinton and Martha Stewart, are featured in chaps. 2 and 5, respectively, of this volume.) Most are by practitioners who carefully screen all options and situations in making their strategic and tactical decisions; for example, Avon (chap. 3), Philip Morris (chap. 4), and Merrill Lynch (chap. 6). A few are demonstrations captured in case studies that build better understanding for the strategies and techniques used in making the public relations efforts successful (e.g., international issue and policy management in chap. 7, internet activism in chap. 8, and employee recruitment in chap. 9). Still others focus on the thought process that leads to decisions and action on effective communications solutions (e.g., the combination of knowledge, discourse, and ethics for proactive public relations in Chapter 10 and the dynamics of harnessing intraorganizational expertise on news in Chapter 11).

With the channels of communication multiplying in quantity and technological innovation, and with more activities and issues competing for the attention of a public that has become more fickle and knowledgeable, the ability of practitioners to effectively use these new and emerging tools will affect the power and results of their communications. From a practical standpoint, practitioners who cannot show or convince senior managers how to muster the power of public relations in a meaningful and cost-effective manner may find their careers limited. However, the practitioner who succeeds in relating the power of public relations to the organizational and personal goals of CEOs will find his or her value enhanced.

Successful practitioners, whether in a consulting firm, large corporation, government agency, or small not-for-profit organization, must understand the multiple disciplines and real-world environments in which they work, if they are to achieve powerful programming that gets desired results. Through the case studies and analyses presented in *Power and Public Relations*, one can gain a better understanding of the thinking and action necessary for creating and implementing effective, ethical, and powerful public relations.

Acknowledgements

We have been privileged to work with some talented people on this project, and we've been blessed to have had the opportunity to do so. We'd like to recognize the people that were helpful to us in so many ways during the course of this project.

We express our sincerest appreciation to the practitioners and scholars who were peer reviewers of chapters submitted for publication in this volume. All together they exhibited a marvelous level of dedication, expertise, and supportiveness that truly helped raise the quality of this book as they each reviewed and commented on multiple chapter manuscripts. Those reviewers were Josh Boyd, Phil Chidester, Bonita Dostal Neff, Vince Hazelton, Keith Michael Hearit, Rachel Holloway, Øyvind Ihlen, Lee Krähenbühl, Dean Kruckeberg, John Llewellyn, Matt Seeger, Jennifer Thackaberry, Jeff Tyus, Rob Ulmer, Susanne Williams, and Joe Zompetti. Thank you all very much!

We are also most grateful to the School of Communication at Illinois State University and the Department of Communication at the University of Wisconsin-Whitewater for their support while we worked on this project. We'll always remember and value the enthusiasm our colleagues and administrations in our respective institutions gave us.

At Hampton Press we could not have had better counsel and guidance through the process. We extend our heartfelt thanks to Gary Kreps for his thorough and thoughtful review of our initial proposal through our final manuscript. To Barbara Bernstein we also express our appreciation for her diligence and dedication in guiding us through the process and seeing the book published in its final form.

Others still provided us with invaluable help or advice in various ways at various times. The high quality and clarity of the final manuscript would not have occurred without the help of Jeff's Seminar in Public Relations Research in Fall 2005. These graduate students not only caught errors in typing and grammar, but they also significantly contributed to the insights added to various chapters. We especially thank Tameem al-Shawaf, a 2005 graduate and incoming master's degree student at Illinois State, for his invaluable assistance in verifying references, ISU graduate student Sara Poggi for her assistance in creating the subject index, Steve Tabels, a 2004 Illinois State graduate, for his keen eye in proofreading the chapters at the end of the editing process, and Sean Vezain of the ISU Center for Teaching, Learning and Technology for the preparation of the appendix in Chapter 11. We also wish to thank Sandra Berkowitz, Carl Botan, Bernie Brock, B. J. Dickson, Bill Elwood, Robert Heath, Allen Hightower, Jim Hikins, Mark Moore, Loren Murfield, Tim Shannon, and Gerald Slaughter for their counsel and encouragement along the way.

Jeff personally would like to thank his parents for their support during the writing of this book. Their love and concern has been more meaningful to him than they'll ever know. Jeff also thanks the members of Northside Church of Christ, especially his fellow music team members and the Baldwin house group, for their love and encouragement from the writing of the proposal to the book's final stages. Pete also expresses his deepest appreciation to his wife, Patty, and sons, Matthew and Jeffrey, for their unending support, love, and understanding throughout and beyond this book project.

chapter 1

"Problems" of Power in Public Relations Theory and Practice

Jeffrey L. Courtright

Peter M. Smudde

The more things change, the more they stay the same—but there is much to learn. A century ago, public relations was just in its infancy as a formal organizational function. The turn of the 20th century was an era marked by the corporate excesses of arrogant robber barons, and government was not always certain what to do about it. Although introductory public relations texts often highlight the role of President Theodore Roosevelt and the U.S. Congress in breaking up monopolies, the Supreme Court's deference to big business during those same years often goes unnoticed. (This was the so-called "Lochner" Era of the Court, so named because *Lochner v. U.S.* was emblematic of a generation of case law in which the Court sided with corporations much more readily than with the public interest.) Activists and millionaires were neither completely vilified nor universally praised. And the world's richest man, John D. Rockefeller, Sr., only turned to public relations once public criticism had grown to such a fevered pitch that it could no longer be ignored.

How things have changed in a century.

But have they?

At the beginning of the 21st century, corporate CEOs fashion golden parachutes for themselves at the expense of employee security, resort to shady accounting practices to inflate investor perceptions, and turn to public relations not only in crisis situations but to provide cover for today's corporate excesses. Public opinion again is divided—some lionize corporate best practices and others extol the importance of activism to help protect the consumer from the effects of corporate ills. And it was not too many years ago that Microsoft did not even show concern for its immediate community in Redmond, Washington, let alone engage in philanthropy to the global degree that it now does. In the face of antitrust action at home and abroad, perhaps Bill Gates, too, began to recognize that public relations might help his dual images of rapacious monopolist and highly admired entrepreneur. (Is it then surprising that *Business Week* compared Bill Gates to John D. Rockefeller, Sr. [Chernow, 1999]?)

POWER, PUBLIC RELATIONS AND SCHOLARSHIP

Although the complexity of media channels and multiple publics has changed considerably the face of public relations practice, one thing has not changed: the concern for the potential power that public relations might give those who can obtain its services. Yet by and large, the extant literature tends to focus on two major themes—the effectiveness of public relations and the relationship between gender and corporate hierarchy.

The effects literature also can be divided in two parts. First, academics have defended the field in terms of the good that public relations' power can achieve (e.g., how to generate and gain power for an organization [Lerbinger, 2001]), how to use access to an organization's "dominant coalition" in order to facilitate conflict resolution (Plowman, 1998), and how public relations can be used to make the organization itself a "valuable public asset" (Levy, 2002). To some extent, positive treatments of public relations' effects relate to political dynamics. Of course, there is no shortage of criticism of the power that public relations might exercise to the detriment of the public interest (and the field's reputation). Although a few academics have sounded an alarm against public relations as it is practiced (e.g., Olasky, 1987; Sethi, 1977), some of the more popular book titles critical of the practice suffice to tell the tale—Stauber and Rampton's (1995) *Toxic Sludge is Good for You*; Ewen's (1996) *PR! A Social History of Spin*; and Tye's (1998) *The Father of Spin: Edward Bernays and the Birth of Public Relations.*

The second half of the majority of the public relations power literature focuses on the power that public relations practitioners themselves hold within organizations (e.g., Holtzhausen & Voto, 2002), agencies, and industries (e.g., Hollywood; cf. Seipp, 1999). Receiving the most coverage is the state of affairs we find between women and men in the profession. In addition to a complete book on the subject (Grunig, Toth, & Hon, 2001), academic articles have covered a wide range of gender-related issues over the past decade (e.g., effects on upward influence [O'Neil, 2003, 2004]; sexual harassment [Serini, Toth, Wright, & Emig, 1998]; perceptions of women in power positions [Choi & Hon, 2002]).

Yet power has more facets than ethics and gender—and is a topic that deserves much greater exploration in public relations. In 2004, *Public Relations Review* issued a call for articles devoted to "public relations effects, power, and influence" ("Call for Papers," 2004, p. 131), but the editor reported to us that not enough manuscripts of quality had been received as of September 2005 to warrant their inclusion as a special section in an issue of the journal (R. Hiebert, personal communication, September 24, 2005). In two special issues of the *Journal of Public Relations Research* in 2005 (Aldoory, 2005; Moffitt, 2005), the subject of power featured prominently in the eight articles published, even though other subjects were covered. Clearly, the time is ripe for a book-length treatment of the subject. In the most recent volume dedicated to the "excellence" model of public relations advanced by James Grunig and Larissa Grunig and their disciples, Toth's (2007) edited book includes chapters, for example, by Bruce Berger and Derina Holtzhausen which focused on theoretical characteristics of power and public relations.

What this book seeks is a deeper analysis of what public relations' power is. We believe this volume is the first to explore simultaneously the theoretical underpinnings and practical applications of power to public relations. Such an approach goes beyond common stereotypes or even accounts and analyses of public relations *in situ*—it demands a balance between theory and practice, as one informs the other for mutual benefit. Power is ubiquitous and, therefore, problematic. This book employs a philosophical framework that sees "problem" in a neutral-to-positive light, not in its usual negative shadow. To this end the central thesis of this book is that the power of public relations is both widely understood and misunderstood, and it is the latter that must be addressed. This book highlights specific cases to explore how public relations' power is obtained, used, and misused to create and recreate worldviews for good or ill. In this way, the book looks at power in terms of both process and outcomes.

PREVIEW OF THIS BOOK'S CONTENT

Public relations is "the measured and ethical use of language and symbols to inspire cooperation between an organization and its publics" (Smudde, 2001, p. 36). This basic premise is implicit throughout *Power and Public Relations,* which, in tune with contemporary rhetorical inquiry, concerns the means by which power constructs, regulates, and perpetuates itself through symbols and the individuals that use them. In Foucault's (1977/1980) words, "It is in discourse that power and knowledge are joined together" (p. 100). Once internalized, individuals regulate their own attitudes and behavior—and those of others—in relation to that power (Foucault, 1989, 1990). *Power and Public Relations* bridges theory and practice to address misunderstandings about PR's power. This bridge-building is enacted through the explication of selected theory- and research-based perspectives on actual cases and examples of public relations' power.

The case studies found in the following chapters include a range of perspectives on power. The variety runs from ideas that have their roots in ancient Greece up to the most current trends of thought coming from the critical studies literature. These chapters were subjected to peer review and are meant to be an introduction to these perspectives, not a daunting "sink-or-swim" immersion in heady technical terminologies. Our hope is to whet your appetite to explore ideas on your own after reading *Power and Public Relations.* In the book's first section, Kathleen German (chap. 2) and Heidi Hatfield Edwards (chap. 3) examine the important relationship between power and image in public relations efforts. German's chapter provides a good example of traditional rhetorical criticism applied to public relations efforts in the political realm with her analysis of Hillary Rodham Clinton's "Talking It Over" newspaper column. Edwards extends traditional and contemporary understandings of a central concept in classical rhetoric, Aristotle's enthymeme, to Avon Products' sponsorship of a Walk for Breast Cancer. The study examines how much organizations and event participants stand to gain through corporate sponsorships.

In the second section the popular topic of crisis communication receives needed attention as to the role of power in responding to crises and restoring the image of public relations. The three cases thus cast new light on three important situations occurring in the first years of the new millennium. In Chapter 4, Amy O'Connor applies key concepts from the writings of Pierre Bourdieu and the issue management literature to the "People of Philip Morris" image campaign. In Chapter 5, Angela Jerome, Mary Anne Moffitt, and Joseph Knudsen, using a combination of principles from Michel Foucault and the image restoration literature, demonstrate how Martha Stewart ceded her power to speak during the insider trading investigation against her, affecting both her personal image as well as that of Martha Stewart Omnimedia. In Chapter 6, Jeffrey Brand applies principles of argumentation to show how Merrill Lynch turned a crisis situation to its advantage and claimed leadership of its industry with changes it made to remedy the crisis.

The next three chapters reveal the power of public relations to control messages and dominate publics. In Chapter 7, Maureen Taylor and Michael Kent apply principles from issue management theories and rhetorical studies to explore how the government of Malaysia managed issues and maintained cultural dominance of Malays in 1987. In Chapter 8, Jeffrey Courtright illustrates the potential power that activists may have through Internet communication, what can happen when an organization legitimizes those activists in other public spheres, and how organizations constrain that power. In Chapter 9, Theresa Russell-Loretz compares employee recruitment videos in 1990 to employee recruitment via the Internet in 2000. Her analysis suggests that the power of organizations to shape perceptions through these channels signals a lack of diversity in employee recruitment.

In the last section of the book the role of power is discussed as it relates to message planning. Peter Smudde explains the core principles of Michel Foucault's approach to message analysis, applies it to a case, and then suggests how that approach may be used to plan campaigns as well as evaluate them. Finally, Katherine Rowan, Teresa Mannix, Timothy Gibson, and Troy Bogino report their study of university media relations specialists and how they deal with science news reporting. The perceived power of management sometimes is sufficient to deter any release of a news story.

In recalling his campaigns that led to women being allowed to smoke in public in 1928 and celebrating the 50th anniversary of Edison's invention of the first incandescent lamp, Edward Bernays responded to the suggestion that public relations gave him the power to influence audiences: "Well, but you see, I never thought of it as power. I never treated it as power. People want to go where they want to be led" (Blumer, Moyers, & Grubin, 1983). We beg to differ. Power is inherent in public relations, whether the practitioner acknowledges it or not. The 10 case studies in *Power and Public Relations* provide an excellent sample of the breadth of perspectives and definitions of power that are available to understand power's role in public relations practice.

REFERENCES

Aldoory, L. (Ed.). (2005). Identity, difference, and power in public relations [Special issue]. *Journal of Public Relations Research, 17*(2).

Berger, B. K. (2007). Public relations and organizational power. In E. L. Toth (Ed.), *The future of excellence in public relations and communication management: Challenges for the next generation* (pp. 221-234). Mahwah, NJ: Erlbaum.

Blumer, R., Moyers, B. (Writer), & Grubin, D. (Producer/Director). (1983). The image makers [Television series episode]. In M. Koplin (Senior Executive Producer), *A walk through the 20th century with Bill Moyers.* New York: Corporation for Entertainment Learning.

Call for manuscripts and abstracts: Public relations effects, power, and influence. (2004). *Public Relations Review, 30,* 121.

Chernow, R. (1999, November 22). The burden of being a misunderstood monopolist. *Business Week, 3656,* 42.

Choi, Y., & Hon, L. C. (2002). The influence of gender composition in powerful positions on public relations practitioners' gender-related perceptions. *Journal of Public Relations Research, 14,* 229-263.

Foucault, M. (1980). *Language, counter-memory, practice: Selected essays and interviews by Michel Foucault* (D. F. Bouchard, Ed.). Ithaca, NY: Cornell University Press. (Original work published 1977)

Foucault, M. (1989). *Foucault live: Interviews, 1966-1984* (J. Johnston, Trans., L. D. Krizman, Ed.). New York: Routledge.

Foucault, M. (1990). *Michel Foucault: Politics, philosophy, culture* (A. Sheridan, Trans., L. D. Krizman, Ed.). New York: Routledge.

Grunig, L. A., Toth, E. L., & Hon, L. C. (2001). *Women in public relations: How gender influences practice.* New York: Guilford.

Holtzhausen, D. R. (2007). Activisim. In E. L. Toth (ed.) *The future of excellence in public relations and communication management: Challenges for the next generation* (pp. 357-380). Mahwah, NJ: Erlbaum.

Holtzhausen, D. R., & Voto, R. (2002). Resistance from the margins: The postmodern public relations practitioner as organizational activist. *Journal of Public Relations Research, 14,* 57-84.

Lerbinger, O. (2001). *Corporate power strategies: Getting the upper hand with interest groups, media and government.* Newton, MA: Author.

Levy, R. N. (2002). Value-added public relations. *Public Relations Quarterly, 47*(4), 34-35.

Moffitt, M. A. (Ed.). (2005). Public relations from the margins [Special issue]. *Journal of Public Relations Research, 17*(1).

Olasky, M. (1987). *Corporate public relations: A new historical perspective.* Hillsdale, NJ: Erlbaum.

O'Neil, J. (2003). An analysis of the relationships among structure, influence, and gender: Helping to build a feminist theory of public relations. *Journal of Public Relations Research, 15,* 151-179.

O'Neil, J. (2004). Effects of gender and power on PR managers' upward influence. *Journal of Managerial Issues, 16,* 127-144.

Plowman, K. D. (1998). Power in conflict for public relations. *Journal of Public Relations Research, 10,* 237-261.

Seipp, C. (1999). The puppet masters. *American Journalism Review, 21*(8), 22-29.

Serini, S. A., Toth, E. L., Wright, D. K., & Emig, A. (1998). Power, gender, and public relations: Sexual harassment as a threat to the practice. *Journal of Public Relations Research, 10,* 193-218.

Sethi, S. P. (1977). *Advocacy advertising and large corporations: Social conflict, big business image, the news media, and public policy.* Lexington, MA: Lexington Books.

Smudde, P. (2001). Issue or crisis: A rose by any other name.... *Public Relations Quarterly, 46*(4), 34-36.

Stauber, J., & Rampton, S. (1995). *Toxic sludge is good for you: Lies, damn lies and the public relations industry*. Monroe, ME: Common Courage.

Toth, E. L. (Ed.). (2007). *The future of excellence in public relations and communication management: Challenges for the next generation*. Mahwah, NJ: Erlbaum.

Tye, L. (1998). *The father of spin: Edward L. Bernays and the birth of public relations.* New York: Crown.

Power and Image

chapter 2

Hillary Rodham Clinton and the Rhetorical Depiction of Family in "Talking It Over"*

Kathleen M. German

Since Martha Washington and Abigail Adams stepped out of the traditional role of wives, first ladies have endured questions and controversy about their relationship to the U.S. president whenever they have engaged in behaviors deemed inappropriate (Anthony, 1991; Campbell, 1996; Caroli, 1987; Watson, 2000; Wertheimer, 2004). A woman who exercises political power (i.e., influence and control over public policy development and the dynamics of governmental or bureaucratic processes) in public view challenges culturally entrenched restrictions on feminine roles and risks being marginalized or publicly censored. There exist unstated but stubbornly entrenched standards of acceptable behavior for first ladies that have frequently constrained the representation of political spouses in public life

---

*An earlier version of this chapter was presented at the Central States Communication Association Convention, St. Louis, MO, April 13, 1997.

(Lewin, 1996; Pinsdorf, 2002; Rifkind, 2000). Hillary Rodham Clinton navigated this terrain as a 20th century first lady functioning in a 19th century role. She presents an interesting case for the construction of public image and a challenge for political practitioners of public relations who seek to harness the power of public opinion.

This analysis explores the rhetorical paradox of the public persona of Hillary Rodham Clinton during the 1996 presidential reelection campaign. In response to criticism, Clinton's public persona was reconstructed as spouse and mother within the conventional definition of family. Among other media outlets, her weekly newspaper column, "Talking It Over," asserted her role as a more traditional first lady through the rhetorical depiction of feminine qualities. This image of Rodham Clinton was crafted without denying her coexisting role as a nonelected public official who wielded considerable power as an important advisor to the president.[1]

Although the employment of public relations professionals by title is generally prohibited for governments and government officials, the use of public relations principles by political professionals is central in modern politics because the skillful use of media is critical to political success (McKinnon, Tedesco, & Lauder, 2001; Seitel, 2001). Whether it is in the construction of the public image of the individual or the organization, it is the projected image on which voters increasingly make decisions in the wake of the decline of the strong party system of earlier decades (Hollihan, 2001). Like corporations and private sector organizations, politicians depend on public relations to create powerful, persuasive, positive personae or images (Heath, 2001). The widespread use of public relations principles in the public sector to secure political power (i.e., to establish one's own level of influence and/or authority about selected issues above most others through acts of public communication), as well as the limited study of this application, warrant further investigation.

By examining one aspect of this successful use of public relations, the construction of the persona of Hillary Rodham Clinton, we can begin to understand its potential in the political arena and further add to the scholarship about women in public roles (Dow & Condit, 2005; cf. L. Grunig, 1988; L. Grunig, Toth, & Hon, 2001). The White House had mastered the art of public relations during much of the second Clinton term, strengthening its political power through public opinion support and providing a model for other political hopefuls to emulate (McKinnon, Tedesco, & Lauder, 2001). Political power is, at least in part, a function of public relations' symbolic power to influence public image, and the construction of image is largely a rhetorical enterprise calling for an appropriate rhetorical perspective (Cheney & McMillan, 1990; Crable, 1990; Heath, 2001; Sproule, 1990).

In particular, the case of Hillary Rodham Clinton provides an illustration of rhetorical paradox at the intersection of gender and political power.

Through a public relations campaign, the image of Rodham Clinton was shifted to align more closely with the expectations of voters, from the appearance of a nonelected partner in the administration to a more traditional first lady. In 1996, voters were encouraged to embrace the incompatible images of Rodham Clinton as public servant and Rodham Clinton as parent by accepting depictions of her as wife and mother. A closer examination of the 1996 presidential campaign and convention will establish reasons why a paradoxical persona was necessary to recapture the political center and the White House.

After introducing the concept of rhetorical paradox, which is central to understanding Rodham Clinton's public relations actions in a political context, this analysis reviews the emergence of the family theme during the 1996 campaign. Then, it examines Rodham Clinton's weekly newspaper column in light of the rhetorical paradox. Ultimately, this study raises issues of power because women have historically been excluded from positions of power, particularly in politics. Public relations' power to craft compelling images, thus, can lead to greater political power.

RHETORICAL PARADOX

Compared to their predecessors, contemporary women have an enlarged sphere of public influence. Their role has expanded in public life, and even the relatively conservative position of first lady reflects this change. First ladies have moved from presiding over ceremonial functions to acting as political surrogates and viable advocates, suggesting that the transition from spouse to political candidate is a logical next step in this evolutionary process. Still, unique challenges face women who enter the political arena, particularly as they negotiate the struggle over the images that form political reality (Meyrowitz, 1985; Mitchell, 1994; Nimmo & Combs, 1983; Parry-Giles, 2000). The rhetorical figure of paradox serves to capture the fundamental conundrum of gender, especially in the case of Hillary Rodham Clinton, who, as is shown, simultaneously enacts the roles of traditional woman and public servant in the texts of "Talking It Over."

The classical figure of paradox functions rhetorically to preserve ostensibly inconsistent positions. Operating through inductive rules of its own, rhetorical paradox "can create, maintain, and mediate the perspectives of reality which control social bindings and social divisions" (Chesebro, 1984, p. 170). It does so by substituting an acceptable position for one that is unacceptable without retracting the unacceptable position. As a result, two seemingly incompatible positions can exist simultaneously without apparent contradiction.

Symbols or public images also function as paradox, selectively establishing a relationship among formerly contradictory images so that they retain their meaning without losing their differences (Chesebro, 1984). Although paradoxes are often created logically, formally, semantically, and ironically, it is clear that mediated images can also produce paradoxes, mainly through rhetorical depiction. That is, narratives about celebrities emphasize qualities valued by audiences. Such narratives assure audiences that the person depicted shares their worldview, even though that person simultaneously retains behaviors and values that clash with those of the audience.

Historically, paradox characterizes the condition of women who have sought to influence public opinion or generate social change. For decades, American women have faced public scrutiny when they stepped outside the private, domestic domain traditionally assigned to them through cultural practices (Jorgensen-Earp, 1990). Women who aspired to political power in the public sector violated perceived feminine roles and often earned social criticism. To this extent, gender roles have limited women's aspirations to political power. The difficulties faced by women who spoke out in public settings have previously been investigated. Sojourner Truth's gender was questioned as she advocated freedom for slaves; Victoria Woodhull faced public censure for her statements regarding the relationships of men and women; Emma Goldman was ultimately deported for her political views; the Grimke sisters were harassed as were Susan B. Anthony, Elizabeth Cady Stanton, and many of the early advocates of women's suffrage (Campbell, 1989). Others were tolerated only when they blunted public condemnation by presenting themselves within the context of the home and family. Margaret Sanger, for instance, surrounded herself with her children whenever she addressed audiences on birth control (Kennedy, 1970). The personal-public division imposed on women by gender is further complicated when the public woman is a political spouse.

THE 1996 PRESIDENTIAL CAMPAIGN

Hillary Rodham Clinton has often been a lightening rod for controversy. This tendency began during the 1992 presidential campaign and continued throughout the first Clinton administration (Miller, 1992). Political commentators expressed anxiety about how much clout Rodham Clinton actually wielded in the White House. As journalists Fineman and Miller (1993) put it, "The only question is when—if ever—Hillary's unique role will raise the issue of who's really in charge in the Oval Office" (p. 18). Soon after, the healthcare reform agenda headed by Rodham Clinton strengthened these concerns. Aside from specific criticism of the healthcare reform proposal, political opponents charged that Rodham Clinton was illegitimately assuming political responsibility without appropriate accountability. As a result, her image hardened in the public eye (Goldman & Miller, 1994).

The public perception of Rodham Clinton's apparent disregard for the traditional supporting role of first lady was an underlying problem stemming from the failure of healthcare reform (Caroli, 1987; Kennedy, 2004; Muir & Benitez, 1996; Pooley & Blackman, 1996; Quinn, 1992; Watson, 2000). Plummeting popularity ratings reflected public concern, revealing a consistent belief that Rodham Clinton hurt her husband's administration (Bennet, 1997; Ebron, 1996; Gates, 1996; Sack, 1996). Her part in spearheading healthcare reform underscored Rodham Clinton's nontraditional role and contributed to her unpopularity. As she reflected, "I regret very much that the efforts on health care were badly misunderstood, taken out of context and used politically against the administration. I take responsibility for that . . . " (Burros, 1995, p. A1). A series of unfolding scandals added to the problem. The low point in Rodham Clinton's ratings occurred in the beginning of 1996 with her grand jury appearance during the Whitewater investigation; her approval rating dropped 17 points within weeks (Burrell, 2000). Following the failure of the Health Care Reform Task Force and the negative publicity linking her to several scandals, Rodham Clinton "focused her advocacy on more traditional issues concerning women and children, and was visible internationally serving as a goodwill ambassador and working on the rights and economic problems of women globally" (Burrell, p. 530).

Rodham Clinton's role in the administration was recast, moving her from center stage to the more benign public role of a spouse whose primary concern was the welfare of families and children (Radcliffe, 1999). As a direct consequence of public perceptions, Rodham Clinton dodged public controversy as "she attempted to add a *softer* dimension to her image during the 1996 presidential campaign" (Rifkind, 2000, p. 614). She began to embrace the twin themes of "community" and "family responsibility" and to avoid potentially damaging political controversies.

Rodham Clinton's "Talking It Over" newspaper column replicates earlier administration themes of family that surfaced in speeches and television appearances at the end of the first Clinton administration and the beginning of the 1996 campaign. The theme of family undergirded the release of *It Takes a Village* (Clinton, 1996a) and its accompanying promotional activities. Although the press made much fun of Rodham Clinton's constantly changing hair styles and dress, this also represented attempts to soften her public image (Kelly, 2001; Parry-Giles, 2000; cf. Dozier, L. Grunig, & J. Grunig, 2001; Heath, 1997). The newspaper column functions as one tactic within a continuing social presence and broader campaign to reshape the first lady. By layering the family theme in various channels from radio to television to newspapers, the administration used redundancy to overcome the noise of competing negative messages and reach varied strata of voters (Graber, 1992; cf. Heath, 1997). By disseminating its family theme through various media, the administration attempted to decrease its vulnerability to public media coverage (Graber, 1992).

In spite of this lower public profile, the healthcare debacle lingered to haunt Rodham Clinton throughout the 1996 campaign (Funk, 1996; McArdle, 1996). Both Bob and Elizabeth Dole frequently referred to it, asserting that Elizabeth Dole would go back to her job at the Red Cross after the election (Bumiller, 1996; Nagourney, 1996). Even Elizabeth Dole's potential conflict of interest as head of an organization that had constant, sometimes adversarial, dealings with federal agencies under the president's control rarely surfaced. The focus remained fixed on Rodham Clinton's nontraditional activities in the White House. As *Time* (Gibbs & Duffy, 1996) summarized the situation:

> Bill Clinton can thank her for his worst failure too: Hillary is the woman to whom the President turned to implement his biggest domestic initiative in 1993, a decision that, apart from its other lessons, proved that the elasticity of the First Lady's role has limits. (p. 26)

As the 1996 presidential race shaped up, Elizabeth Dole effectively created an image of the traditional supportive wife (Eddings & Barone, 1996). Polls reflected a 2-to-1 approval rating for Elizabeth Dole over Hillary Rodham Clinton. Taking advantage of this positive public response, the GOP engineered Dole's image to contrast sharply with Rodham Clinton's, "keeping her largely in a world of women and spotlighting her helpmate role rather than her other identity as a political heavy-weight" (Goldberg, 1996, p. A11). In July, the contrast was parodied by a *Time* magazine cover face-off of Hillary and "Liddy." Others suggested that a debate between the two candidates' wives would provide more fireworks and insight than a debate between the candidates themselves. The media continued to exploit the contrast, measuring both Dole and Rodham Clinton against a yardstick of traditional, expected behaviors (Rifkind, 2000; Toner, 1992).

During the Democratic National Convention, the family theme peaked as a nostalgic return to the 1950s, the time of a better America (Gibbs & Duffy, 1996; Klein, 1992; Mitchell, 1995; Toner, 1996). This sentimental yearning for the ideal family tapped concerns about the future and the kind of world our children would inherit (Barone, 1996; Golay & Rollyson, 1996; Pear, 1997: cf. Depoe, 1990; Furstenberg, 1988). It also struck the themes that would shape Rodham Clinton's public role. From opening night, the convention featured women and families in appearances laden with emotional overtones (Nagourney, 1996; Roberts & Barone, 1996). Christopher Reeve (1996) broadened the appeal with a newer, more inclusive definition of family in the phrase, "We are all family," which encouraged identification of family values with the Democratic Party, a broader view of family consistent with Rodham Clinton's messages.

Three advantages accrued from highlighting family values during the convention. First, Clinton appeared to be more centrist and conservative as a result of honoring families. This heightened his attractiveness for independent voters and generated positive support among conservative voters (Alter, 1996/1997). Second, Democrats anticipated that women would respond to the convention theme of family (Mitchell, 1995; Quirk & Cunion, 2000; Roberts & Barone, 1996) in the hope of increasing female voter turnout, which hurt the Democrats substantially during the 1994 congressional elections (Borger, 1996; Clift, 1994; Turque & Cohn, 1995). Finally, the family theme also countered the increasing pressure of scandals associated with the White House. Whitewater, Travelgate, Paula Jones, the Rose Law Firm billing records, the FBI files, and Rodham Clinton's solarium séances, one after another, scandals plagued the Clintons and captured front page headlines, threatening to eclipse the campaign message (Alter, 1996/1997; Duffy & Pound, 1996; Goldman & Mathews, 1992; Isikoff & Klaidman, 1996). The wholesome family appeal functioned to neutralize the increasingly negative news environment and augment the family theme that dominated Rodham Clinton's public relations campaign.

Administration advisors advocated a lower public profile more consistent with the public expectation of a traditional first lady (Burrell, 2001). In order to support her husband's presidential bid without rekindling the dormant antagonism concerning her quasi-official status, Rodham Clinton adopted the strategy of rhetorical paradox following the convention. She managed the tension between her private and public functions by reconstructing her public persona as a traditional woman and concealing her part in policy management (Campbell, 1996). Her speeches featured family issues and avoided overt policy suggestions that might remind voters of her role in the healthcare controversy, and she dodged hostile encounters by addressing mostly supportive audiences in preselected cities (Brant, 1996; Lawrence, 1996). For certain groups, Rodham Clinton's attraction remained strong. In spite of her negative national ratings, she excited ardent support among a loyal faction of Democratic women (Borger, 1996; Brant, 1996). She also drew more media attention than other candidates' spouses and surpassed some of the candidates themselves in media coverage (Burrell, 2001).

THE WEEKLY NEWSPAPER COLUMN

Throughout the campaign, Rodham Clinton also avoided national journalists and television news coverage (Church & Blackman, 1996). There was one exception, her weekly newspaper column, "Talking It Over." It was couched as a nonpartisan message that reached a more heterogeneous group of voters than other, more limited forums.

For this analysis, 31 columns syndicated to appear weekly from July 1995 through March 1996 in newspapers across the country during the campaign were examined. Over this period of 9 months, Rodham Clinton discussed a variety of family-friendly topics such as quality day care, the v-chip, and television programming for children. Conclusions were drawn from a close textual analysis of all of the columns as they appeared during the campaign, although, for the sake of brevity, only selected illustrations are included.

Rodham Clinton's column, "Talking It Over," was inspired by Eleanor Roosevelt.[2] The column appeared in more than 100 newspapers and magazines beginning July 30, 1995, and continuing through March 1996. During this period, it is estimated, based on general circulation figures, that 56 million subscribers, or 58.45% of total adult voters, received newspapers with the syndicated column (Newspaper Association of America, 2004). Although it is impossible to know how many people actually read the column, it certainly reached more voters than her limited public appearances. Reader responses in the form of letters to the editor also suggest that the first lady's column was widely read by both supporters and nonsupporters ("Readers Respond," 1995).

The column was designed specifically to enhance Rodham Clinton's appeal to women and minority voters whose support President Clinton needed for reelection (Purdum, 1995). This venue for reconstructing her public persona deserves particular attention because it is unusual. The medium of print allowed Rodham Clinton to develop a public persona more directly under her control than the quick soundbites pulled from speeches or other public appearances. The column allowed her to exploit the tendency of media to frame news in a way that highlights personal behavior and motives, focusing on personal character over substance (Cappella & Jamieson, 1997; West, 2003). This strategy also highlighted her character rather than her political positions, a necessary approach in an age when voters rely on personality indicators to make political decisions (Hollihan, 2001).

The newspaper column fits within an overall public relations campaign to disperse messages about the first lady. First, it offered a controlled media source in a negative news environment. Amid the general news coverage of scandals, it represented a positive view of the administration. In addition, the news column was more insulated from negative attack than straight news as it was unfettered by the constraints of objectivity and format (Graber, 1992). It was monologic in form, rather than dialogic, further insulating it from negative feedback. This was particularly attractive in an administration that mistrusted the press (Hayden, 2002).

The column provides the illusion of reader participation. Its images are homespun and tap a common denominator of experience for many readers. The narrative structure offers a story that engages the reader in the unfolding of events in which the first lady plays a vital role. In addition, it appears to be "talking it over"—as a dialogue with a friend, although it is actually a highly controlled one-way communication that mimics interpersonal conversation. The column's placement in the society/lifestyle sections of newspapers frames it as nonpolitical (Mickey, 2003). The column presents the first lady as a mother, wife, and parent—vulnerable to the fears and insecurities of daily life, thus entrenching her within the realm of the personal and further diverting attention from the political.

The column placement, appearing in family and leisure sections of newspapers and providing personal vignettes featuring the first lady, was consistent with her subdued role in the campaign (Purdum, 1995). The newspaper column, as part of the overall public relations effort, softened Rodham Clinton's image, even though her role in the administration paradoxically remained the same. Osborn (1986) identified five functions of rhetorical depiction, which is the use of rhetoric to construct a portrait of a person or position. I adapt these five functions to analyze the rhetorical construction of Rodham Clinton's image in "Talking It Over": a personable style, the use of synecdoche, appeals to identification, recommendations for audience action, and the celebration of fundamental American rituals. These five functions formed an overlapping matrix in each weekly column. The result was the rhetorical depiction of Rodham Clinton as a more traditional first lady, allowing her to simultaneously maintain a separate persona as a first lady involved in politics and public affairs.

Function One: Personable Style

"Talking It Over" presented Rodham Clinton in a personable style. In its first installment, Rodham Clinton framed the column as an informal conversation engaging readers with her in dialogue (cf. Anderson, 2002; Branham & Pearce, 1996). She concluded the July 30, 1995, column by writing, "This column will give me the chance to talk things over in the hope that some of you will join the conversation. So, let's talk again next week" (p. 2E). The title of the column, "Talking It Over," adds to the illusion of a friendly, personal conversation (cf. Keeter, 1987). To foster this impression, Rodham Clinton shares her thoughts framed by routine, domestic scenarios like working out, planning vacations, making New Year's resolutions, and talking with her family. Throughout the columns, she emphasizes the informality of her White House role when she describes her interactions with heads of state, family friends, and others in informal situations. She chats, for example, with Mother Theresa about their common concern for the adoption of unwanted children (Clinton, 1995b). Similarly, her role in negotiations for a television rating system is shared in these terms: "As one of the few mothers in the room when the President met with leading entertainment executives at the White House recently, I can tell you how encouraging the discussion was" (Clinton, 1996j, p. 2E). Thus tone, language choices, structure, and placement are more than layout choices; they serve to establish a relationship of familiarity with the target public.

In each column, Rodham Clinton's language is informal; she highlights the personal side of public events. She tells her readers, for example, "I am writing this aboard Air Force One, traveling home with my husband after attending funeral services for Yitzhak Rabin. . . . I want to share some of the feelings and questions this awful experience raised for me" (1995p, p. 8E). Even this state event is cast as an intimate moment of reflection between Rodham Clinton and her readers. She highlights personal moments that position her as a wife, rather than a political figure: "I am very fond of Leah Rabin and always treasured the time I spent with her and the prime minister, even when he kidded me for not letting him smoke in the White House" (1995p, p. 8E). This intimacy also situates the reader within her circle of confidence. As Branham and Pearce (1996) suggested, "A rhetorical transaction may be framed as broadly conversational in a deliberate attempt to construct or reconstruct the public identity of the speaker and to reshape or disguise the hierarchical relationship between speaker and audience(s)" (p. 435). This reshaping of Rodham Clinton's public identity embraces her readers as personal acquaintances.

Function Two: Synecdochic Instances

The synecdoche is a classical figure of speech in which a part of something substitutes for the whole thing, as in "wheels" when referring to an automobile. Synecdochic instances reduce complex issues to a few examples that stimulate broad recognition among readers (Osborn, 1986). Rodham Clinton encourages this affiliation by beginning most of her columns with specific instances. In particular, Rodham Clinton's daughter Chelsea is featured prominently in many of the columns. Instances such as learning to feed her newborn daughter unquestionably define Rodham Clinton as a mother. Her panic as she notices foam in Chelsea's nose is reassuringly maternal: "I pushed every call button within reach. When the nurse arrived, she assured me that I was simply holding the baby at an awkward angle, making it difficult for her to swallow the milk she took in" (1995j, p. 2E).

Other family members also reinforce Rodham Clinton's supportive roles as mother, wife, and daughter. Visiting nephews lead to this revelation: "We took turns telling Tyler that he shouldn't throw his food on the floor and carrying Zach around when he needed comforting" (Clinton, 1996c, p.

2E). Such references to nurturing actions articulate her identity as part of the family unit.

Memories of their courtship and Bill's proposal, as well as a "secret" celebration of their 20th wedding anniversary, provide a feeling of camaraderie with the reader: "I know it sounds corny, but we love each other more now than when we married" (Clinton, 1995k, p. 2E). The reader gets the details of the courtship, the proposal, and their first house: "[Bill] had gone to Wal-Mart and bought sheets with green and yellow flowers. To this day, he still jokes that he doesn't know what he would have done with that house if I had said no" (Clinton, 1995k, p. 2E).

Rodham Clinton (1995n, 1995t) also stimulates affiliation with her readers by downplaying her career and highlighting common experiences. References to her legal career are incidental to Rodham Clinton's relationship to her daughter. In one column, the focus is on the frantic, last minute search for child care during an emergency: "And, like any working mother, I can tell you about the times I have had to leave at midday or miss work altogether because of a family emergency" (Clinton, 1995c, p. 3E). Her career as a lawyer is subordinated to her primary concern with parenting. Such personal details of motherhood spark recognition and alter Rodham Clinton's relationship with the reader, who discovers, for example, that Chelsea "is a *Sesame Street* kid" who learned to count with Big Bird (1995d, p. 2E). In this way, ordinary experiences from daily life foster familiarity. In particular, motherhood becomes the synecdoche for broader public concerns. Each anecdote highlights an issue facing women such as, in the previous examples, quality child care and television programming. The column thus intensified her relationship to readers through synecdochic instances with brief but potent examples that fell within the experience of most readers.

Function Three: Identification

"Talking It Over" also offered readers their own values highlighted in cultural types (Campbell, 1996; Osborn, 1986). In her first column, common experiences that represent fundamental American values are depicted. For example, Clinton writes about taking the car out for a drive, eluding her Secret Service detail: "For several hours, I enjoyed a marvelous sensation of personal freedom" (1995a, p. 2E). The car represents freedom in a uniquely American way. We associate feelings of independence with the automobile, and Rodham Clinton's momentary escape from her extraordinary life appeals to this fundamental icon.

Elsewhere, she recognizes the "anxious mom" phenomenon, as millions of women everywhere dial home at 3 o'clock just to make sure the kids have returned safely from school (Clinton, 1995c). This directly confirms community identification with collective values and subtly asserts the common problem of child care. Also, she recognizes the inspiration of common American heroes. Rodham Clinton cites extraordinary public figures like Eleanor Roosevelt, Martin Luther King, Lady Bird Johnson, and Christopher Reeve as heroic trailblazers (1995l, 1996d, 1996g, 1996k).

Much of the reader's identification Rodham Clinton tries to prompt comes via the emotions associated with family life. The nostalgia of past vacations, milestones in children's lives, and the personal rewards of American freedom are fundamental. Thinking about Chelsea at the start of another school year when "her dad and I would make her pose for the ritual picture before driving her to school," Rodham Clinton (1995h, p. 3E) reveals her gratitude for the educational opportunities offered in a democracy. Similarly, she writes jokingly of their trip to South Asia: "As the mother of a teenager, I felt very lucky indeed that my 15-year-old was willing to spend 10 days with me" (1995r, p. 4E). She concludes more seriously,

> I was glad Chelsea was with me so she could see for herself how other people live and work around the world. . . . We have so many blessings here in the United States—mostly because millions of other people paid the price for the life we enjoy today and because we have a stable democratic government that provides public services which benefit us all. (p. 4E)

In other columns, Rodham Clinton expresses her concern with the effects of product advertising on young minds, children growing up in war zones, the hard work it takes to nurture a family, the effects of divorce on children, and the pain of inadequate pediatric medical care. Each column is grounded in common cultural values like peace, commitment to family life, hard work, and charity.

Function Four: Recommendations for Audience Action

Throughout the columns, Rodham Clinton introduces relatively noncontroversial opinions on various issues. Yet "Talking It Over" endorsed partisan programs by suggesting specific behaviors, focusing on individual action rather than policy proposals. For example, she endorses public television, the V-chip to block violent television programming, women's suffrage, universal human rights, and routine mammograms (1995d, 1995f, 1995g, 1995m, 1996j). She defends the United Nations as a peacekeeper in the world because "it offers a forum where talking instead of fighting is valued" (1995o, p. 23) and rejects the expulsion of HIV positive personnel from jobs because they have devoted an average of "10 years of their lives to the military" (1996h, p. 2E). These positions require wider policy initiatives; however, Rodham Clinton does not seek them. Occasionally, she proposes specific, innocent, individual actions, implying support for more controversial policies (1995i, 1995q, 1996e, 1996f). For example, she requests that readers send letters and holiday gifts "no larger than a shoe box" to soldiers serving in Bosnia (1995u, p. 2E). This request presumes her support of the Bosnian troop deployment but couches it within a personal gesture.

In the same manner, Rodham Clinton inserts the issue of equality for women as she discusses Chelsea's 16th birthday. The birthday celebration reminds Rodham Clinton of past days, when adolescence seemed easier but more restricted for girls, when "Television was limited to three networks . . . and *The Patty Duke Show* was the raciest program we saw" (1996i, p. 2E). Rodham Clinton adds that she was rejected for the NASA space program because the program did not enroll women: "Now, girls can realistically dream of flying in space, piloting jet fighters and running Fortune 500 companies . . . or they can choose full-time motherhood and homemaking. The point is, it's now a choice" (p. 2E). In the midst of new choices, she reassures her readers that we have not abandoned basic values. These traditional beliefs still guide us in a new era. Expressing the fears of hundreds of parents, Rodham Clinton (1996b) concludes, "For my part, when my daughter jumps behind the wheel of the car and takes off on her own soon, I'm sure I'll be filled with excitement at her newfound independence. I'll also take a deep breath—and hope for the best" (p. 2E).

Function Five: Celebrating Common Rituals

A final function of the columns is to endorse middle-class values through a celebration of the past. "Talking It Over" celebrated fundamental American rituals, such as holidays, landmarks, and transitional events.

Sometimes the very triteness of the experience secures our common feelings of nostalgia. For example, Rodham Clinton reminisces about summer automobile vacations during her childhood. She fought with her brothers for space in the back seat, played word games to ease the boredom, and complained about the endless hours in the car (1995e). While her life has changed, the memory of those vacations remains, along with an appreciation of simpler days, as she relates: "Even now, I can shut my eyes and see my father driving through the night or my mother laying out a picnic at the side of the road" (1995e, p. 3E).

The Clintons celebrate milestones in ways that bind families. They mark the first day of each new school year with a picture of Chelsea (Clinton, 1995h). As she turns 16, Chelsea's passage from childhood into adulthood is observed with a special family celebration. Rodham Clinton plans a White House Christmas and lists her resolutions for the new year (1996b). She describes the seasonal celebration and thanks hundreds of

Americans who designed decorations for 30 trees in the White House. She writes, "I hope you will have a chance to visit, if not this year, then some other holiday season," (1995s, p. 4E) as though the reader is simply dropping in on a neighbor.

A significant part of the celebration of common rituals is the emotions they evoke. Rodham Clinton emphasizes these emotions throughout the columns. For example, she expresses nostalgia for childhood, pride in America, indignation at unscrupulous advertisers, parental concern for children, and impish rebellion against the constraints of her public life. As she couples emotional appeals with common rituals, Rodham Clinton places herself squarely within the symbolic community of traditional Americans.

Together, the five functions of rhetorical depiction in the "Talking It Over" columns help Rodham Clinton cultivate an ostensibly personal relationship with the reader. The columns portray a first lady who appears traditional, caring for her family and possessing little political power. In reality, Rodham Clinton controlled the relationship with her readers and, to that extent, retained the power to influence them. First, the style of the columns created an interpersonal relationship as Rodham Clinton chatted informally with readers as though they were friends and not constituents. Second, she also related to her readers through common experiences like courtship, family life, parenting, and child care. By sharing such informal and private experiences with Rodham Clinton, readers are more likely to disregard her role as a public policymaker. Third, Rodham Clinton invoked fundamental American values, such as personal freedom, peace, hard work, and charity, which are difficult to refute. She associated herself with basic American ideals. Fourth, Rodham Clinton strategically avoided controversial positions that would remind readers of her past political advocacy. Finally, Rodham Clinton stirred emotions like nostalgia and pride by recalling common American celebrations. In reality, the power Rodham Clinton exercised in the White House had not changed, only the public depiction of it.

IMPLICATIONS FOR PUBLIC RELATIONS

Three related implications can be drawn from the rhetorical depiction of Hillary Rodham Clinton within the context of the traditional family in "Talking It Over." First, "Talking It Over" located Rodham Clinton squarely within the overall theme of family endorsed during the presidential campaign of 1996. Second, her evocation of traditional definitions of womanhood, achieved through the five functions of rhetorical depiction, occurred simultaneously with her continued advocacy of public issues, a contradictory position acceptable within the logic of paradox. By highlighting her roles as mother and wife, Rodham Clinton drew attention to herself as a traditional first lady and redirected public concerns about the power she wielded as a nonelected official. Finally, the success of the strategy provided a foundation for her transition into elected political office. Most immediately, the public relations campaign to reinvent Rodham Clinton had a strategic effect on the reelection and established a logic of paradox that served as a foundation for transition into public office.

Strategic Effect

As a key component of the reelection strategy, Rodham Clinton modified her direct advocacy of public policies in an effort to appeal to women's concerns with home and family rather than other issues, avoiding controversy over her status as a nonelected public servant (Golay & Rollyson, 1996; Mitchell, 1995; Roberts & Barone, 1996). According to Auster (1996), she "learned to lower her profile, pick her fights and be more effective" (p. 26).

Although the effectiveness of Rodham Clinton in the 1996 campaign cannot be assessed directly through standard polling measures, there are indirect indications that this strategy was successful. Postelection research revealed the largest gap in voting records between men and women in recent history. The gender gap appeared in all age groups, in all education categories, and among Black women as well as White women. Pleck (1996) concluded that the gender gap was key to the 1996 election results. Rodham Clinton contributed to the reelection campaign to the extent that she convinced women to turn out and vote for Clinton. Generally, Watson (2000) concluded that she "contributed to a slight increase in her husband's overall public approval rating" (p. 158).

More specifically, ratings of Hillary Rodham Clinton followed the same pattern as ratings of her husband rather than diverging as before the campaign. Opinion polls revealed a strong preference among women for both Rodham Clinton and her husband (Newport, 1996; Short-Thompson, 1997). Although it is impossible to claim a direct correlation between Rodham Clinton's columns and her ratings, she was perceived positively among women, which was something Democrats desperately needed following the 1994 congressional elections.

Fundraising results offer another indication that Rodham Clinton was a pivotal figure in the campaign (Burrell, 2001). She was the principal fundraiser for the president among Democratic women, single-handedly raising $5 million, "a historic high for women" (Auster, 1996, p. 26). To the extent that political power rests on financial resources, Rodham Clinton demonstrated her ability to tap monetary assets.

"Talking It Over," as part of a broader public relations campaign, allowed Rodham Clinton to symbolically reclaim conservative ground. She defined herself and, as a consequence, her husband in terms of traditional roles. This appeal to tradition undoubtedly tapped that potent reservoir of feelings described by Hobsbawm and Ranger (1983): "It also seems clear that the most successful examples of manipulation are those which exploit practices which clearly meet a felt—not necessarily a clearly understood—need among particular bodies of people" (p. 307). The felt need among voters resonated with the centrality of family communicated by Rodham Clinton. Arturo Corona's letter to the editor provides anecdotal evidence of this phenomenon:

> I can't tell you how impressed I was with Hillary Clinton's column. . . . It has completely changed my mind about her. I had a one-sided perception of what type of person she is. She is really trying to get down to the people. ("Readers Respond," 1995, p. 2E)

Although not all readers responded as positively, most wrote that they enjoyed seeing the "human side" of the first lady ("Readers Respond," 1995, p. 2E). The human side of Rodham Clinton was captured in her personalized narratives as wife and mother. To the extent that Rodham Clinton was perceived in more feminine terms, she was able to reconcile previously unacceptable views of her highly public role in the administration with her private role as wife and mother. This reorientation of images occurred without sacrificing her public activities. Consequently, Rodham Clinton both fractured and recreated her public image as first lady.

Specifically, the columns downplayed Rodham Clinton's connections to political power through their informal, chatty style. Feminine feelings and actions delineated Rodham Clinton as a mother and wife, reducing complex issues to a few synecdochic instances dependent on common affiliation. The columns also highlighted identification among Rodham Clinton and her readers by relying on cultural values. Rather than directly supporting policy initiatives as she had done in the past, Rodham Clinton asked for personal gestures and individual actions. These served as noncontroversial oblique endorsements of issues. Finally, Rodham Clinton fulfilled her role as America's hostess, celebrating common national rituals in the White House and defining her activities in terms of family milestones.

As suggested, the primary strategic accomplishment of the redefinition of Rodham Clinton within the domestic sphere occurred as she talked about the personal rather than the political. This rhetorical depiction of traditional feminine interests functioned to accent politically conservative values. By stressing her role as wife and mother, Rodham Clinton redirected voters from her past activities as a corporate lawyer risen to nonelected policy maker, driven by unprincipled professional ambition. Rodham Clinton refuted Republican attackers by appropriating their symbolic ground; she subverted their attacks by associating herself symbolically with their values. By doing so, she deprived political conservatives of arguments against her while advancing the agenda of the Clinton reelection campaign.

The Logic of Paradox

Beyond the direct impact of the rhetorical depiction of the first lady on the 1996 campaign, Rodham Clinton's exploitation of traditional definitions had additional ramifications for women in public roles. In many ways, the tension between Rodham Clinton's private and public lives reflects the double bind (cf. Jamieson, 1995) that constrains all women in the public eye. Women who do not display feminine behaviors are criticized for overstepping their boundaries (Bostdorff, 1991; Mattina, 2004; Spitzack & Carter, 1987; Tuchman, Daniels, & Benét, 1978). In her attempt to reconcile this tension during the 1996 presidential campaign, Rodham Clinton displayed accommodation to voter expectations rather than confrontation (Sullivan & Turner, 1996). She downplayed nontraditional characteristics that alienated voters by describing herself in traditionally feminine ways as wife and mother. Her private role determined by the family structure thus dominated the narrative structure of her public discourse. However, Rodham Clinton did not abandon her advocacy of public issues. She merely reframed them in culturally acceptable ways. In this political milieu Rodham Clinton was able to reconcile power and gender by adopting a position within traditional gender roles from which to speak.[3]

Perhaps the most important idea embedded in this description is that ambiguous definitions allowed Rodham Clinton to straddle paradoxical positions. This is particularly useful for women who often find themselves faced with the contradictory demands of private and public expectations (Zarefsky, 1986). Certainly, the double bind inherent in the position of first lady was eased by defining Rodham Clinton in terms of her traditional family roles.

In this case, the use of persuasive definition pleaded several causes for the first lady. The depiction of Rodham Clinton as wife and mother attempted to activate latent values. These traditional images coalesced positive virtues (cf. Agranoff, 1972). The image of Rodham Clinton as wife and mother provided a vehicle for readers to objectify their feelings, as the myth of family is one of the most potent in American culture (Adams, 1983; Nimmo & Combs, 1980). The family image encouraged a camaraderie that stimulated trust and affirmed her credibility for readers. It aroused feelings of identification that were not associated with specific ideas or controversial policies but rested on generic emotional responses.

Second, Rodham Clinton served as a character witness for her husband. In the same manner, Elizabeth Dole humanized her husband by revealing the personal side of an otherwise prickly public persona (Seelye, 1996; cf. Campbell, 1996). For President Clinton, the portrait of family deflected character questions. He took on the characteristics of a loyal husband and proud parent as Rodham Clinton emphasized the family unit.

Third, the family theme functioned as a nostalgia-laden retrocampaign (Coontz, 1996). The voter was reminded of life in the good old days, and the candidate avoided problems of the present. During the 1996 campaign, the family portrait cultivated in the "Talking It Over" column placed Rodham Clinton in a publicly acceptable position and supported the broader public relations campaign to redefine the first lady as a traditional woman while simultaneously allowing her to advocate public policies. As Burrell (2000) concluded after an analysis of public opinion polls, "Her relationship with the public was a fascinating mixture of public and private roles and complex reactions to her" (p. 533). In sum, she was highly influential in the presidential election of 1996 (Burden & Mughan, 1999; Burrell, 2000).

Foundation for Transition

In the years since her role in the Clinton administration, Rodham Clinton has served as a transitional figure, successfully negotiating the transformation from the largely feminized role of first lady to that of an elected senator. The restoration of her popularity in 1996 provided a base of public support that she used to become a key figure in the 1998 election campaign. As Burrell (2000) concluded, "In 1998, Hillary was a formidable force in the Democratic campaign strategy of that midterm election" (p. 538). In the 2000 New York senatorial campaign, Rodham Clinton gained momentum as a viable political candidate opposing first New York City mayor Rudolph Giuliani, who dropped out of the race to be replaced by Republican Congressman Rick Lazio.

The progression of Rodham Clinton from first lady to senator is complex but hinges on redefinition within the family theme embraced by the Clinton administration and clearly observed in her weekly newspaper column. It allowed her to appropriate the conservative symbol of the family and establish herself within more traditional definitions of gender through incremental erosion (Heath, 1997). Anderson (2002) extended the analysis: "Although the story of first lady Hillary Rodham Clinton revolved around questions of gender, news about candidate Hillary was more concerned with issues of place" (p. 125).

Soon after she announced her intention to run for the Senate seat in New York, Rodham Clinton was labeled a carpetbagger, a reminder to voters that she had only recently become a resident of the state. She defused the carpetbagger charge with rhetorical depictions that placed her directly within the realm of families. Throughout the Senate campaign, Rodham Clinton continued to couch her policy platform in nonthreatening, and often domestic, narratives characteristic of her newspaper column. Her speeches frequently began with anecdotes that placed her in personal situations, much like her columns. Her speaking employed concrete language, a personal tone, and anecdotal evidence (cf. Blankenship & Robson, 1995; Campbell, 1989; Dow & Tonn, 1993; Jamieson, 1988). Anderson (2002) observed:

> As Clinton laid them out, she eschewed the policy tone that characterized her speeches during the health-care reform campaign and adopted a more personal, narrative mode. She began each paragraph with phrases like, "When I ate lunch with teachers at a school in Queens," and "when I sat on porches in backyards from Elmira to New Rochelle." (p. 115)

This technique of sandwiching issues within homey narratives combined the personal narrative with typically male political strategies, creating a complex political persona that resonated positively with New York voters.

Rodham Clinton's adoption of rhetorical strategies associated with traditional roles for women has shifted the directness with which she approached policy initiatives and tempered the appearance of political power wielding (Hernandez & Healy, 2005). By celebrating her familial place, Rodham Clinton claimed a territory from which she could launch her foray into the political sphere. As she did so, she located herself within the culturally acceptable realm of the domestic, tapping feelings of trust and caring resonating from that image, thus offsetting, to some extent at least, the suspicions of dishonesty that plagued her. The symbol of family provided a potent framework from which Rodham Clinton could more easily formulate effective messages that transcended differences without changing her policy positions or challenging the patriarchal, political power structure (Graber, 1992; Sapienza, 1987).

CONCLUSION

First ladies have struggled to define their roles as nonelected but highly visible public figures since Martha Washington accompanied the troops led by her husband during the Revolutionary War (Anthony, 1991). Since those days, the ambiguous position of the first lady has generated tension between private and public roles for the women who have occupied the position.

Rodham Clinton's attempts to negotiate the public and private duality of her image as first lady have been no exception. Although her newspaper column, "Talking It Over," served the predominantly pragmatic function of raising political support among women during her husband's 1996 reelection campaign, it also affirmed cultural symbols derived from the rhetorical depiction of Rodham Clinton as a traditional woman. It presented Rodham Clinton in a personable framework that intensified her relationship to readers through synecdochic instances, common cultural values, and American rituals. The column allowed her to endorse partisan policies within a non-controversial format, thus pursuing a contradictory position acceptable within the logic of paradox.

Rodham Clinton's advantage over Martha Washington and other first ladies is the rhetorical power of public relations to shape public image. The deft balancing act between politico and mother accomplished through "Talking It Over" suggests several advantages that the rhetorical figure of paradox might afford public relations practices in general. Primarily, rhetorical paradox provides flexibility in image-making: The speaker may emphasize one role at one point time and a different role at another. The end result over a campaign's timeframe may be to become both at the same time—without drawing attention to the paradox at any particular point in time.

Similarly, different images often are presented to different publics, often without those publics challenging the contradiction. The practitioner must be careful not to push the paradox too far, however. All the same, organizations sometimes manage stark contrasts in image within the very same message: for example, the CEO who becomes closer to his employees by holding a "Town Hall" meeting in which he actually is speaking one to many; or the consolidated bank that is "large enough to meet your needs" but "small enough to know you personally" simply because of the friendliness of employees in "hometown" branches across the country. Clearly, Hillary Rodham Clinton (or the staffers who assisted her with the articles) knew not to push the paradoxes presented in "Talking It Over" too far.

In the short term, the "Talking It Over" column reached millions of print readers across the nation, portraying the first lady as a confidant, someone just like them, concerned with the problems of everyday life and successful parenting. In the longer term, it was part of a broader public relations campaign to soften the public image of Hillary Rodham Clinton, which foreshadowed her successful New York Senate campaign and, in the future, may provide the public support to launch a national presidential bid. As one columnist noted, the columns reflect an adaptation of her rhetorical choices to those traditionally acceptable for women, redirecting her to adopt "an incremental approach to social progress, using the White House pulpit to lay issues before the public and urging others to find solutions" (Broder, 1997, p. A24).

It is likely that the political function of gender in relationship to power will continue to defy easy explanations (Kahn & Goldenberg, 1991; Purnell, 1978). It is the politicization of gender roles through cooptation that continues to restrict women to the private realm (Jablonski, 1988). Edelman (1988) summarized the challenge women face in public life: "It is as if women can prove their fitness for high office only by demonstrating their allegiance to patriarchal norms" (p. 61). This double bind of private and public personas for women who aspire to public office will undoubtedly remain fruitful grounds for research, as will the role of rhetorical paradox in public relations image-making.

NOTES

1. Consistent with the Associated Press and American Psychological Association style guides, in this chapter "first lady" is never capitalized; "president" is only capitalized when it is used as a title immediately preceding the office holder's name. Capitalization of these titles occurs when direct quotations incorrectly employ it.
2. Six days a week, between 1936 and 1945, Eleanor Roosevelt wrote a syndicated newspaper column titled "My Day." The column was a chatty letter to readers—part diary, part chronicle of her daily routine, and part commentary on current events. As a response to public criticism of her influence in the White House, Eleanor Roosevelt used the column to elaborate on her activities and opinions (Campbell, 1996).
3. Zarefsky's (1986) comments on definition in the modern presidency can be applied profitably to Rodham Clinton: "To choose a definition is to plead a cause. Indeed, the skillful choice of definitions can enable a rhetor simultaneously to plead more than one cause, as audiences with different interests and agendas are attracted to different aspects of a definition" (pp. 8-9).

REFERENCES

Adams, J. (1983). The familial image in rhetoric. *Communication Quarterly, 31*, 56-61.

Agranoff, R. (1972). *Campaign media in the age of television.* Boston: Holbrook.

Alter, J. (1996/1997). Thinking of family values. *Newsweek, 128*(27), 30-32, 35.

Anderson, K. V. (2002). From spouses to candidates: Hillary Rodham Clinton, Elizabeth Dole, and the gendered office of U.S. president. *Rhetoric & Public Affairs, 5*, 105-132.

Anthony, C. S. (1991). *First ladies: The saga of the presidents' wives and their power, 1789-1961* (Vol. 1). New York: William Morrow.

Auster, B. B. (1996). The first lady picks her battles. *U.S. News & World Report, 121*(9), 26-27.

Barone, M. (1996). The year of the great parental pitch. *U.S. News & World Report, 121*(10), 6-7.

Bennet, J. (1997, January 20). Hillary Clinton, an evolutionary tale. *The New York Times*, p. A14.
Blankenship, J., & Robson, D. C. (1995). A "feminine style" in women's political discourse: An exploratory essay. *Communication Quarterly, 43,* 353-366.
Borger, G. (1996). What will the first lady do now? *U.S. News & World Report, 120*(24), 45.
Bostdorff, D. M. (1991). Vice-presidential comedy and the traditional female role: An examination of the rhetorical characteristic of the vice presidency. *Western Journal of Speech Communication, 55,* 1-27.
Branham, R. J., & Pearce, W. B. (1996). The conversational frame in public address. *Communication Quarterly, 44,* 423-439.
Brant, M. (1996). Cashing in on letting Hillary be Hillary. *Newsweek, 128*(10), 24.
Broder, J. M. (1997, October 24). Clinton pledges $300 million toward improving child care. *The New York Times,* p. A24.
Bumiller, E. (1996, July 16). Elizabeth Dole is eager to keep strength subtle. *The New York Times,* pp. A1, A14.
Burden, B. C., & Mughan, A. (1999). Public opinion and Hillary Rodham Clinton. *Public Opinion Quarterly, 63,* 237-250.
Burrell, B. C. (2000). Hillary Rodham Clinton as first lady: The people's perspective. *Social Science Journal, 37,* 529-546.
Burrell, B. C. (2001). *Public opinion, the first ladyship and Hillary Rodham Clinton.* New York: Routledge.
Burros, M. (1995, January 10). Hillary Clinton asks help in finding a softer image. *The New York Times,* pp. A1, A15.
Campbell, K. K. (1989). *Man cannot speak for her* (Vol. 1). New York: Praeger.
Campbell, K. K. (1996). The rhetorical presidency: A two-person career. In M. J. Medhurst (Ed.), *Beyond the rhetorical presidency* (pp. 179-195). College Station: Texas A & M University Press.
Cappella, J. N., & Jamieson, K. H. (1997). *The spiral of cynicism: The press and the public good.* New York: Oxford University Press.
Caroli, B. B. (1987). *First ladies.* New York: Oxford University Press.
Cheney, G., & McMillan, J. J. (1990). Organizational rhetoric and the practice of criticism. *Journal of Applied Communication Research, 18,* 93-114.
Chesebro, J. W. (1984). The symbolic construction of social realities: A case study in the rhetorical criticism of paradox. *Communication Quarterly, 32,* 164-171.
Church, G. J., & Blackman, A. (1996). Hushed on the stump. *Time, 148*(17), 48.
Clift, E. (1994). Hillary: Humbled, bitter and "shellshocked." *Newsweek, 124*(12), 31.
Clinton, H. R. (1995a, July 30). Talking it over: Column to showcase first lady's insights. *Dayton* (OH) *Daily News,* p. 2E.
Clinton, H. R. (1995b, August 6). Talking it over: Children's home signifies beginning. *Dayton* (OH) *Daily News,* p. 3E.
Clinton, H. R. (1995c, August 13). Talking it over: Family-friendly workplace should be goal. *Dayton* (OH) *Daily News,* p. 3E.
Clinton, H. R. (1995d, August 20). Talking it over: Public TV provides lifeline to country's kids. *Dayton* (OH) *Daily News,* p. 2E.
Clinton, H. R. (1995e, August 27). Talking it over: Vacation memories a lasting reality. *Dayton* (OH) *Daily News,* p. 3E.

Clinton, H. R. (1995f, September 3). Talking it over: All should recall hard-fought suffrage victory. *Dayton* (OH) *Daily News,* p. 2E.
Clinton, H. R. (1995g, September 17). Talking it over: Human rights the focus as first lady answers the conference call. *Dayton* (OH) *Daily News,* p. 3E.
Clinton, H. R. (1995h, September 24). Talking it over: Start of school triggers thoughts of kids. *Dayton* (OH) *Daily News,* p. 3E.
Clinton, H. R. (1995i, October 1). Talking it over: Don't like the advertiser's message? Then don't buy. *Dayton* (OH) *Daily News,* p. 2E.
Clinton, H. R. (1995j, October 8). Talking it over: Health of new mom, baby should be top priority, first lady says. *Dayton* (OH) *Daily News,* p. 2E.
Clinton, H. R. (1995k, October 15). Talking it over: Celebrating a milestone. *Dayton* (OH) *Daily News,* p. 2E.
Clinton, H. R. (1995l, October 22). Talking it over: Eleanor Roosevelt was a trailblazer and role model to remember. *Dayton* (OH) *Daily News,* p. 2E.
Clinton, H. R. (1995m, October 29). Talking it over: Save your life, get a mammogram. *Dayton* (OH) *Daily News,* p. 2E.
Clinton, H. R. (1995n, November 5). Talking it over: Readers respond to first lady's column. *Dayton* (OH) *Daily News,* p. 4E.
Clinton, H. R. (1995o, November 12). Talking it over: Misunderstood United Nations works to keep its place in history. *Dayton* (OH) *Daily News,* p. 23.
Clinton, H. R. (1995p, November 19). Talking it over: Rabin's death a blow to democratic ways. *Dayton* (OH) *Daily News,* p. 8E.
Clinton, H. R. (1995q, November 26). Talking it over: Monetary cuts at children's hospitals pain all involved. *Dayton* (OH) *Daily News,* p. 2E.
Clinton, H. R. (1995r, December 3). Talking it over: First family thankful to live in America. *Dayton* (OH) *Daily News,* p. 4E.
Clinton, H. R. (1995s, December 10). Talking it over: Months of planning bring glorious Christmas tree to life. *Dayton* (OH) *Daily News,* p. 4E.
Clinton, H. R. (1995t, December 17). Talking it over: Many "remarkable" people work to bring peace to Ireland. *Dayton* (OH) *Daily News,* p. 2E.
Clinton, H. R. (1995u, December 24). Talking it over: Military families rally for support during Bosnia deployment. *Dayton* (OH) *Daily News,* p. 2E.
Clinton, H. R. (1996a). *It takes a village and other lessons children teach us.* New York: Simon & Schuster.
Clinton, H. R. (1996b, January 7). Talking it over: First lady: Make lists her resolutions, hopes for '96. *Dayton* (OH) *Daily News,* p. 3E.
Clinton, H. R. (1996c, January 14). Talking it over: It takes hard work to nurture and raise a family. *Dayton* (OH) *Daily News,* p. 2E.
Clinton, H. R. (1996d, January 21). Talking it over: King's message rings true in today's world. *Dayton* (OH) *Daily News,* p. 4E.
Clinton, H. R. (1996e, February 4). Talking it over: First lady, make divorce harder when kids are involved. *Dayton* (OH) *Daily News,* p. 2E.
Clinton, H. R. (1996f, February 11). Talking it over: Groups interact to work toward peace in Bosnia. *Dayton* (OH) *Daily News,* p. 3E.
Clinton, H. R. (1996g, February 18). Talking it over: Reeve's courage sends strong message to those in power. *Dayton* (OH) *Daily News,* p. 3E.
Clinton, H. R. (1996h, February 25). Talking it over: Promising military careers cut short by unfair AIDS policy. *Dayton* (OH) *Daily News,* p. 2E.

Clinton, H. R. (1996i, March 10). Talking it over: Adolescent girls face wealth of opportunities, risks. *Dayton* (OH) *Daily News,* p. 2E.

Clinton, H. R. (1996j, March 17). Talking it over: V-chip new beginning for parents. *Dayton* (OH) *Daily News,* p. 2E.

Clinton, H. R. (1996k, March 31). Talking it over: Lady Bird's environmentalism still blooming across nation. *Dayton* (OH) *Daily News,* p. 2E.

Coontz, S. (1996). In search of the American family: Where are the good old days? *Modern Maturity, 39*(3), 36-43.

Crable, R. E. (1990). Organizational rhetoric as the fourth great system: Theoretical, critical, and pragmatic implications. *Journal of Applied Communication Research, 18,* 115-128.

Depoe, S. P. (1990). Requiem for liberalism: Therapeutic and deliberative functions of nostalgic appeals in Edward Kennedy's address to the 1980 Democratic National Convention. *Southern Communication Journal, 55,* 175-190.

Dow, B. J., & Condit, C. M. (2005). The state of the art in feminist scholarship in communication. *Journal of Communication, 55,* 448-478.

Dow, B. J., & Tonn, M. B. (1993). 'Feminine style' and political judgment in the rhetoric of Ann Richards. *Quarterly Journal of Speech, 79,* 286-302.

Dozier, D. M, Grunig, L. A., & Grunig, J. E. (2001). Public relations as communication campaign. In R. E. Rice & C. K. Atkin (Eds.), *Public communication campaigns* (3rd ed., pp. 231-248). Thousand Oaks, CA: Sage.

Duffy, B., & Pound, E. T. (1996). Summer on the grill. *U.S. News & World Report, 121*(1), 24-26.

Ebron, A. (1996). Power, personality, politics, what you told us. *Family Circle, 109*(15), 16.

Eddings, J., & Barone, M. (1996). Eyes on the prize. *U.S. News & World Report, 121*(7), 22-29.

Edelman, M. (1988). *Constructing the political spectacle.* Chicago: University of Chicago Press.

Fineman, H., & Miller, M. (1993). Hillary's role. *Newsweek, 121*(7), 18-25.

Funk, C. L. (1996). The impact of scandal on candidate evaluations: An experimental test of the role of candidate traits. *Political Behavior, 18,* 1-24.

Furstenberg, F. (1988, September 1). The family since '80: Rhetoric vs. reality. *The Wall Street Journal,* p. A16.

Gates, H. L., Jr. (1996). Hating Hillary. *The New Yorker, 72*(2), 116-121, 123-128, 130-133.

Gibbs, N., & Duffy, M. (1996). Just heartbeats away. *Time, 148*(2), 24-26, 28.

Golay, M., & Rollyson, C. (1996). *Where America stands 1996: What Americans think and need to know about today's most critical issues.* New York: Wiley.

Goldberg, C. (1996, August 14). Dole's wife and daughter push for their candidate. *The New York Times,* p. A15.

Goldman, P., & Mathews, T. (1992). The specter of scandal. *Newsweek, 120*(27), 32-36.

Goldman, P., & Miller, M. (1994). The message struggle. *Newsweek, 124*(19), 38-40.

Graber, D. A. (1992). *Public sector communication: How organizations manage information.* Washington, DC: Congressional Quarterly.

Grunig, L. A. (1988). A research agenda for women in public relations. *Public Relations Review, 14*(3), 48-57.

Grunig, L. A., Toth, E. L., & Hon, L. C. (2001). *Women in public relations: How gender influences practice*. New York: Guilford Press.

Hayden, J. (2002). *Covering Clinton: The president and the press in the 1990s.* Westport, CT: Praeger.

Heath, R. L. (1997). *Strategic issues management: Organizations and public policy challenges.* Thousand Oaks, CA: Sage.

Heath, R. L. (2001). A rhetorical enactment rationale for public relations: The good organization communicating well. In R. L. Heath (Ed.), *Handbook of public relations* (pp. 31-50). Thousand Oaks, CA: Sage.

Hernandez, R., & Healy, P. D. (2005, July 13). From seeking big change to taking smaller steps: The evolution of Hillary Clinton. *The New York Times,* p. B1.

Hobsbawm, E. J., & Ranger, T. O. (Eds.). (1983). *The invention of tradition.* Cambridge, England: Cambridge University Press.

Hollihan, T. A. (2001). *Uncivil wars: Political campaigns in a media age.* Boston: St. Martin's.

Isikoff, M., & Klaidman, D. (1996). Hillary's other side. *Newsweek, 128*(1), 20-23.

Jablonski, C. J. (1988). Rhetoric, paradox, and the movement of women's ordination in the Roman Catholic Church. *Quarterly Journal of Speech, 74,* 164-183.

Jamieson, K. H. (1988). *Eloquence in an electronic age: The transformation of political speechmaking.* New York: Oxford University Press.

Jamieson, K. H. (1995). *Beyond the double bind: Women and leadership.* New York: Oxford University Press.

Jorgensen-Earp, C. (1990). The lady, the whore, and the spinster: The rhetorical use of Victorian images of women. *Western Journal of Speech Communication, 54,* 82-98.

Kahn, K. M., & Goldenberg, E. N. (1991). Women candidates in the news: An examination of gender differences in U.S. senate campaign coverage. *Public Opinion Quarterly, 55,* 180-199.

Keeter, S. (1987). The illusion of intimacy: Television and the role of candidate personal qualities in voter choice. *Public Opinion Quarterly, 51,* 344-358.

Kelly, C. E. (2001). *The rhetoric of first lady Hillary Rodham Clinton: Crisis management discourse.* Westport, CT: Praeger.

Kennedy, D. (2004, January 22). The two faces of Hillary Rodham Clinton: Boston, Phoenix. Retrieved February 9, 2005, from http://weeklywire.com/ww/06-21-99/boston_feature_1.html

Kennedy, D. M. (1970). *Birth control in America: The career of Margaret Sanger.* New Haven, CT: Yale University Press.

Klein, J. (1992). On the road again. *Newsweek, 120*(7), 31, 33.

Lawrence, J. (1996, September 25). On the road, spouses making strides. *USA Today,* pp. A1, A4.

Lewin, T. (1996, March 27). Americans attached to traditional roles for sexes, poll finds. *The New York Times,* p. A15.

Mattina, A. F. (2004). Hillary Rodham Clinton: Using her vital voice. In M. M. Wertheimer (Ed.), *Inventing a voice: The rhetoric of American first ladies of the twentieth century* (pp. 417-433). Lanham, MD: Rowman & Littlefield.

McArdle, T. (1996, November 1). When a Democrat goes wrong. *Investor's Business Daily,* pp. 1-2.

McKinnon, L., Tedesco, J.C., & Lauder, T. (2001). Political power through public relations. In R. L. Heath (Ed.), *Handbook of public relations* (pp. 557-564). Thousand Oaks, CA: Sage.

Meyrowitz, J. (1985). *No sense of place: The impact of electronic media on social behavior.* New York: Oxford University Press.

Mickey, T. (2003). *Deconstructing public relations: Public relations criticism.* Mahwah, NJ: Erlbaum.

Miller, M. (1992). Lessons of a lightning rod. *Newsweek, 120*(27), 11.

Mitchell, A. (1995, July 29). On issue of family values, Clinton unveils an agenda of his own. *The New York Times,* p. A6.

Mitchell, W. J. T. (1994). *Picture theory: Essays on verbal and visual representation.* Chicago: University of Chicago Press.

Muir, J. K., & Benitez, L. M. (1996). Redefining the role of the first lady: The rhetorical style of Hillary Rodham Clinton. In R. E. Denton, Jr., & R. L. Holloway (Eds.), *The Clinton presidency: Images, issues, and communication strategies* (pp. 139-158). Westport, CT: Praeger.

Nagourney, A. (1996, August 29). One convention goal: Displaying party's advantage with women. *The New York Times,* p. A1.

Newport, F. (1996). *Gender gap continues to benefit Clinton.* Retrieved February 9, 2005, from http://www.gallup.com/poll/releases/pr960612.asp

Newspaper Association of America. (2004). *Facts about newspapers: A statistical summary of the newspaper industry.* Retrieved February 9, 2005, from http://www.naa.org/info/facts04/circulation-daily.html

Nimmo, D., & Combs, J. E. (1980). *Subliminal politics: Myths and mythmakers in America.* Englewood Cliffs, NJ: Prentice-Hall.

Nimmo, D., & Combs, J. E. (1983). *Mediated political realities.* New York: Longman.

Osborn, M. (1986). Rhetorical depiction. In H. W. Simons & A. A. Aghazarian (Eds.), *Form, genre, and the study of political discourse* (pp. 79-107). Columbia: University of South Carolina Press.

Parry-Giles, S. J. (2000). Mediating Hillary Rodham Clinton: Television news practices and image-making in the postmodern age. *Critical Studies in Mass Communication, 17,* 205-226.

Pear, R. (1997, October 23). Child care talks return first lady to spotlight. *The New York Times,* p. A24.

Pinsdorf, M. K. (2002). Greater dead heroes than live husbands: Widows as image-makers. *Public Relations Review, 28,* 283-299.

Pleck, E. (1996, November 15). Gender gap [Message 13]. Message posted to http://www.h-net.org/~women/threads/disc-gendergapcontd

Pooley, E., & Blackman, A. (1996). Reinventing Hillary. *Time, 148*(25), 37.

Purdum, T. S. (1995, July 24). The first lady's newest role: Newspaper columnist. *The New York Times,* p. A10.

Purnell, S. E. (1978). Politically speaking, do women exist? *Journal of Communication, 28,* 150-155.

Quinn, S. (1992). Beware of Washington. *Newsweek, 120*(26), 26, 28.

Quirk, P. J., & Cunion, W. (2000). Clinton's domestic policy: The lessons of a "new Democrat." In C. Campbell & B. A. Rockman (Eds.), *The Clinton legacy* (pp. 200-225). New York: Chatham House.

Radcliffe, D. (1999). *Hillary Rodham Clinton: The evolution of a first lady.* New York: Warner Books.

Readers respond to column. (1995, September 3). *Dayton* (OH) *Daily News,* p. 2E.

Reeve, C. (1996). Speech at the 1996 Democratic National Convention. Retrieved February 9, 2005, from http://www.chrisreevehomepage.com/sp~dnc1996.html

Rifkind, L. J. (2000). Breaking out of the circle: An analysis of the gendered communication behaviors of Hillary Clinton and Sarah Netanyahu. *Social Science Journal, 37,* 611-618.

Roberts, S. V., & Barone, M. (1996). Lookin' good. *U.S. News & World Report, 121*(10), 20-26.

Sack, K. (1996, August 27). Mrs. Clinton invokes memories of famed and faulted. *The New York Times,* p. A11.

Sapienza, A.M. (1987). Image-making as a strategic function: On the language of organizational strategy. In L. Thayer (Ed.), *Organizational communication: Emerging perspectives II* (pp. 3-20). Norwood NJ: Ablex.

Seelye, K. Q. (1996, October 5). On the trail, Dole's wife seeks votes of women. *The New York Times,* p. A10.

Seitel, F. (2001). *The practice of public relations* (8th ed.). Upper Saddle River, NJ: Prentice-Hall.

Short-Thompson, C. (1997, April). *The "gender gap" in 1996: Explorations and explanations.* Paper presented at the annual meeting of the Central States Communication Association, St. Louis, MO.

Spitzack, C., & Carter, K. (1987). Women in communication studies: A typology for revision. *Quarterly Journal of Speech, 73,* 401-423.

Sproule, J. M. (1990). Organizational rhetoric and the rational-democratic society. *Journal of Applied Communication Research, 18,* 129-140.

Sullivan, P. A., & Turner, L. H. (1996). *From the margins to the center: Contemporary women and political communication.* Westport, CT: Praeger.

Toner, R. (1992, August 20). Republicans send Bush into the campaign under a banner stressing "family values." *The New York Times,* pp. A1, A18.

Toner, R. (1996, June 28). Democrats' new goal in congress: Modesty. *The New York Times,* p. A26.

Tuchman, G., Daniels, A. K., & Benét, J. (1978). *Hearth and home: Images of women in the mass media.* New York: Oxford University Press.

Turque, B., & Cohn, B. (1995). Hillary shores up a shaky base for '96. *Newsweek, 125*(23), 29.

Watson, R. P. (2000). *The presidents' wives: Reassessing the office of first lady.* Boulder, CO: Lynne Rienner.

Wertheimer, M. M. (2004). First ladies' fundamental rhetorical choices: When to speak? What to say? When to remain silent? In M. M. Wertheimer (Ed.), *Inventing a voice: The rhetoric of American first ladies of the twentieth century* (pp. 1-15). New York: Rowman & Littlefield.

West, D. M. (2003). Responsibility frenzies in news coverage: Dissecting a Hillary Clinton rumor. *Harvard International Journal of Press/Politics, 8,* 104-114.

Zarefsky, D. (1986). *President Johnson's war on poverty: Rhetoric and history.* University: University of Alabama Press.

chapter 3

Avon Calling—You! The Influence of Corporate Sponsorship of the 3-Day Walk for Breast Cancer

Heidi Hatfield Edwards

Between 1998 and 2002, Avon, the cosmetics company, sponsored a series of extreme fundraising events to raise money for breast cancer.[1] The scope of the Avon 3-Day Breast Cancer Walks was massive, including thousands of participants, contributors, and spectators. In 4 years, more than 58,000 participants (for all events, including repeat walkers) walked in the 3-day, 60-mile event in cities throughout the United States, including Atlanta, Boston, Denver, Los Angeles, Miami, New York, San Francisco, and Washington, DC. With each walker required to raise almost $2,000 each, the event series raised almost $186 million[2] for breast cancer education, programs to help medically underserved groups, and breast cancer research (Avon, 2002b; Pallotta Teamworks, 2001a. 2001b).

This chapter looks at the Avon 3-Day Walk case as a ceremonial event in which a company reaches outside its established enterprise and engages in a dialogue with an active public about a social issue. The recent growth of corporate involvement in social issues is a noteworthy phenomenon in today's strategic business practices. What was once called *philanthropy* or *corporate citizenship* is now part of a larger strategic plan that is widely publicized with direct links between a cause and a corporation. Little research has directly tackled the impact of the corporate voice on how society deals with issues such as health, education, and the environment (e.g., Gwinner, 1997; Pope & Voges, 1999; Rifon, Choi, Trimble, & Li, 2004; Smith, 2004), and it has been advanced largely from the fields of advertising and marketing. This case study addresses how the experience shared by Avon and a highly involved public shaped participants' perspectives on breast cancer and personal efficacy. The chapter then focuses on critical concerns regarding power and corporate involvement in social issues, particularly an organization's ability to control others' contributions toward those issues, the potential for corporations to define policy or solutions to an issue, and the questionable outcomes for corporations using causes to build new-member identification.

CORPORATE ADVOCACY, CEREMONIAL DISCOURSE, AND ENTHYMEMES

Cheney's (1991) work on organizational communication extended the traditional definition of the *rhetorical speaker* to include contemporary organizations. In his view,

> the contemporary bureaucratic organization is fundamentally a rhetorical enterprise. The organization seeks to establish or reinforce certain value premises in the minds of its audiences so that members of the audience will make decisions in accord with the preferences of the controlling members of the organization. (p. 8)

He argued further that in our society, corporations (or organizations) have historically been granted legal status as "legal persons" who may speak with only slightly limited First Amendment freedom. When organizations defend themselves in courts of law, lobby policymakers, and make ceremonial statements, they are speakers, sources of messages, and public rhetors.

Rhetorical analyses of public relations practice tends to focus on the communicator and message. Recognition of the role of audience—or targeted public—as an active participant in the communication process is largely absent in studies of organizational rhetoric (Toth, 1992; cf. Crable & Vibbert, 1983). "A rhetorical paradigm of public relations," Heath (1993) wrote, "captures the meaning that shapes the social reality by which people have similar thoughts, contest points of view, make judgments, and regulate their behavior and that of others" (pp. 142-143). The absence of audience roles in studies about corporate rhetoric may be due to the way power in organizational relationships is assumed to be held almost entirely by an organization, not individuals. Tompkins and Cheney (1985) defined *organizational power* as the "ability or capacity of a person or persons to control the contributions of others toward a goal" (p. 180). The object of an organization's control, that is, the audience of its rhetoric, is the people who can help the organization reach its goals. If power is held by the organization, it should always reach its objectives.

Yet we know by failed ventures and other internal and external organizational failures that organizations do not always succeed in attaining goals. They cannot necessarily "control the contributions of others" because the audience has the ability and will to interpret messages and make decisions that may or may not benefit the organization. In fact, the audience may manifest itself as a new organization in varying degrees of structure that can create dynamic power relationships between a corporation and its stakeholders. That is not to say the audience has complete power either, but that the network of power relations is complex. Fiske (1987) and Condit (1989) argued that audience members are empowered by the ability to construct meaning from texts, but that empowerment is limited:

> The structure of meanings in a text is a miniaturization of the structure of subcultures in society—both exist in a network of power relations, and the textual struggle for meaning is the precise equivalent of the social struggle for power. (Fiske, 1987, p. 392)

Condit (1989) warned against overstating the audience's will and influence and urged researchers to consider the audience as variable and part of the whole communication process:

> The audience's variability is a consequence of the fact that humans, in their inherent character as audiences, are inevitably situated in a communication *system*, of which they are a part, and hence have some influence within, but by which they are also influenced. (p. 120)

This communication system or process that promotes give and take between both a speaker and an audience is an important concept in understanding the power of corporate rhetoric. For a corporation that fosters dialogue with its publics, that organization is imbued with a kind of communication power because it values and shares points of reference that engenders *identification* with its publics. Organizational members are key to making this happen. To reach its goals, an organization must not merely have its own identity, but it must also have members who identify *with* it. According to Tompkins and

Cheney (1985), "A decision maker identifies with an organization when he or she desires to choose the alternative that best promotes the perceived interests of that organization" (p. 194). Tompkins and Cheney were referring specifically to internal organizational members; however, this also applies to external publics, like consumers, policymakers, and, in this case, event participants.

Notice that identification takes us beyond mere persuasion, which typifies many public relations texts. Burke (1950) argued that identification does not come by way of individuals aligning their goals and ideals with an organization, but rather by the organization showing how its values align with those invited to identify with it. Further, strong identification with one group means dissociation with other groups (Burke, 1950). In the political arena one is either a Democrat or Republican (or Libertarian, Independent, etc.). In marketing, brand loyalty illustrates this concept. Are you a Coke person or Pepsi person? In a restaurant that only serves Pepsi, the devoted Coke drinker opts for water. To identify with one group and therefore dissociate with other groups has important implications for choices individuals make in regard to those organizations with which they choose to identify.

Identification is achieved through the use of *enthymemes* (Tompkins & Cheney, 1985), which are the premises drawn from audience values and beliefs and used by the speaker to make an argument (Aristotle, 1991). Identification is more ephemeral than persuasion based on enthymemes. Audiences participate in their own persuasion by thinking about their own commonplace beliefs and inserting those beliefs into the speaker's argument. Tompkins and Cheney (1985) argued that Aristotle's definition of enthymeme must be operationalized differently when discussing how it is used by organizations. The difference is the source of major audience premises.

For Aristotle's definition, distinguished by Tompkins and Cheney as enthymeme$_1$, "premises are *assumed* to be in the mind and the messages of the 'audience'" based on a "variety of socializing forces" and previous experience (1985, p. 189). That is, emphasis is on the public's values and how well they match the organization's values, whereas in ethymeme$_2$, the organization is one of those socializing forces, influencing values and beliefs in its members. Therefore, as a premise source the emphasis of the secondary enthymeme is on the organization's values and the decision-making premises it teaches, either explicitly or implicitly. In socializing its members, the organization may first draw on ethymeme$_1$ to build identification, but to reach its goals it uses ethymeme$_2$ to create new shared values and encourage members to make decisions consistent with organizational objectives. An organization may be able to inspire publics to accept its position and values, unless the target public already holds those enthymemes in some shape or form. This suggests that ethymeme$_2$ does not work in its purest form except in dealing with organizational members per se. The key to ethymeme$_2$ is that, over time, organizational members make decisions without realizing that the underlying rationale may have been inculcated by the organization in the first place. Therefore, the most powerful identification messages combine the two enthymematic approaches so the values sources blend until they are barely distinguishable (Tompkins & Cheney, 1985).

The power relationships between an organization and its publics, then, constantly shift back and forth as a public negotiates and interprets meanings (Condit, 1989; Fiske, 1987) based on enthymematic messages (Tompkins & Cheney, 1985). The power of both the corporate speaker (or rhetor) and the audience is limited by the social constructions they both must use to understand each other within the communication process. Studying the process as a whole allows us to better understand the rhetorical process by which organizations build identification with publics and through which publics contribute to the dialogue.

The study of the Avon Breast Cancer 3-Day Walk offers a unique analysis of how an organization worked with an external public and used ethymeme$_1$ and ethymeme$_2$ to manage the public's identity with the organization and thus reach the organizational goals related to the event. It is an analysis of the public's role as an organization member and how it negotiated the organizational rhetoric and created meaning that was oftentimes, but not always, consistent with Avon's epideictic goals. The remainder of this chapter explores some of the findings from a study of the Avon Walk and implications for corporations that choose to participate in social issue advocacy. Evidence presented here is from data collected using multiple qualitative methods. I begin with a description of Avon's involvement in the breast cancer issue, followed by its discourse regarding the 3-Day Walk and participants' experiential understanding of that discourse, and finally a discussion of Avon's communicative power and its limitations.

AVON'S VALUES—A COMPANY FOR WOMEN

Avon began employing "Avon ladies" to sell cosmetics door-to-door in 1886. It now has 3.9 million representatives in 143 countries and sales of more than $6 billion per year. Widely recognized as a "woman's company," Avon has cultivated that image through comprehensive corporate outreach campaigns targeted toward women's issues: breast cancer (Breast Cancer Crusade), fitness (Avon Running—Global Women's Circuit), entrepreneurship (Women of Enterprise Progam), and overall health (Worldwide Fund for Women's Health) [Avon Annual Report, 2002a]. All of these programs are administered by the Avon Foundation, which was founded in 1955 to "provide much needed services and financial support in the cities, towns and villages where Avon does business." The Foundation's mission is to "improve the lives of women and their families" (Avon Foundation, 2005).

Avon's link to primarily female issues is a deliberate effort to address its constituents' needs and interests, a clear example of ethymeme.$_1$ Through research, Avon determined that health issues, particularly breast cancer, resonated with its key publics. In a 1994 interview, a company spokesperson noted, "We felt the sincere need, almost an imperative, to continue to find ways to give back to the people who have sold our products for 108 years and to the people who have bought them" (Larson, 1994, p. 17). Using ethymeme,$_2$ the spokesperson attributed the success of Avon's outreach to how well the causes match company values, which, according to its website, are "trust, respect, belief, humility and high standards" (Avon Products, 2002b). Thus, Avon began its communication about breast cancer by coordinating its values with those of its consumers and strengthening its persuasive messages by using both types of enthymeme to encourage member identity.

The largest of the Foundation's programs, the Avon Worldwide Fund for Women's Health, began in 1992, and has fundraising initiatives in 40 countries, on four continents. Most of the $250 million raised for the Fund has been through its U.S.-based Avon Breast Cancer Crusade, which began in 1993. The cause-marketing campaign raises money for breast cancer education programs, patient services for medically underserved women (low-income, un- and underinsured), and breast cancer research. Avon raises funds for the Crusade by selling "pink ribbon products," and sponsoring breast cancer walks (Avon Foundation, 2001). In 2001, Avon expanded its pink ribbon product line, launching the "Kiss Goodbye to Breast Cancer" campaign: lipsticks with names like Courageous Spirit, Crusade Pink, Strength, and Triumph. It also introduced a new fragrance, Little Black Dress, in conjunction with an online charity auction of celebrity dresses (Avon, 2002b). Sales of Avon's "pink ribbon products," including Courageous Spirit, Crusade Pink, Strength, and Triumph lipsticks, contributed more than $6.5 million in 2004, compared to $5.1 million in 2003 (Avon Foundation, 2005).

The issue of breast cancer adds to the complexity of the identification process because it is through this issue that the organization reaches out to a particular constituency using both enthymematic premises to draw in new members. Avon defines the issue in its terms, but the values of the breast cancer cause become the defining elements for enthymematic arguments originating from both the organization and the audience.

The bulk of the funds raised for the crusade came from the 3-Day Walks. Avon partnered with Pallotta Teamworks (henceforth identified as Pallotta), a for-profit cause-marketer specializing in extreme events, for the first Walk in October 1998. More than 2,000 people walked from Santa Barbara to Malibu, California, raising $4.2 million for the breast cancer cause (Pallotta, 2001). In 1999, the company sponsored four Walks in cities across the United States; it sponsored nine in 2001 and hosted 13 in 2002 before dropping its sponsorship of the 3-Day and subsequently creating a new, comparable event for 2003.

The Walks are challenging, both physically and emotionally. In order to participate, walkers had to raise $1,900. Then they walked an average of 20 miles for each of three consecutive days. In four years, more than 58,000 walkers raised almost $186 million for breast cancer education, programs to help medically underserved groups gain access to mammograms and other services to enhance early detection of the disease, and, since 2000, for research (Avon, 2001; Pallotta Teamworks, 2001a).

The relationships that exist within this cause-marketing event are complex and vast in number. Walkers volunteer their bodies and their fundraising capabilities, and they spend months preparing to walk in the name of breast cancer for Avon. Training in Avon t-shirts and wearing "Ask me about the 3-Day" buttons, walkers became spokespeople for the event, breast cancer, and Avon. They become extensions of the organization. The following demonstrates how Avon uses enthymematic arguments to suggest beliefs the audience already holds which create a community of organizational members making decisions and helping the organization reach its goal to raise money for breast cancer. Although recruitment begins with enthymeme_1 premises, enthymeme_2 messages quickly emerge in Avon's sponsorship, symbols linking the company to the cause, and control of how monies are used.

The next section explains how the walkers negotiate Avon's discourse to create their own understanding of how they fit within the organization, and how this negotiation takes place in context with walkers' competing identities and goals. It also illustrates how the power of an organization to persuade member identification may be limited by intervening enthymematic arguments within the context of the third element in this organization-public relationship, the cause.

THE AVON 3-DAY WALK

The Avon Breast Cancer 3-Day Walk is painstakingly orchestrated—from beginning to end—by Avon and the event producer, Pallotta Teamworks. In artfully crafted language, they construct a very particular representation of the Walk as physically challenging, emotionally rewarding, and as an event that past participants insist was "the greatest experience of their lives"

(Pallotta Teamworks, 2001b, p. 17). This use of ethymeme$_1$ is complemented by messages implementing ethymeme$_2$: Avon and Pallotta (because Pallotta was the producer behind the scenes, I refer to the messages as coming from Avon) recruit "mainstream citizens" to accomplish "powerful things" with them (p. 6).

When walkers registered, Avon's use of enthymeme$_2$ actively increased, whereas enthymeme$_1$ premises remained constant. The organization sent them an Avon 3-Day t-shirt and a binder full of material to help them prepare for the event. Part of the binder was fundraising information: sample letters, suggestions, tips, creative ideas, and information about breast cancer. The other part was an introduction to the basics of the Walk—what to expect, how to prepare—and a training guide. The training guide included a mileage chart, suggestions for how to build up to long distances over several months, and information on nutrition, stretching, equipment, and safety. The contents of the binder and guide contained the messages that emphasized both types of enthymematic arguments in an effort to get walkers to approach training and fundraising in such a way as to meet organizational objectives.

Enthymeme$_2$ is at work when the walker is inexperienced or unaware of the importance of training and safety issues. Avon becomes the source of good health and safety information. Enthymeme$_1$ is at play for those walkers who already participate in walks or other forms of exercise. Avon reemphasized this information in monthly newsletters, which also contained lists of locally organized training walks and inspirational messages from survivors. Walker coaches contacted participants by telephone and email, checking their training and fundraising. Evidence that participants relied on and welcomed this constant flow of information as they prepared for the Walk appeared throughout conversations with them. For example, Frankie[3] noted that on her long training walks, she "followed every guideline that they had mailed me or put in that brochure."

Avon's use of enthymeme$_1$ and enthymeme$_2$ (same message with different enthymematic meaning depending on the walker's background) gave participants literal guidelines on how to become members of the organization in a sense. Walkers chose to accept these guidelines as signified by their participation. Thus, this self-selection ensured participants began the experience with a set of premises (enthymeme$_1$) consistent with organizational premises (enthymeme$_2$) and, through the socialization process, were perhaps more inclined to make decisions consistent with organizational objectives in terms of training and fundraising (Tompkins & Cheney, 1985). Yet it was only when walkers began to implement the guidelines and merge these premises did they begin to construct a collective identity, defining themselves within the 3-Day community. Interestingly, however, identification was not with Avon. Enthymeme$_2$ as envisioned by Tompkins and Cheney does not seem to work in this setting the same way it does in the workplace where organizational membership is a direct outcome of the identification process.

The Shared Experience of the 3-Day— Constructing a Collective Identity from Identities

Participants came to the 3-Day with a wide range of individual motivations and expectations, and from different places in their lives; for each, the Walk fulfilled a personal need. These formed the foundation for ethymeme$_1$ arguments about the day and participants' role in it. For some, it was a need to fight against a disease that had taken something from them: their own health, a loved one, their self-confidence. Frankie said, "It has given me the opportunity to 'slay the dragon'. . . . It has given me the opportunity to fight back." For Frankie and other survivors, the Walk was a way to take action against a disease over which they seemingly have no control. For others, participation was a way to feel strength, access inner resources, and build self-esteem. Sylvia said she signed up for the Walk as a way to focus on herself, her well-being. It began as a way for her to adopt a healthier lifestyle and lose weight. Through participation in the 3-Day, she could be "selfish," but with a greater purpose—raising money for breast cancer. The fact that there was a cause legitimated the time she was taking for herself.

Thus, the 3-Day began as an individual experience, and Avon used traditional enthymematic arguments (enthymeme$_1$) to begin the identification process. Walkers made a decision to walk drawing on personal reasons. Many discussed how they started training by walking alone or with a friend a couple of miles a day. Then, following the Avon 3-Day guidelines, their once solitary training expanded to include other walkers.

> Adelaide: I can remember being daunted by thinking that I had to walk seven or eight miles. How am I going to do that? . . . So I would start out and then go a little longer and . . . I met some other people and we all exchanged email addresses. Then this whole email exchange started happening and there were a few of us that decided to make our training a little bit more formal. Instead of just training by ourselves, we would meet. . . . Then the group starting growing and growing and before long . . . there were between 10 and 14 of us who trained together.

Shared walks were a sensible way to train. Here, in the coming together of walkers, was the beginning of a community—in some sense, not yet a community, but a group of people brought together by practical necessity. Other walkers had the same individual goals: finishing the Walk and raising money. They had the same time frame, they faced the same long training sessions.

Walking together, they were more likely to adhere to Avon's training suggestions, reminding each other to stretch, hydrate, wear proper shoes, be safe. "Train with other walkers. Meet on the weekend—at the library, at Stone Mountain, wherever. Here's a list of training walks," Avon advised. Carey (1975) called our attention to the importance of these everyday activities in the creation and maintenance of culture. He noted:

> The activities we collectively call communication–having conversations, giving instructions, imparting knowledge, sharing significant ideas, seeking information, entertaining and being entertained–are so ordinary and mundane that it is difficult for them to arrest our attention. (p. 11)

"Bring your water bottle, energy bars, an extra pair of socks." The sentiment is so ordinary and mundane, and yet, in these activities, community is created, for Avon might have added: "Bring your stories and a listening ear, and maybe a tissue or two. There's plenty of time, when you're walking seven or eight or ten or fifteen or twenty miles, to listen and share." And so, training took on new dimensions: storytelling, friendships, and bonding:

> Adelaide: We have so much fun on those [training] walks. We talk about everything under the sun, from recipes to husbands, to you name it. . . . I mean meeting the women from all different walks of life that I would have never come in contact with otherwise has been really amazing. That has been great—the camaraderie that has come out of it. . . .

What had begun as an individual project became a shared one, no longer a community of practical necessity, but one of ritual. Walkers, talking as they walked, shared values and stories about their lives, the Walk, and breast cancer. Two- and three-time walkers shared their experiences, giving advice and telling the first-timers what to expect. Thus, enthymeme$_2$ emerged in walkers' discussions as they blended their own motivations with the corporate communications and shared them with each other.

As a motivational tool, Avon materials distributed to walkers reminded them to remember why they were walking: "You are making a powerful statement, raising money and awareness for all the people who have, have had, or will have breast cancer." Similar to the training regimen, enthymematic focus depended on walkers' motivations. Some came to the Walk motivated by the cause, therefore, enthymeme$_1$ came into play. For many, breast cancer was peripheral and messages about the cause were founded in enthymeme$_2$ premises. But participants said that as they shared with other walkers, their understanding of "what they were doing" and "why they were doing it" changed.

As their understanding changed, the two types of enthymematic premises became intertwined. For example, Eileen trained with a large group and in doing so, she came to think of her participation not as her personal "sacrifice" for a cause, but as part of a group effort to reach a common destination:

> Eileen: There is a lady that walks around Stone Mountain who will be at the 3-Day Walk and she has one leg. She uses a prosthetic leg . . . and seeing that gave me even more incentive to keep going because she can do it with one leg and I am doing it on two. So I am thinking it is really making me a stronger person and making me realize the sacrifices in life that you have to do to achieve your common goal.

Eileen was making choices—in her words, sacrifices—that were consistent with organizational goals (enthymeme$_2$). Eileen's increased self-awareness was a feeling expressed by many study participants. They talked of becoming aware of breast cancer, its dimensions, and its effects, as they strode side-by-side with a survivor, with a survivor's sister, mother, or friend. Katie said she was raising money for "everybody"—the nameless, faceless people with breast cancer—until she started training with several survivors and heard their stories. Mary Katherine, too, talked of intensely emotional stories told by a training partner that changed her perspective on the disease and on those who struggled to survive:

> Mary Katherine: To hear her stories about thinking that it was going to be her last Christmas . . . and giving ornaments and telling her husband, . . . "I don't mind if you get married again, but . . . make sure that my daughters get these ornaments." I still have cold chills about that, when she told me that. She is a remarkable lady.

As these stories unfolded and became part of the folklore within the 3-Day community, walkers began claiming these premises as their own—enthymeme$_1$—and adding their own stories to the collective consciousness. Linda said she became friends with the mother of a young woman with breast cancer, and during their training walks she listened to her new friend share her concerns, feelings, and frustrations as she watched her daughter battle the disease. The young woman died. Linda went to the funeral; she comforted her friend. Suddenly, for Linda, as for so many others, breast cancer was no longer statistics on a piece of paper, no longer the story of a stranger in a newsletter. It was real. It had a face. It was her friend. Linda had gone from considering the cause as an afterthought, to viewing her participation in the 3-Day as a personal statement about breast cancer. For her, the 3-Day now had a different meaning.

Training together, sharing their stories, and creating rituals, moved walkers from their individual motivations to experiencing collective inspiration, but it was just one step in the identification process. As they continued preparing for the Walk through fundraising, the conflation of relationships and enthymematic premises became ever greater, the walkers' identities more focused. Yet, the data indicate this identification was not with Avon but with the other walkers, the event, and the cause. Avon's fundraising and training suggestions invited participants to create their own enthymematic arguments, building on ethymeme$_1$ presented in the recruiting stage, whereas ethymeme$_2$ arguments were limited to premises regarding the Walk and breast cancer and could also be coopted by the walkers, who created their own enthymematic premises in the context of the "new" organization.

Enthymeme$_1$ was employed even further in reaching out to potential donors. Avon's literature suggested walkers ask potential donors to share their stories. "Give people a personal reason—remind them of the importance of the issue through their own experiences, urge them to make a personal connection, and they will give"—ethymeme$_1$. It was, in essence, issuing an invitation to join the 3-Day community and, in doing so, participate in the fight against breast cancer. "Share your stories with me," walkers said in their letters. "Let me walk for you, for someone you care about. Give me names to carry with me on the Walk. Let me represent *your* stories."

This tactic of inviting contributors to share stories had powerful implications beyond the expediency of fundraising. First, donor stories were now added to and mixed with the folklore of the Walk. Walkers drew on this folklore, weaving it into narratives to sustain the community—to build identification with each other using the traditional enthymeme. When Elizabeth's training group started to complain, frustrated at all the time given up, and sometimes at the pain, she motivated them with stories that came from donors, friends, and family, using enthymeme$_1$ tools provided by donors to motivate her fellow walkers:

> Elizabeth: I could only listen to them whine a little bit, and I would say, "This is why we are doing it: because we have a good friend who is 45 and is dying of breast cancer and we have to do this for her and for everybody else, and for you, and for our daughters. . . ."

Susan wrote the names her donors sent her on a t-shirt. During the Walk, people wore t-shirts and buttons with names and pictures of people with breast cancer, stories made visible in material artifacts.

The more stories walkers shared, the more people they perceived themselves to be walking for on behalf of others. They were training with survivors, getting names, and hearing stories from their donors and their friends' donors. Each story added another face to the disease. With each new face, the walkers' relationships to the cause also seemed to strengthen:

> Joyce: Since I have done this walk, I have come across people that are close to me who, either their mothers [or] friends are going through it now and it is hitting home. I am just hoping, and like I said praying, that . . . we raise enough money to make a difference. So that next year if I decide to walk that hopefully I won't have to know that somebody's mother is taking chemo and that somebody else's mother, who they opened up . . . and then closed her right back up because they couldn't do anything.

Equally important, the accumulated stories raised awareness of the magnitude of the problem.

> Franklin: It was just incredible the type of stories I got from people that gave me money because, I hadn't known their mothers had breast cancer or died from breast cancer. And I did not really know it from knowing them, but they then donated and told me things like that.

Breast cancer touches a lot of people. Of course, 3-Day literature says that—with numbers: "This year, approximately 182,000 women in the United States will be diagnosed with invasive breast cancer" (Pallotta Teamworks, 2001b, p. 16). As well, newsletters have stories about walker survivors. And, walkers expect some of the people they walk with will be survivors. But walkers have a list, sometimes a very long list, of people they know, or feel as though they know, who have experience with the disease, and they are walking for them.

As walkers described their experiences, a subtle shift occurred in how they talked about themselves in the early days of their involvement, after months of training and fundraising, and after having completed the walk. Over time they constructed a "walker identity" that became more well defined with each new experience. Yet, this was not an *Avon* walker identity, which is an important distinction. Perhaps as a socializing agent, Avon's discourse was not socializing participants into organizational membership or brand loyalty, but rather it socialized participants into a new identity more closely associated with the cause than with the company.

Initially, participants had viewed themselves merely as individuals "walking in the 3-Day." In the process of the 3-Day, they became "3-Day walkers" joined in symbolic community. Assuming this walker identity, they dissociated themselves from those outside the 3-Day community. Walkers trained and raised money, and with their commitment to meeting the demands of the Walk, they formed a rich folklore, shared values, and created rituals. By the time of the actual Walk, they were different from who they were when they first registered. They became a community, the "experienced rubric in and through which people read, think, feel, love, and plan" (Jensen & Pauly, 1997, p. 158), formed through an ongoing, dynamic process. They are members of the 3-Day organization (but not necessarily Avon)—in essence building a new organization that has its own enthymematic arguments that could be designated as $enthymeme_2$, but that are separate from the corporate sponsor.

Through identification and socialization, the walkers' "vision is narrowed" (Tompkins & Cheney, 1985) so when making decisions they were more likely to consider values and knowledge and behavioral alternatives that corresponded with the organization's interests. Members held multiple identities (with other groups, family, etc.) that they drew on to make decisions, and sometimes these identities competed, especially when priorities conflicted. Avon strengthened the relationships among walkers' identities by using already-held beliefs and values to help build the walker identity; thus, walkers were more likely to make decisions consistent with 3-Day organizational goals. Therefore, training and safety became important to walkers, as did community, kindness, and raising money for specific breast cancer initiatives. Avon's goals for combating the disease became walkers' goals. Avon attained "organizational power" as defined by Tompkins and Cheney (1985) in its ability to control the contributions of walkers toward 3-Day Walk objectives. Yet, from a public relations perspective, its power as a company was limited because of the conflated identities—it was not building membership or brand loyalty in Avon the company, but rather in the Avon Breast Cancer 3-Day Walk.

This power shift shows the tenuous nature of corporate power when the organization steps out of its natural role as a product or service provider and tries to build identification primarily through shared cultural values. In this instance, $enthymeme_1$ and $enthymeme_2$ are fluid to the point that the premises originating from the organization ($enthymeme_2$) are carried by employees and walkers who become representatives of the cause (and the company that sponsored the Walks). These premises are indistinguishable from those initiated from the audience ($enthymeme_1$) and become part of a larger cultural context that manifests itself in identification with the socially redeeming image of the breast cancer fight and Avon's role in it. A new organizational membership is born and the Tompkins and Cheney $enthymeme_2$ is no longer the corporation's premise (that is, Avon's) but an identification enthymeme related to the new organization—the Walk, which benefits from the many identities participants enacted with it. The company was building goodwill with the walker community, the breast cancer community, and the communities within which it conducted the Walks.

Using enthymemes as Avon did has the potential to disrupt an organization's communicative power adversely. As Foucault (1980) argued, power is based on human relationships and negotiated through discourse. "Discourse transmits and produces power; it reinforces it, but also undermines and exposes it, renders it fragile and makes it possible to thwart it" (Foucault, 1978, p. 101). Walkers were able to take Avon's messages—its guidelines, suggestions, motivators—and appropriate them for their own use. As Bakhtin (1981) asserted, "Prior to this moment of appropriation, the word . . . exists in other people's mouths, in other people's contexts, serving other people's intentions: it is from there that one must take the word, and make it one's own" (pp. 293-294). This "responsive understanding" (p. 280) creates the dialogue through which power is negotiated. Walkers made Avon's discourse their own, and in the process, created an identity separate from Avon.

In the Avon case, even though organizational power may be thwarted if walkers do not identify with Avon the company, corporate power is not benign. In focus groups, participants revealed their impressions of the company as the sponsor of the event. They each made a connection between Avon (the "cosmetic company") and breast cancer (a "women's issue"). Although many credited Avon for its philanthropy, they recognized the company's involvement was not purely altruistic. "I am sure they have some kind of belief in it," said Susan, "but I would think it is a good, positive message to be involved with women and women's issues." Sharon connected the company's history of giving to women's causes to its current involvement in breast cancer issues, but also made a link to the positive publicity that comes from the event:

> Sharon: Avon has been sponsoring women's events for a long, long time . . . I used to play competitive golf, so I have known that Avon has always been involved in women's athletics and been a big sponsor of that. But, I think they have probably gotten more press because they don't just say the 3-Day. They say, oh, you are doing the *Avon* 3-Day. . . . Everybody knows that it is associated with Avon. . . .

As corporations embrace causes, defining them and the answers to social problems, they are exerting power beyond the scope of their original functions because of their alliance with the cause. Literature focused on societal implications of corporate involvement in social issues is primarily critical of the practice, wary of corporate motives and raising legal and ethical questions. Critics point to questionable corporate relationships (Salmon & Sun, 2002), the impact on giving by individuals (e.g., Parpis, 2000), methods by which funds are disbursed and beneficiary decisions are made (Briggs, 2001; Groves, 2002; Morello, 2001), political implications of corporate giving

(Plys, 2001a, 2001b), and the potential for commercialization of disease (Ehrenreich, 2001; Lieberman, 2001; Taylor, 1994).

The Avon case exemplifies some of the problems associated with corporate involvement in social issues. It also illustrates much of the dynamics of organizational power through public relations efforts. Perhaps as a consequence of Avon's inability to observe or measure direct results of its efforts to build corporate identification through the 3-Day, the company discontinued its sponsorship of the event and shortly after started a new, very similar event. Its withdrawal from the 3-Day threw the charity event into chaos, and, although problems were eventually resolved, the power of Avon to disrupt ongoing fundraising activities for breast cancer is evidence supporting critics' concerns—and the subtlety of enthymeme$_2$ as a means of image building.

CONCLUSION

This research has implications for the study of relationships between corporations and active publics, particularly as they relate to corporate involvement in social issues. As discussed earlier in this chapter, the increasing presence of the corporate voice in social issues places those companies engaging in cause-related corporate outreach outside their traditional domain and into the "business" of shaping socially constructed values. These findings suggest that within the context of their relationships with a cause-related corporate outreach effort, audience members construct their realities, define their identities, and shape a community based on the corporation's communication and use of enthymeme$_1$ and enthymeme$_2$. In the Walk experience, the folklore and rituals walkers create outside of *Avon* provide another powerful frame of reference—enthymemes—which they use to build their identities within the 3-Day community. This implies the company's messages about breast cancer resonate within a larger social context. However, its messages may not build brand loyalty to the company, but rather are more reflected by new members' identification with the cause and/or the charitable event. The link between the sponsor's image and its brand and products seems tenuous.

Companies thinking about creating a corporate outreach program must seek to understand the role they play, constructing (or merely adapting to) community values about the issues they choose to address. As they work to improve society, striving to be good corporate citizens, corporate involvement in causes raises both practical and ethical issues. First, as suggested by these findings and earlier case studies (cf. Adkins, 1999; Sagawa & Segal, 2000), successful campaigns depend on how well company values match the values of both the cause and society. Because Avon encouraged the blending of enthymematic arguments, it gave up some of its message control and, therefore, some of its power to assimilate identification through the pure form of enthymeme$_2$. The Avon 3-Day Walk flourished in part because the company ensured its key messages (using enthymeme$_1$ and enthymeme$_2$) were reinforced by walkers' interactions within a larger cultural frame.

Second, companies that engage the public in their cause-related corporate outreach efforts have a weighty responsibility when they choose an issue. They prescribe how society should address that issue when they designate how funds are used. They must not only choose a cause that matches their corporate ethos, but they must also examine the societal implications of their prescribed "solutions" and be ready to adjust the messages they send to better fit the "responsive understanding" (Bakhtin, 1981, p. 280) of their publics.

Finally, companies must also consider their own motivations for engaging in cause-related corporate outreach. If the organization is seeking to draw new members who identify with it because of its relationship to a social issue, attaching itself to a cause may be counterproductive. Identification occurs but, as shown here, perhaps not with the sponsoring company but with a "new" organization—the 3-Day Walkers. When faced with choices, the new members will most likely make decisions that are more aligned with the cause or event than with the company's goals if those goals conflict, resulting in a loss of communicative power for the organization.

This study is an example of how public relations, when viewed as dialogue, is a constant negotiation between an organization and its publics. The communicative power within those relationships is adaptable, as enthymematic premises fluctuate with the audiences' interpretations. Whereas organizations gain power through use of enthymeme$_2$ (Tompkins & Cheney, 1985), audiences or publics are empowered by their ability to interpret organizational messages (Condit, 1989; Fiske, 1987). Although Condit and Fiske both warn that publics' power or influence is limited by the social system within which they must maneuver, the same can be said of the corporation. To borrow from Condit (1989), corporations are also "inevitably situated in a communication *system*, of which they are a part, and hence have some influence within, but by which they are also influenced" (p. 120). By taking itself out of its traditional role as product or service provider and more fully inserting itself into the social system by taking on a social issue that has its own enthymematic appeals, the corporation gave up some of its control to those who led a social cause. Objectives shifted from organizational goals to those of the cause, which could be in conflict because the company was not in business to facilitate action on social causes. If the company was trying to build brand loyalty through its association with a cause, it could have been on a precarious path toward dilution of the brand, confused identity, and mixed messages about what is important for organizational success.

NOTES

1. In May 2002, bowing to shareholder and public criticism that too little of the proceeds have gone to breast cancer (net proceeds averaged 63% of monies raised), Avon announced it would withdraw as sponsor of the Breast Cancer 3-Day Walk, breaking ties with event producer Pallotta Teamworks, but fulfill its obligation to the remaining 2002 Walks. Two months later it announced a new fundraising event—the Avon Walk for Breast Cancer—a 2-day walk strikingly similar to the 3-Day.
2. The net donation to charity from the walks was $116,979,000, or 62.82% of the $186 million raised.
3. The names of all quoted participants are pseudonyms.

REFERENCES

Adkins, S. (1999). *Cause related marketing: Who cares wins*. Boston: Butterworth-Heinemann.

Aristotle (1991). *On rhetoric: A theory of civic discourse* (G. A. Kennedy, Trans.). New York: Oxford University Press.

Avon Foundation, Inc. (2005). *2004 Avon Foundation full audited results.* Retrieved October 15, 2005, from http://www.avoncompany.com//women/avonfoundation/2004_audited_financial_statement.pdf

Avon Products, Inc. (2002a). *Avon annual report 2001*. Retrieved May 20, 2002, from http://www.avoncompany.com/investor/annualreport/2001index.html

Avon Products, Inc. (2002b). *Avon Foundation*. Retrieved May 20, 2002, from http://www.avoncompany.com/women.

Bakhtin, M. M. (1981). *The dialogic imagination* (C. Emerson & M. Holquist, Trans.). Austin: University of Texas Press.

Briggs, B. (2001, August 3). Critics: Cancer walk shortchanges charity; Avon says event's higher costs justified. *The Denver* (CO) *Post,* p. A01.

Burke, K. (1950). *A rhetoric of motives*. New York: Prentice-Hall.

Carey, J. W. (1975). A cultural approach to communication. *Communication, 2,* 1-22.

Cheney, G. (1991). *Rhetoric in an organizational society: Managing multiple identities*. Columbia: University of South Carolina Press.

Condit, C. M. (1989). The rhetorical limits of polysemy. *Critical Studies in Mass Communication, 6,* 103-122.

Crable, R. E. & Vibbert, S. L. (1983). Mobil's epideictic advocacy: "Observations" of Prometheus-bound. *Communication Monographs, 50,* 380-394.

Ehrenreich, B. (2001). Welcome to Cancerland: A mammogram leads to a cult of pink kitsch. *Harper's Magazine, 303*(1818), 43-53.

Fiske, J. (1987). *Television culture*. New York: Methuen.
Foucault, M. (1978). *The history of sexuality: An introduction* (Vol. 1) (R. Hurley, Trans.). New York: Pantheon Books.
Foucault, M. (1980). *Power/knowledge: Selected interviews and other writings, 1972-1977* (C. Gordon, Ed. & Trans.). Brighton, England: Harvester Press.
Groves, M. (2002, January, 15). Los Angeles; Judge allows AIDS rides by rival groups. *The Los Angeles Times,* p. B4.
Gwinner, K. (1997). A model of image creation and image transfer in event sponsorship. *International Marketing Review, 14*(3), 145-158.
Heath, R. L. (1993). A rhetorical approach to zones of meaning and organizational prerogatives. *Public Relations Review, 19,* 141-155.
Jensen, J., & Pauly, J. J. (1997). Imagining the audience: Losses and gains in cultural studies. In M. Ferguson & P. Golding (Eds.), *Cultural studies in question* (pp. 155-169). London: Sage.
Larson, J. (1994). If you're not committed, don't bother. *American Demographics, 16*(12), 16-17.
Lieberman, T. (2001, December 17). Companies too often look for "safe" causes: Many seek to avoid linking product sales to "scary" issues. *The Los Angeles Times,* p. S3.
Morello, C. (2001, June 20). Fundraiser with a marketer's touch: Treks stress "human potential" at cost to charities, some say. *The Washington Post,* pp. A1, A16.
Pallotta, D. (2001). *When your moment comes: A guide to fulfilling your dreams by a man who has led thousands to greatness.* San Diego, CA: Jodere Group.
Pallotta Teamworks (2001a). *Pallotta Teamworks record of impact.* Retrieved March 1, 2001, from http://www.pallottateamworks.com/pdf/1202PTWROI2001.pdf
Pallotta Teamworks (2001b). *Pallotta Teamworks catalog of 2002 events.* Los Angeles: Author.
Parpis, E. (2000). Consumer republic. *Adweek* (Eastern Edition), *41*(2), 20.
Plys, C. (2001a, February 9). Urge to do good can leave you feeling bad. *The Chicago Sun-Times,* p. 39.
Plys, C. (2001b, February 16). Even pure intentions tarnished by association. *The Chicago Sun-Times,* p. 37.
Pope, N. K. L. & Voges, K. E. (1999). Sponsorship and image: A replication and extension. *Journal of Marketing Communications, 5,* 17–28.
Rifon, N. J., Choi, S. M., Trimble, C. S., & Li, N. (2004). Congruence effects in sponsorship: The mediating role of sponsor credibility and consumer attributions of sponsor motive. *Journal of Advertising, 33*(1), 29-42.
Sagawa, S., & Segal, E. (2000). *Common interest, common good: Creating value through business and social sector partnerships.* Boston: Harvard Business School Press.
Salmon, J. L., & Sun, L. H. (2002, January 14). Charities reap millions from tie-ins: Marketing agreements worry some watchdogs, but that doesn't deter shoppers. *The Washington Post,* p. A10.
Smith, G. (2004). Brand image transfer through sponsorship: A consumer learning perspective. *Journal of Marketing Management, 20,* 457-474.
Taylor, J. S. (1994). Consuming cancer charity: Ugliness the illness, cosmetics the cure. *Z Magazine, 7*(2), 30-33.

Tompkins, P. K. & Cheney, G. (1985). Communication and unobtrusive control in contemporary organizations. In R. McPhee & P. K. Tompkins (Eds.), *Organizational communication: Traditional themes and new directions* (pp. 179-210). Beverly Hills, CA: Sage.

Toth, E. L. (1992). The case for pluralistic studies of public relations: Rhetorical, critical and systems perspectives. In E. L. Toth & R. L. Heath (Eds.), *Rhetorical and critical approaches to public relations* (pp. 3-16). Hillsdale, NJ: Erlbaum.

Power in Crisis Communication

chapter 4

A Resource Capital Analysis of Philip Morris' Values Advocacy Campaign, 1999-2001*

Amy O'Connor

Nowhere in the annals of U.S. business does a case exist like that of the tobacco industry, generally, and Philip Morris, specifically. Over the last three centuries, the pendulum has swung back and forth regarding public sentiment toward tobacco. At the end of the 19th century, less than 1 in 100 Americans used cigarettes regularly (Hilts, 1996; Kluger, 1996). By the mid-20th century, more than 50% of the adult population smoked (Hilts, 1996). Now, in the early part of the 21st century, cigarette smoking has declined to 25% of the adult population (Roper Center, 2001). In response to the changing patterns in U.S. tobacco consumption, Philip Morris[1] has worked feverishly to diversify its holdings and improve its corporate identity while retaining its commitment to tobacco.

*This chapter is part of the author's dissertation completed at Purdue University under the direction of Carl Botan. The author would like to thank Patrice Buzzanell and Josh Boyd for their support of this research.

To understand how Philip Morris has risen from the ashes of tobacco to be one of the largest and most profitable consumer packaged goods companies in the United States, this chapter first reviews the company's history as one of America's most reviled *and* revered businesses, thereby providing an historical context to analyze Philip Morris' contemporary use of values advocacy and capital. Second, the chapter offers a theoretical construct that illuminates Philip Morris' use of public relations in the form of values advocacy as a means to convert capital into forms that reinforce its desired corporate citizen persona. In doing so, this chapter examines the 1999-2001 *Working to Make a Difference: The People of Philip Morris* values advocacy campaign through the lens of capital accumulation theory and the corporation's ability to construct a narrative of social responsibility. Finally, the chapter exposes the underlying power premises inherent when corporations convert economic capital and use values advocacy campaigns as a form of public relations. For the purposes of this chapter, power is viewed as residing in "every perception, every judgment, every act" (Deetz, 1992, p. 252). In this sense, power is an invisible web supported by social structures rather than legal and judicial rules (cf. Foucault, 1980, 1982, 1986). Through this lens, the chapter is able to explore the creation, maintenance, and dissolution of philanthropy, public relations, and power and the potential social consequences of corporate largesse.

BACKGROUND

During the first half of the 20th century tobacco reigned supreme. In those heady days, the tobacco companies enjoyed profits *and* popularity. Americans associated smoking with status, sex appeal, youth, and adventure. Cigarettes were a symbol of American culture. Soldiers were given cigarettes as a part of their rations; government hospitals distributed them free to patients; and movie stars and athletes touted their goodness (Hilts, 1996; Kluger, 1996).

In 1952, however, concerns about the safety of smoking began to be raised. That year, *Reader's Digest* ran a story entitled "Cancer by the Carton," and 40% of Americans believed smoking caused lung cancer (Hilts, 1996). After the publication of the article connecting cigarette smoke to tumor growth in the journal *Cancer Research*, the major tobacco companies took an unprecedented step and met to make policy. On the morning of December 15, 1953, the leaders of the biggest tobacco companies (Philip Morris, R.J. Reynolds, Brown and Williamson, American Tobacco, U.S. Tobacco, Benson and Hedges, and Lorillard) secretly convened at the Plaza Hotel in New York City (Hilts, 1996; Kluger, 1996). The purpose of this meeting was singular: to determine a strategy to counter recent claims that smoking caused cancer. Fearful of having to acknowledge the hazards of smoking and the possibility of tobacco becoming regulated by the government, the executives agreed to collaborate for the betterment of all. Only Lorillard declined to participate, believing that silence was better than mounting a massive public relations campaign (Hilts, 1996; Kluger, 1996).

Joining the executives that historic day was John Hill, founder of the public relations firm Hill and Knowlton. He suggested that the industry could launch a massive counterattack against its critics rather than acknowledge the risks of smoking (Hilts, 1996). To accomplish such a feat, the executives agreed to pool their resources and establish an informal committee to execute the public relations functions for the industry. The committee charged with defending tobacco was named the Tobacco Industry Research Committee (TIRC). The TIRC's primary aim was the establishment of a "public relations campaign, which is positive in nature and entirely pro-cigarettes" (Hilts, 1996, p. 34). The massive, do-no-harm public relations campaign was possible due to the deep financial reservoirs of the tobacco industry and their singularity of purpose.

Economic Powerhouse

Economically, Philip Morris and the other tobacco companies did very well throughout the 20th century. In 1968, Philip Morris' operating revenues exceeded $1 billion (Philip Morris, 2002a). Then, in 1969, Philip Morris acquired Miller Brewing Company in what was to become the first of many astute acquisitions. During the 1970s, the cigarette industry continued to grow. By 1972, Philip Morris' revenues had climbed to $2 billion. By the end of the decade, revenues had quadrupled to $8 billion (Philip Morris, 2002a). These increases in revenue positioned Philip Morris to reach beyond tobacco and acquire businesses in other areas of the consumer packaged goods industry. In 1985, Philip Morris purchased General Foods for a record $5.6 billion (Kluger, 1996; Philip Morris, 2002a). The acquisition represented the largest non-oil purchase in U.S. history. This record, however, was quickly shattered in 1988 when Philip Morris acquired Kraft Foods for $13.6 billion (Kluger, 1996; Philip Morris, 2002a). Combined in 1989, Kraft and General Foods created the largest food company in the United States. Finally, in 2000 Philip Morris acquired Nabisco from rival R.J. Reynolds, further extending its reach into American households (Altria Group, 2004).

In addition to revenue generated from acquisitions, tobacco companies saw their tobacco interests increase substantially due to hefty price increases. Between 1981 and 1985, the average price for a pack of cigarettes in the United States rose from 67¢ to $1.03. By the end of the decade, Philip Morris held 42% of the overall cigarette business (Kluger, 1996). At the same time,

Philip Morris' stock price soared, and investors reaped handsome dividends. During the 1980s, the annual per-share gains, in net figures, were more than 20%. Thus, one share of Philip Morris stock bought in 1966 was worth 1,992 shares in 1989 dollars (Kluger, 1996). This growing dominance provided Philip Morris with the opportunity to transform its corporate identity.

Image Cultivation

The economic dependency of so many individuals and organizations on the cigarette industry—tobacco growers, manufacturers, investors, and governments—allowed Philip Morris to pursue a new corporate identity through cultural channels. Leading Philip Morris through its corporate metamorphosis were George Weissman (president and CEO, 1978-1983), Hamish Maxwell (CEO, 1984-1990), and Geoffrey Bible (CEO, 1991-2002). Under their leadership, Philip Morris began to use its economic capital to establish itself as a modern-day Daddy Warbucks.

Weissman cultivated a public relations campaign centered on corporate citizenship, thereby associating Philip Morris with positive social values, institutions, and ideas. He characterized Philip Morris sponsorship as follows: "We hope people will come away with a favorable impression of the company—that we are cultured human beings like everybody else, not a bunch of barbarians" (quoted in Kluger, 1996, p. 488). Through its massive public relations and philanthropic efforts, Philip Morris was largely successful in holding back the cultural tidal wave of antitobacco sentiment throughout the 1980s and early 1990s. Under Weissman's direction, Philip Morris had established cultural legitimacy in certain circles of society and increased its corporate presence among opinion and political leaders. By the late 1980s, social philanthropy was estimated at $50 million a year (Philip Morris, 2002a; Kluger, 1996). Events such as the exclusive sponsorship of the Vatican treasures (1983), the Bill of Rights Tour (1990), and the inclusion of art from the Whitney Museum in its corporate atrium for public viewing (1983), led the *Wall Street Journal* to proclaim Philip Morris "a 20th century corporate Medici, the art world's favorite company" (Freedman, 1988, p. 22, cited in Kluger, 1996, p. 619). While Philip Morris was receiving accolades from the arts community, dissent was growing within the community of suffering smokers and their attorneys.

Medici or Menace?

The "no harm from cigarettes" public relations campaign worked for nearly 40 years. In that time, the government enacted virtually no legislation that Philip Morris did not endorse, the public grew tired of the debate about cigarettes, and no plaintiff won a penny from a tobacco company in court (Hilts, 1996). The success of the campaign was described in a company memo: "Suspicion is still widespread but the lynching party seems to have been called off, at least temporarily. . . . Even adverse stories now tend to carry modified statements" (p. 17). The relative success of the massive public relations endeavor allowed Philip Morris to continue its tobacco operations relatively unhindered while expanding its influence in new directions. The industry's confidence in its public relations efforts led to an astounding amount of internal documents being centrally archived (Hilts, 1996; Orey, 1999). It was these documents that would challenge the company's public relations statements and define its communication strategy for the 21st century.

The first wrinkle in the carefully woven public relations effort came in the form of Merrell Williams, a 50-year-old paralegal with Brown and Williamson's home counsel of Wyatt, Tarrant, and Combs in Louisville, Kentucky. He was the first person to provide tobacco documents to the press. Williams described the papers this way: "The ones I picked were always the kind of things that there was just no way of denying it. . . . I had the biological studies on the hazards of smoking" (Hilts, 1996, p. 134). Shortly after the Williams documents surfaced, another Brown and Williamson employee made headlines. Jeffrey Wigand, PhD, was the chief researcher for Brown and Williamson (1989-1993) who testified to Congress and appeared on *60 Minutes* to discuss the tobacco industry's research on the negative health effects associated with smoking, the role of nicotine in cigarettes, the relationship between tar and nicotine, and industry procedures that control the level of nicotine available in different brands (Hilts, 1996; Kluger, 1996; Orey, 1999).

The information released decimated the public relations strategy of Philip Morris and the tobacco industry. First, the company would have difficulty defending its "cigarettes do no harm" mantra in the face of industry documents stating otherwise. Second, public relations efforts that presented Philip Morris as a concerned corporate citizen could now be interpreted by publics as a smokescreen rather than an act of corporate kindness. The tension between these conflicting public relations images presented itself on April 14, 1994, when executives from the tobacco companies appeared before U.S. Representative Henry Waxman's Senate Subcommittee on Health and the Environment (United States, 1995). All seven executives (Donald S. Johnston, American Tobacco Company; Thomas E. Sandefur, Brown and Williamson Tobacco Corporation; Edward Horrigan, Liggett Group, Inc.; Andrew Tisch, Lorillard Tobacco Company; Joseph Taddeo, U.S. Tobacco Company; James W. Johnston, R. J. Reynolds; William I. Campbell, Philip Morris) raised their right hands and swore to tell the truth. They each declared, as William Campbell of Philip Morris did, "I believe nicotine is not addictive" (Hilts, 1996, p. 115). At the end of the hearings it was clear that it did not matter to Congress what tobacco industry executives believed. By 1998, the aims, objectives, and strategies of the power relationship between Americans and the tobacco industry were being rewritten.

The Master Settlement Agreement

In November 1998, the nation's leading cigarette manufacturers, including Philip Morris, signed the Master Settlement Agreement (MSA)[2] with the attorneys general of 46 states and five territories. The stated goal of the agreement is to reduce youth smoking and promote public health (*Master Settlement*, 2002). The MSA, along with earlier agreements with Mississippi, Florida, Texas, and Minnesota, has changed the way tobacco products are advertised, marketed, and promoted in the United States. In total, the MSA will provide the States with over $200 billion over 25 years (*Master Settlement*, 2002). Of the total judgment, Philip Morris is responsible for 50% (*Master Settlement*, 2002; Philip Morris, 2002b). In addition to the financial settlement, the MSA addresses many of the contentious issues between tobacco and its critics. These issues include marketing and advertising practices, the supervisory role of state and federal government, and corporate accountability for the production of cigarettes. Table 3.1 outlines some of the agreement's central elements.

The agreement is historic for several reasons. First, it offers sweeping reform of an industry that for decades had been largely unchallenged. Second, the financial amount of the initial settlement, $200 billion over 25 years, is unprecedented in U.S. business litigation. Under the agreement, the payments are to be made in perpetuity. Third, the MSA provides $250 million over 10 years for the American Legacy Foundation, an independent national foundation that studies ways to reduce youth smoking and conducts research into ways to prevent diseases connected to tobacco use. In addition, the companies are required to pay the foundation $1.45 billion to conduct a national public education campaign to educate consumers about the dangers of smoking and discourage youth tobacco use. These endeavors represent the largest single public health campaign in U.S. history (*Master Settlement*, 2002). Fourth, the MSA requires cigarette companies to change their corporate culture. Under the agreement, the companies are required to make youth smoking prevention a central corporate goal and regularly communicate corporate principles that demonstrate a commitment to complying with the terms of the agreement. Finally, and arguably most significant to the purposes of this chapter, the agreement signals a shift in the power relations between the tobacco companies and the American public. This is particularly evident in the historic limitations placed on corporate communication (including public relations).

TABLE 3.1. Overview of the Master Settlement Agreement Provisions

MARKETING RESTRICTIONS

1. Prohibits the use of cartoon characters in the advertising, promotion, packaging or labeling of tobacco products.
2. Prohibits most forms of outdoor advertising including: billboards, signs and placards in arenas, stadiums, shopping malls and video arcades.
3. Bans transit advertisements including buses and taxis, and limits ads at trains stations, airports, and similar locations.
4. Prohibits tobacco companies from paying for product placements in movies, television shows, performances, or video games.
5. Limits each manufacturer to a single brand-name sponsorship in any 12-month period. Events in adult-only facilities are not considered sponsorships under the agreement. Sponsorships cannot be of concerts, events in which minors are a significant percentage of the intended audience, and events in which any paid participants or contestants are minors.
6. Prohibits manufacturers from brand-name sponsorship of athletic events between opposing teams in any football, baseball, basketball, soccer, or hockey league.
7. Manufacturers are banned from distributing free samples of tobacco products, except in adult-only facilities.

LEGISLATIVE AND ADMINISTRATIVE RESTRICTIONS

The MSA lists eight types of state or local legislative or administrative proposals that cigarette manufacturers may not oppose. They include:

1. Limitations on youth access to vending machines.
2. Inclusion of cigars within the definition of tobacco products.
3. Enhanced efforts to identify and prosecute illegal sales to minors.
4. Increased use of technology to verify the age of potential purchasers.
5. Limitations on the use of tobacco products as prizes.
6. Penalties for minors for possession or use of tobacco.
7. Limitations on tobacco advertising on school property, or wearing of tobacco branded merchandise on school property.
8. Limitations on non-tobacco products designed to look like tobacco products, such as bubble gum cigars and candy cigarettes.

PUBLIC DISCLOSURE OF DOCUMENTS AND RESEARCH

The settlement requires the tobacco industry to make many of its previously non-public documents available to the public. The industry archive created by this provision of the agreement is located in Minnesota. In addition, nonprivileged, non-confidential documents produced in future civil actions will be made available to the public.

Source: *Master Settlement Agreement* (2002).

The MSA demonstrates how a public policy initiative can recast power relations and reframe an issue through public relations; whereas, public relations activities serve to "orient attention in one way rather than another, to perceive this rather than that" (Deetz, 1992, p. 253). The power of the MSA is in its ability to focus attention away from the "do no harm" campaign onto the unethical communication claims and culpability in the deaths of hundreds of thousands of Americans. As such, Philip Morris embarked on the largest values advocacy campaign in U.S. history in an attempt to turn attention away from the MSA and resurrect and revamp its corporate citizenship persona established in the 1980s.

WORKING TO MAKE A DIFFERENCE: THE PEOPLE OF PHILIP MORRIS

CEO Geoffrey C. Bible summed up the new public relations strategy, thereby signaling the dawn of a new relationship between Philip Morris and Americans:

> There is going to be a day of judgment. And you are going to ask yourself, "Well, what did I achieve in my life?" It's not about how much money you've made or how big a house you've got, or how many cars. It's about what you did for your fellow man. "What did I do to make the world better?" That's what it's going to come down to. (quoted in Bryne, 1999b, p. 178)

The MSA had given Philip Morris a preview of judgment day, so the tobacco giant looked to its charitable contributions and diversified holdings as a way to atone for its sins. Philip Morris found itself in a unique position relative to other tobacco companies in trying to rebuild its corporate identity in the wake of the MSA and growing public outrage. First, Philip Morris is one of the largest consumer products companies in the world. As such, it has deep financial reservoirs to finance a corporate makeover. Second, through diversification, Philip Morris has acquired more socially acceptable brands than cigarettes. In addition to Marlboro, the Philip Morris family of companies includes many other well-known brands (e.g., Velveeta® cheese, Maxwell House® coffee, and Oreo® cookies). Third, Philip Morris is one of the largest philanthropic organizations in the United States. With 178,000 employees in over 140 countries, its 1999 charitable contributions exceeded $60 million (Bryne, 1999b). Philip Morris' corporate size, product diversity, and philanthropic tradition provided it with points of identification beyond tobacco. Accordingly, Philip Morris officials decided to talk about the company's philanthropy, *not* its product. This decision resulted in the largest values advocacy campaign in U.S. history, *Working to Make a Difference: The People of Philip Morris* ("Big Tobacco Seeks," 1999; Bryne, 1999a).

Unveiled in October 1999, the cornerstone of the $150 million campaign was a series of television commercials touting the philanthropic commitments of Philip Morris and its subsidiaries Kraft Foods and Miller Brewing (Elliot, 1999). The campaign included numerous print advertisements, speaking engagements by senior executives, and a corporate website (J. S. Poole, personal communication, November 2, 2001). The goal of the *Working to Make a Difference: The People of Philip Morris* campaign was clear and concise: "To rebuild Philip Morris' rightful place in society as a respected consumer-products company" (Steven C. Parrish, quoted in Byrne, 1999a, p. 192).

Perceptions of the campaign's purpose varied. Philip Morris executives characterized the campaign as "an honest, good-faith effort to get people to understand what we are" (Lindeman, 1999, p. B10). Insiders reported that the campaign was in response to a 1998 employee survey that suggested senior management work to improve organizational image (Byrne, 1999a). Critics of the industry, however, argued that the campaign was an unabashed attempt to influence litigation—a charge Philip Morris denied: "For many years, we've let our critics define us. This is not a litigation strategy. This is a communications strategy," said Mike Pfeil, spokesperson for Philip Morris (quoted in Byrne, 1999b, p. 178). No matter the intent, the campaign provided a new look at an old American institution, thus orienting public attention toward images beneficial to Philip Morris.

The ads were based on Philip Morris' activities in preventing domestic violence, feeding the hungry, providing disaster relief, and giving humanitarian assistance. All advertisements begin with the words, "Based on a true story," in type at the bottom of the screen and offer testimonials from the benefactors of Philip Morris' benevolence. For example, the domestic violence prevention ad tells the story of "Laura" and how she left her abusive husband in order to protect herself and her children. The visual is of a pregnant woman who has been beaten. The narrator states: "All across the country battered women and children are starting new lives—thanks in part to Philip Morris, one of the largest supporters of programs that feed, clothe and shelter victims of domestic violence" (Philip Morris, 1999a).

Subsequent advertisements depict Philip Morris employees engaging in corporate philanthropy and volunteerism. In "Corey's Story" (Philip Morris, 2000a), a Kraft employee's dedication to Chicago's Off-the-Street Club is demonstrated. The young man she tutored provides the following account:

> Chris was like my shadow. She's always there. For three years, she'd drive down from her job at Kraft to tutor me. . . . When she left to have a baby, I told her I hoped she'd have a daughter. She already did a great job of helping raise a son.

These advertisements represent an attempt by Philip Morris to associate itself with widely supported social issues. In doing so, the company demonstrates its emotional and financial support of the causes noted. The values advocacy campaign does not simply invoke shared values in principle. Rather, the advertisements show each shared value and Philip Morris in action together to solve issues of concern to Americans.

The philanthropy-in-action theme is demonstrated in the advertisements' common components. First, the majority of the television ads feature women and children as the primary characters. Of these women, two are visibly pregnant, and the other women are either positioned as the source of comfort or as the person needing help. Second, all the advertisements are based on true stories. This approach provides the advertisements with a sense of legitimacy. Third, the causes supported are well-known and noncontroversial in nature. Specifically, the advertisements avoid charities that could have negative political associations or appear to benefit only an elite group (e.g., support of the arts). For example, in "Tangerine" (Philip Morris, 1999b), an elderly Black woman is shown as the beneficiary of fresh fruit from a local food bank. She offers this comment about the tangerine in her hand: "I've been sick and they've been such a wonderful surprise."

The new campaign, which is summarized in Table 3.2, was not based on blind benevolence alone, however. In 1993, a Cone/Roper poll found that two-thirds of consumers considering similar products at a similar price would switch to the brand that was associated with a better citizen (Gladstone, 2001). Similarly, a poll conducted in late October 2001 indicated that, after the attacks on September 11, Americans expected companies to take an active part in solving the needs of society. In addition, Americans would reward socially responsible companies with "their purchases as a consumer, their references in the community, and their investments as a shareholder" (Gladstone, 2001). These data indicate that there are opportunities for companies to align themselves with charities and possibly distance themselves from controversial products. Geoffrey Bible, CEO of Philip Morris, noticed the significance of being a good corporate citizen in the mid-1990s. It was then he told board members, "Instead of always being defensive—we're right and you're wrong—we need to align ourselves with society" (Bryne, 1999b). This approach was adopted and advertised everywhere Philip Morris conducted business.

TABLE 3.2. Description of 1999-2001 Philip Morris Values Advocacy Television Advertisements.

TITLE	VISUAL	AUDIO
"Laura's Story"	Black and white police photos show pregnant woman who has been beaten. Next frame shows the woman and her children safe at a shelter. Ad ends with display of 800 number to seek help if needed.	All across the country battered women and children are starting new lives—thanks in part to Philip Morris, one of the largest supporters of programs that feed, clothe, and shelter victims of domestic violence.
"Elba, Alabama"	Film of the flood damage. Local residents talking about the flood and the disaster clean water from Miller.	Miller, part of the Philip Morris family of companies, donated thousands of gallons of drinking water to victims last year. For decades, Philip Morris has assisted communities in distress all across the world.
"Tangerine"	An elderly Black woman holding a tangerine. She is alone in her kitchen.	For over 20 years Kraft, part of the Philip Morris family of companies, has been a leader in the fight against hunger. After all, who's better suited to feed the hungry than America's largest food company.
"Corey's Story"	Professional, pregnant, White woman tutoring a Black, male high school student.	The Philip Morris companies, including Kraft Foods, give back to our communities through corporate contributions and volunteerism. In the last 40 years, Philip Morris has given hundreds of millions of dollars to programs like Chicago's Off-the-Street Club that make a difference in people's lives.
"Throwaways"	Teens living under bridges on streets, and in cars. Executive Director gives testimonial about the grant Philip Morris gave to the shelter.	The Philip Morris companies know there are many people in jeopardy, that's why over the last four decades, we've contributed hundreds of millions of dollars to programs that can make a difference in someone's life.

"Molly's Story"	Refuge camp in Kosovo during winter. Philip Morris worker shown delivering food and aiding refuges in a mess tent.	For 40 years, the Philip Morris companies have been one of the largest corporate contributors to disaster relief efforts in the United States and around the world.
"Jerry's Story"	Man arrives in a van while elderly woman looks out the window. He brings lunch and sings Italian love songs to her.	In cities across the country, Philip Morris provides grants to Meals on Wheels programs to eliminate waiting lists. So that thousands of additional seniors can have a hot meal and a visitor. Philip Morris and Meals on Wheels are fighting more than hunger. We're fighting loneliness.

Source: (Philip Morris, 1999a, 1999b, 2000a, 2000b, 2000c, 2000d, 2001).

THEORETICAL FRAMEWORK

In contemporary American society, corporations provide more than a source of employment. It is often the corporation that is the source of child care, healthcare benefits, and retirement income, in addition to funding the arts, schools, and parks when local, state, and federal governments are unwilling or unable to do so (Deetz, 1992). Virtually every sports stadium has a corporate name attached (Boyd, 2000); the federal government is considering allowing corporate sponsorship of our national parks (U.S. Dept. of the Interior, 2003); and some public schools are operated by for-profit corporations (Edison Schools, 2004). This chapter suggests that the ability of public relations to communicate the nature of such relationships between corporations and publics demonstrates the way power acts as a process that operates continually in the relational interplay of entities. To support this premise, values advocacy and capital accumulation theory are offered as a framework for understanding the connection among public relations, power, and corporate social responsibility.

Values Advocacy

Values advocacy (Bostdorff & Vibbert, 1994) is conceptualized as the communication of commonly shared values. It differs from traditional advocacy in that the organization seeks to find areas of commonality with publics rather than just stating its position on a contested issue. In addition, the areas of agreement are not necessarily directly related to a corporation's core business. Values advocacy messages often use a corporation's philanthropic endeavors, employee activities, and commitment to upholding social mores to create a context of shared values. Through the communication of shared values, values advocacy is a means "(1) to enhance the organization's image; (2) to deflect criticism of the organization and/or its policies, products, and services; and (3) to establish value premises that can be used in later discourse" (Bostdorff & Vibbert, 1994, p. 141). The first two strategic uses of values advocacy address the immediate needs of an organization. Specifically, enhancing image and deflecting criticism implies that the organization has particular issues it needs to address.

In this sense, values advocacy addresses the socially vital dimensions of an issue without directly stating the central problem. For example, traditional advocacy would clearly outline an organization's position on an issue. Philip Morris engaged in this type of advocacy with its advertisements about the provisions of the 1998 MSA. Conversely, Philip Morris' values advocacy messages do not mention public concern about tobacco. Rather, the advertisements speak only of the corporation's commitment to worthy social causes, thereby avoiding the topic of tobacco completely and bolstering its contributions as a good corporate citizen. Bostdorff and Vibbert (1994) suggested that values advocacy allows the corporation to "wrap itself in the flag of virtue" (p. 145), thus distracting publics from potentially more substantive issues.

Although the first two objectives address specific needs, the third objective of premise establishment alludes to values advocacy as an ongoing effort. Corporations pursuing values advocacy in this vein lay a foundation of positive identification that may be drawn on in times of trouble. In other words, a corporation actively fills the reservoir of goodwill while it simultaneously primes the pump of public sentiment (Bostdorff & Vibbert, 1994).

In addition to values advocacy campaigns occurring over time, the third objective hints at the way power is manifested in the relationship between publics and corporations. Specifically, if organizations are seeking to lay a foundation for future dialogue, it is conceivable that values advocacy can serve to manipulate publics' understanding, interest, and critical thinking about issues related to the corporation and its position in society with the outcome being attitudes and behaviors favorable to the corporation. As with traditional advocacy, critics contend that advocacy allows corporations to dominate the social and cultural landscape with messages that fail to address public concerns while positioning the corporation as a vital and worthwhile member of society (Deetz, 1992).

For example, the "Throwaways" advertisement demonstrates how power is exercised in the "reciprocal relations of the haves and have-nots"

(Deetz, 1992, p. 253). Domination occurs out of the differentiation communicated via values advocacy that shows Philip Morris supporting social programs while its corporate contemporaries are not. The advertisement features Donna Spence, Executive Director of Crossroads Teen Shelter in Lansing, Michigan. She offers the following testimonial:

> I didn't know where to turn. That's when I called the Philip Morris Company. They sent us an early Christmas present. It covered everything. . . . Philip Morris didn't forget about us either. Whenever we've needed support they've come through. They helped me turn a homeless teen shelter into a home. (Philip Morris, 2000)

The advertisement demonstrates how Philip Morris uses values advocacy as a way of gaining social advantage over other organizations both in terms of showing support for a particular philanthropy and distinguishing itself from other corporations.

Power relations as such arise out of intentional aims and objectives (Foucault, 1980) and allow a narrative of social responsibility to be articulated. Over time publics gradually accept a system in which a good corporate citizen is dominant over its competition. This acceptance is possible because publics look favorably on corporate philanthropic efforts and may not consider alternatives to the norm of corporate funding presented. In this way values advocacy advertisements disperse the process of power into the desired norm of corporate citizenship. As the advertisements show, being a good corporate citizen is the norm by which Philip Morris engages with different communities. The narrative is extended through interviews with the CEO and different news media that report on the corporation's benevolence. As part of the normative process, power relations are viewed as reciprocally beneficial. To understand how the power relations are constituted on economic grounds, this chapter now turns to the theory of capital accumulation to illustrate the role of capital in creating and maintaining power relations and values advocacy campaigns.

CAPITAL ACCUMULATION THEORY

Values advocacy is largely the domain of resource-rich corporations. An organization must possess the capital necessary to financially support socially sanctioned values and fund a communication campaign. The emerging power of a corporate rhetor results in a corporate voice that largely silences other voices that have less capital. In other words, the organizational voice is a scream in a sea of whispers. To examine power as a way to secure advantage through values advocacy, this chapter turns to the theory of capital accumulation (Bourdieu, 1986). The advantage of using capital accumulation theory as a lens to view values advocacy is twofold. First, primacy is given to the role of capital in creating opportunities for corporations to create, maintain, and alter power relations. Second, once the power relations are exposed we can gain a better understanding of how values advocacy influences social and cultural norms.

In his seminal work on the subject, Bourdieu (1986) offered three forms of capital (i.e., economic, social, and cultural) and described the process by which capital is acquired, reproduced, and used as a force that makes everything not equally possible or impossible. As such, capital in all its forms is a reflection of the social world in which it is placed and its influence on that social world. The case of Philip Morris reflects Bourdieu's claims and highlights the role of capital accumulation and its communication outcome, values advocacy, in the power process.

Economic Capital

Bourdieu (1986) posits that economic capital is the root from which other forms of capital grow. In this sense, economic capital is necessary for the formation and maintenance of both social and cultural capital. As organizations engage in external communication activities, economic capital is required to pay for the time, space, and talent to produce messages. The expense of corporate communication campaigns serves to exclude organizations with less economic capital. As such, the disparity in economic capital creates the potential for a wealthy organization to influence the social construction of its identity and do so largely unopposed. Philip Morris' campaign offers such an example: *Working to Make a Difference* was estimated to cost $150 million annually (Elliot, 1999).[3] Philip Morris's voice essentially was louder than that of its opponents (e.g., American Cancer Society, the Legacy Foundation), even though the opponents' voices were still very much part of the chorus of voices on the issue. Ironically, the ability of antitobacco messages to be heard increased only marginally after the Master Settlement Agreement. Reports indicate that less than 4% of the settlement funds to be used for antitobacco communication efforts have been spent in a manner that helped raise the volume for the opposition's voices (Coleman, 2004).

The power of economic capital in the construction of organizational identity is not limited to communication activities, however. In the case of Philip Morris, economic capital allowed the corporation to acquire other businesses with positive social identities (e.g., Miller and Kraft), develop extensive congressional lobbies, and contribute substantially to political campaigns. Even though the majority of Americans are concerned about the health implications of tobacco (Bryne, 1999a), Philip Morris, through its economic capital, attempted to change its image as a merchant of death to one of a merchant of mercy. The power of economic capital is found in the ability to direct attention toward one thing (e.g., social responsibility) and away from another (e.g., cancer), thereby framing the relationship between the corporation and public in a specific way (Deetz, 1992; Foucault, 1980).

Positively, every act of philanthropy gives way to power that "enables and makes positive" (Deetz, 1992, p. 252) the corporate presence in the public sphere. Negatively, however, the ability of a corporation to direct attention to this and not that serves to marginalize or exclude other issues. In the case of Philip Morris the power to direct publics' attention to generous financial contributions (economic capital) to domestic violence shelters, providing food for the hungry, and aiding victims of disaster may serve to marginalize the corporations lack of contributions to charities that provide assistance to publics ravaged by effects of tobacco. The possession and distribution of economic capital alone, however, were insufficient to obtain the type of transformation Philip Morris sought. Specifically, the organization also needed social and cultural capital to link itself to the social values presented in the advertisements.

Social Capital

Economic capital paves the way to social and cultural capital. Bourdieu (1986) discussed social capital in relation to the "network of connections that can be mobilized and the amount of capital possessed by those in the network" (p. 245). The depth of corporate entrenchment can be measured by the extent of its connections with, for example, politicians, media practitioners, scholars, and community groups (Ihlen, 2004). Social capital is important for organizations because it offers a network of other organizations from which the organization can draw resources, thereby demonstrating support within the larger social fabric. Such relationships need not supply additional economic capital; the mere association of one organization's name with another (e.g., the sponsorship of a fundraising event for a nonprofit organization) could result in other types of capital (e.g., cultural capital, to be discussed in the next subsection).

Again, consider the case of Philip Morris. Using its economic capital, Philip Morris has been able to expand its network beyond tobacco. In addition to the acquisitions of Kraft Foods, Nabisco, and Miller Brewing Company, Philip Morris has added to its social network Meals on Wheels, United Way, and domestic violence shelters across the United States (Philip Morris, 2001). These connections now can be mobilized to help the tobacco giant construct its narrative of social responsibility. For example, in "Molly's

Story," a Philip Morris employee is shown distributing food in a Kosovo refugee camp. The advertisement offers the following testimonial from "Molly":

> We at Philip Morris felt we had to do something. So, we sent five tons of food and I went along to see that it got there. . . . You know it's funny, I thought I was coming all this way to do something that would touch their lives. But it turns out; they were the ones who touched mine. Philip Morris, 2001)

From the seed of economic capital grows a network of social capital that reproduces the organizational imperative in a manner unattainable to an organization with limited economic and, therefore, social capital.

Values advocacy campaigns communicate membership within the social group. Power is realized through the separation of values, in this case helping Kosovo refugees and cigarette dangers, and creating one of the two as more desirable (Foucault, 1980). Publics choose where to direct their attention, thus pitting one value (e.g., refugee aid) against the other (punishing Philip Morris for producing cigarettes). Power is exercised by Philip Morris in the framing of the relation between the two values. Social capital is part of the process by which power is exercised as it provides Philip Morris with a network of other organizations and values as points of separation from tobacco. Although the conversion of economic to social capital allows power to be exercised through an extended network, this chapter argues that, with the addition of cultural capital, an organization can obtain even greater strength.

Cultural Capital

Cultural capital, as defined by Bourdieu (1986), differs from economic and social capital in the way it is developed and transferred. Cultural capital demonstrates that achievement and position are linked to how a corporation enacts these elements rather than the mere possession of them. Because cultural capital is intricately tied to the fundamental being of a person or organization, it is often unrecognizable as capital. In essence, it may be viewed as legitimate competence. Further, cultural competence (such as charitable donations) derives a scarcity value and yields profits of distinction (Bourdieu, 1986). Economic and social capital therefore precede cultural capital. Specifically, an organization must have the (economic) means and the (social) networks for the transmission and acquisition of cultural capital. As Bourdieu (1986) suggested, cultural capital is the most insidious of the three forms of capital because the root of economic capital is hidden and the organization's activities may therefore be recognized as legitimate competence.

In "Jerry's Story" (Philip Morris, 2000c), an elderly woman enjoys the food and friendship given by a Meals on Wheels volunteer. The narrator states, "Philip Morris and Meals on Wheels are fighting more than just hunger among the elderly. We're fighting loneliness." The ad ends with the woman and "Jerry" clasping hands. The advertisement depicts more than a financial contribution to Meals on Wheels; it shows Philip Morris providing friendship.

In the case of Philip Morris, cultural capital was obtained through its philanthropic gifts. Annually, the company contributes $60 million to a variety of charities (Bryne, 1999). Due to the amount of its contributions, Philip Morris has derived cultural capital based on Bourdieu's concept of scarcity of value. In turn, this has provided the company with social distinction, within certain segments of society, for its efforts. Philip Morris's advertisements communicated the value to society of the organization's charitable contributions.

As organizational identity becomes tied to social distinction and scarcity, an organization can become inoculated against negative public opinion. This result is largely due to public concern about losing the cultural capital the organization provides and demonstrates power as an advantaging practice. Given the prevailing legislative climate, it is reasonable to interpret these advertisements as a reminder of the cultural capital that would disappear if the organization was forced out of business. Thus, Philip Morris became an organization we cannot live without. The irony, of course, is that 350,000 Americans a year cannot live with them either (Orey, 1999). It is precisely through this tension that we can see the way power is enacted. Although cultural capital alone has influence in the construction of organizational identity and demonstrating support for socially sanctioned values, an organization's power to form and maintain identities that enhance its legitimacy and influence public value premises is strongest when all three forms of capital intersect.

The convergence of economic, social, and cultural capital provides an organization with immense power. It has diversified and solidified at the same time. Specifically, an organization's economic, social, and cultural capital is diverse enough to sustain it in times of difficulty and with multiple stakeholders. Through this diversity, the organization solidifies its ability to acquire the three forms of capital. As discussed earlier, economic, social, and cultural capital are interdependent. As the organization acquires more capital (in all forms) it increases in strength and its ability to get more capital. The Philip Morris campaign provides an example of how the cycle of capital is reinforced. An advertisement for Philip Morris (2000e) reads:

> In celebration of Citymeals' 20th anniversary, Philip Morris will match your gift to Citymeals-on-Wheels. Our long-standing support of this

> exemplary organization is an important part of our commitment to fight hunger across America. With your help, we can give our city's seniors the food and care they need. (*New York Times*, p. A13)

The advertisement features a response coupon for individuals to use when making their contributions. This advertisement demonstrates the convergence of all three forms of capital.

First, Philip Morris has the money to fund an advertisement and provide matching gifts (economic capital). Second, social networks connecting Philip Morris with Citymeals-on-Wheels, seniors, and New York City are explicitly stated in written and visual contexts, and a new network with the reader is being established (social capital). Finally, the generosity of the gift demonstrates cultural competence (cultural capital). Philip Morris, in using its economic, social, and cultural capital, attempts to show its commitment to and competence with socially sanctioned values that are not necessarily in concert with its core business.

Indeed, Philip Morris CEO George Weisman foreshadowed the link between the different forms of capital and public relations in the early 1980s. At that time, Weisman explained the corporation's philanthropy as a "triple helix; an interweaving of interests whereby the arts needed the financial support of business, business needed the arts to improve the quality of its life, and the community at large needed both" (Kluger, 1996, p. 489).

Organizations that command deep reservoirs of economic, social, and cultural capital are able to communicate to publics in a multitude of venues. The corporate voice becomes omnipresent. To this end, power is enacted through the corporate ability to direct public attention toward images and ideals that are beneficial to the corporation. Values advocacy is the communication outcome of capital accumulation and a public display of power as an advantaging practice. In the case of Philip Morris, the very framing of its narrative of social responsibility overshadows the seed from which the philanthropy was possible—tobacco.

CONCLUSION

Individually, power, public relations, and capital are frequently discussed by scholars, practitioners, and everyday people. In recent years, the role of the corporation in the lives of Americans has dominated headlines and commanded our collective attention in movies, sitcoms, and late night comedy routines. Public relations campaigns such as the *Working to Make a Difference: The People of Philip Morris* seek to direct public attention to certain corporate values while masking other, perhaps less desirable, corporate behavior. Hence, power is present in each communication and the corresponding distribution of capital.

Foucault (1980) conceptualized power, perhaps better than anyone else, in a way that can be applied to the field of public relations to understand how campaigns act as an advantaging practice in which every asymmetry is power. By viewing power as an ongoing process, Foucault (1980) suggested that power is not possessed by an individual or organization; rather it is constituted in norms, values, and practices that are enacted through relationships. This chapter connects the work of Foucault (1980) and Deetz's (1992) application of Foucault to corporations to the process of public relations and capital accumulation in values advocacy campaigns. In doing so, it suggests that the power in values advocacy campaigns can be best understood as the ability of corporations to convert capital in ways that enhance the corporation's ability to privilege certain values and norms while marginalizing others. In the case of Philip Morris, large philanthropic contributions may act as social and cultural forms of control (Deetz, 1992), whereby public institutions normalize corporate presence. As corporate presence is normalized in the forms of social and cultural capital, increased economic capital is realized via public support of the corporation and its presented values (Bourdieu, 1986), thus completing the process of accumulation.

CAMPAIGN UPDATE

Several changes have taken place in the organizational structure of Philip Morris since the campaign debuted. First, in 2000, Philip Morris companies acquired Nabisco Foods from rival R. J. Reynolds (Altria Group, 2005b). The Nabisco brands were integrated into the Kraft Foods business worldwide. Second, in 2002, Philip Morris Companies merged Miller Brewing with South African Breweries to form SABMiller, the world's second largest beer company (Altria Group, 2005b). Third, in 2002, Louis C. Camilleri was named chairman and CEO of Philip Morris, replacing Geoffrey Bible. Fourth, in 2003, the Philip Morris board of directors approved a name and logo change for the parent company. Philip Morris and its holdings are now known as Altria Group (2005a). The cigarette business continues, however, to be named Philip Morris. Fifth, the company was threatened by bankruptcy based on a 2003 Illinois class-action lawsuit verdict of $12 billion. Philip Morris claimed the full verdict bond needed to file an appeal would represent a financial hardship and potentially bankrupt the company. An Illinois judge denied their claims and the tobacco giant filed their appeal without filing for bankruptcy (Philip Morris, 2004).

The *Working to Make a Difference* campaign ran from October 1999 to April 2001 on national television and in magazines. The annual cost of the campaign, $150 million, dwarfed the company's yearly philanthropic commitments of $60 million for the same time period. The power of the campaign lies in what the public's attention is directed toward (corporate social responsibility) and the distance the messages put between Philip Morris as merchant of mercy and Philip Morris as merchant of death images.

NOTES

1. In 2003, Philip Morris changed its name to Altria. Altria serves as a holding company for Kraft Foods, Nabisco, and Philip Morris USA (Altria Group, 2005a).
2. The summary presented in this chapter represents only some of the provisions of the Master Settlement Agreement. It is not intended to alter, interpret, or supersede any of the terms of the Agreement. For complete discussion of the Agreement, readers are encouraged to go to http://www.naag.org/issues/issue-tobacco.php
3. This figure represents the cost of the media placement and does not reflect other promotional activities done in support of the campaign.

REFERENCES

Altria Group, Inc. (2004). *Annual reports.* Retrieved September 28, 2005, from http://www.altria.com/investors/02_01_AnnualReport.asp

Altria Group, Inc. (2005a). *The Altria Group story.* Retrieved June 25, 2005, from http://www.altria.com/about_altria/01_05_01_altriastory.asp

Altria Group, Inc. (2005b). *Our history.* Retrieved June 28, 2005, from http://www.altria.com/about_altria/01_05_OurHistory.asp

Big tobacco seeks to improve image. (1999). *Tobacco Retailer, 2*(6), 8.

Bostdorff, D., & Vibbert, S. L. (1994). Values advocacy: Enhancing organizational images, deflecting public criticism, and grounding future arguments. *Public Relations Review, 20,* 141-158.

Bourdieu, P. (1986). The forms of capital. In J. Richardson (Ed.), *Handbook of theory and research for the sociology of education* (pp. 241-258). Westport, CT: Greenwood Press.

Boyd, J. (2000). Selling home: Corporate stadium names and the destruction of commemoration. *Journal of Applied Communication Research, 28*(4), 330-346.

Byrne, J. A. (1999a). Dismantling a bunker mentality. *Business Week, 3657,* 192.

Bryne, J. A. (1999b, November 29). Philip Morris: Inside America's most reviled company. *Business Week, 3657*, 176-192.

Citymeals 20th anniversary (2000, December 12). *The New York Times*, p. A21.

Coleman, C. (2004, Sept. 22). *Tobacco lawsuit.* Retrieved September 28, 2004, from http://www.npr.org/templates/story/story.php?storyId=3931141

Deetz, S. A. (1992). *Democracy in an age of corporate colonization: Developments in the communication and the politics of everyday life.* Albany: State University of New York Press.

Edison Schools (2004). *Edison Schools.* Retrieved November 2, 2004, from www.edisonproject.com

Elliot, S. (1999, November 11). Tired of being a villain: Philip Morris works on its image. *The New York Times*, p. C12.

Foucault, M. (1980). *Power/knowledge: Selected interviews and other writings, 1972-1977* (C. Gordon, Ed. & Trans.). Brighton, England: Harvester Press.

Foucault, M. (1982). The subject and power. In H. Dreyfus and P. Rabinow (Eds.), *Michel Foucault: Beyond structuralism and hermeneutics* (pp. 208-226). Brighton, England: Harvester.

Foucault, M. (1986). Disciplinary power and subjection. In S. Lukes (Ed.), *Power* (pp. 226-241). Oxford: Blackwell.

Freedman, A. M. (1988, June 8). Tobacco firms, pariahs to many, still are angels to the arts. *Wall Street Journal,* pp. 1, 22.

Gladstone, J. (2001, December 14). *Post 9/11 business and philanthropy.* Retrieved December 15, 2001, from http://www.npr.org/templates/story/story.php?storyId=1134816

Hilts, P. J. (1996). *Smoke screen: The truth behind the tobacco industry cover-up.* Reading, MA: Addison-Wesley.

Ihlen, Ø. (2004). Norwegian hydroelectric power: Testing a heuristic for analyzing symbolic strategies and resources. *Public Relations Review, 30,* 217-223.

Kluger, R. (1996). *Ashes to ashes: America's hundred-year cigarette war, the public health, and the unabashed triumph of Philip Morris.* New York: Knopf.

Lindeman, T. F. (1999, October, 22). Philip Morris seeks to change its image with new advertising campaign. *The Pittsburgh* (PA) *Post-Gazette*, p. B10.

Master Settlement Agreement (2002). Retrieved December 15, 2002, from http://www.naag.org/upload/1109185724_1032468605_cigmsa.pdf

Orey, M. (1999). *Assuming the risk: The mavericks, the lawyers, and the whistle-blowers who beat big tobacco.* New York: Little, Brown.

Philip Morris Companies (1999a). *Laura's story* [Broadcast advertisement]. New York: Leo Burnett.

Philip Morris Companies (1999b). *Tangerine* [Broadcast advertisement]. New York: Leo Burnett.

Philip Morris Companies (2000a). *Corey's story* [Broadcast advertisement]. New York: Leo Burnett.

Philip Morris Companies (2000b). *Elba, Alabama* [Broadcast advertisement]. New York: Leo Burnett.

Philip Morris Companies (2000c). *Jerry's story* [Broadcast advertisement]. New York: Leo Burnett.

Philip Morris Companies (2000d). *Throwaways* [Broadcast advertisement]. New York: Leo Burnett.

Philip Morris Companies. (2000e, December 12). *It's more than food* [Print advertisement]. *The New York Times*, p. A13.

Philip Morris Companies (2001). *Molly's story* Broadcast advertisement. New York: Leo Burnett.

Philip Morris Companies. (2002a). *History*. Retrieved December 12, 2002, from http://www.philipmorris.com/about_us/history.asp

Philip Morris Companies. (2002b). *Our commitment.* Retrieved March 25, 2002, from http://www.philipmorris.com/about_us/our_commitment.asp

Philip Morris USA (2004). *Price plaintiffs ask Illinois Supreme Court to ignore lay in order to uphold $10.1B class action verdict.* Retrieved July 22, 2004, from http://www.philipmorrisusa.com/en.pressroom/content/press_release/articles/pr_july_142004_ppaisciloubcav.asp

The Roper Center for Public Opinion Research. (2001). *Measuring the stakeholder power of corporate philanthropy.* Retrieved on October 8, 2004, from www.stakeholderpower.com/story.cfm?article_1d=185

U.S. Department of the Interior. National Park Service. (2003). *Director's order #21: Donations and fundraising*. Retrieved November 4, 2004, from www.nps.gov/policy/DOrders/DO21-reissue.html

United States. House of Representatives. (1995). *Regulation of tobacco products* (Part 1) [Hearings before the Subcommittee on Health and the Environment of the Committee on Energy and Commerce, 103rd Congress, 2nd session] (Serial No. 103-149). Washington, DC: U.S. Government Printing Office.

chapter 5

Understanding How Martha Stewart Harmed Her Image Restoration through a "Micropolitics" of Power

Angela M. Jerome

Mary Anne Moffitt

Joseph W. Knudsen

In late December 2001, allegations of insider trading against Martha Stewart set in motion a chain of events that severely harmed her image and eventually led to her imprisonment. The ordeal that led to Stewart's public relations nightmare began with her relationship with Sam Waksal, a close friend and the CEO of Imclone, a pharmaceutical company that was in the application process to begin the sale of a new cancer drug, Erbitux. On approval from the Food and Drug Administration, Imclone's stock was expected to rise significantly due to consumer demand (Allen, 2003).

However, on December 26, 2001, when Waksal received news that the FDA would not approve the sale of Erbitux, he allegedly began telling friends and family that the stock would drop drastically due to the FDA's rejection. The next day, Stewart sold 3,928 shares of her Imclone stock worth $228,000 (Byrnes, 2003). Waksal's and Stewart's sale of stock, combined with the drop in Imclone's stock, sparked interest for federal investigators as a possible case of insider trading. During the initial stages of the investigation Stewart justified her trade of stock by explaining that the share price dropped below $60 and her broker knew of her wishes to sell the stock when the value dropped below that price. Despite this explanation, the investigation continued. On June 6, 2002, Stewart's sale of the Imclone stock was disclosed to the public.

Although the notion of celebrities overcoming negative press is not new, Stewart's case is unique because her name is also a corporate brand. In addition to her role as a television celebrity, she operates Martha Stewart Living Omnimedia (MSO), which markets her goods through Kmart. In other words, "Martha Stewart's company is only worth what Martha Stewart is worth" (Acki & Robertson, 2003, p. A1). Her actions in response to the insider trading allegations and the media frenzy surrounding this crisis left Stewart needing to repair her personal image and the image of MSO.

Complicating Stewart's image crisis even more is the fact that her crisis had both legal and public relations components. In fact, not surprisingly, many see her case as a legal matter first and a public relations crisis second (Emling, 2003), making her response full of legal implications. Therefore, this case is especially interesting to public relations strategists who struggle to work with a client's attorneys and build or repair a client's corporate image. The issue of public relations strategy versus legal strategy recently has emerged as a significant issue facing public relations communication today (Cameron, Cropp, & Reber, 2001; Parkinson, Ekachai, & Hetherington, 2001; Reber, Cropp, & Cameron, 2001, 2003).

The Stewart case captured the attention of a national audience for more than 3 years. The public interest in the case against Stewart has a huge significance to public relations practitioners. Given that this is one of the most publicized legal cases against a prominent public figure within recent years, it is important to ask how public relations practitioners can learn from this complicated legal and corporate image controversy, particularly the ways that power operates in such situations.

It is important to note here that the longevity of this case makes it impossible to analyze both Martha's pretrial and posttrial responses. We focus on her earliest responses to this crisis because this early period set the rhetorical trajectory (Griffin, 1984) for her image restoration campaign.

This study examines the interplay of public relations and legal functions through the case study of Martha Stewart, a national figure (and her corporation) facing both a crisis of image and one of alleged criminal intent. This study utilizes Benoit's (1995) image restoration framework and other crisis communication models to interpret and analyze the image restoration strategies that Stewart employed in her pretrial crisis. Additionally, consistent with each of Stewart's response strategies, a look at Foucault's (1980b) micropolitics of power explains how her continual reluctance to respond to her strongest and most vocal critics in a timely manner undermined her image restoration attempts. For the public relations professional, this case study demonstrates and confirms the importance of a corporation's timely public answers and honest responses to all relevant audiences during the course of a crisis—even when legal counsel might suggest otherwise.

We acknowledge the image restoration strategies used by Stewart to be those of denying wrongdoing, attacking accusers, and differentiating her case from others that were much worse (cf. Benoit, 1995)—all of which were clearly meant to culminate in the public's perception of Stewart as victim. However, we argue that another of her response strategies—her reluctance to immediately go public and answer her critics and the negative media coverage in a timely manner—represented a strategy of nonresponse, a strategy that did extensive damage to her personal and corporate images and her legal case. This strategy of nonresponse, almost certainly conceived by her attorneys, in the end effectively transferred her power to influence her image over to the attorneys, the media, and the many other audiences she sought to influence. As demonstrated in the ultimate conclusion to this case, which was Stewart's imprisonment, the legal tactic of nonresponse severely harmed her image personally and professionally.[1] Further, her nonresponse or silence, in essence, transferred any power she had to repair her image over to others advising and communicating with her.

THEORETICAL FRAMEWORK

The theoretical framework for this chapter presents several interpretive frames for analyzing the failures of Stewart's image restoration campaign. An examination of the public relations and legal functions in this case illustrates one of the most important issues facing public relations today—the conflict and tension between those functions in a corporation facing a crisis. Benoit's image restoration model provides the terminology and the tools for interpreting the public relations/legal struggle contained in the Stewart image crisis. Other models of crisis communications by Coombs (1995) and Hearit (1995) add further stability to the analysis. Finally, to enhance and deepen the understanding of Stewart's image restoration strategies, we look at Foucault's (1972, 1980b) micropolitics of power to add a critical perspective that focuses on power relations inherent in a corporation's image restoration struggle.

Dynamics between Public Relations and Legal Functions

The Martha Stewart case stands as a perfect example of the tension that can emerge between the legal and public relations departments of a corporation in crisis. The tension that can emerge is easy to understand: Attorneys want as little information as possible released in order to limit potential for legal arguments, and public relations professionals want to release as much information as possible to reassure their multiple audiences that the crisis is under control (Cameron et al., 2001; Parkinson et al., 2001; Reber et al., 2001, 2003).

A significant line of research recently has emerged to study this conflict of interests in crisis management. This research suggests how little public relations knows about the legal function and how little the legal function knows about public relations. Parkinson et al. (2001) found that, when working with important clients, public relations practitioners rarely feel the need—or are required—to become familiar with the client's guidelines on legal disclosure and policies. Furthermore, public relations practitioners need to educate themselves more on legal issues. It is important for public relations professionals to learn to work closely with corporate attorneys to ensure that legal principles guide public relations strategies and communication about legal issues (Parkinson et al., 2001).

Other research into the nexus of legal and public relations communication indicates that both functions are beginning to recognize the importance of knowing each other's role in corporate communication. Cameron et al.'s (2001) seminal study documented the tension and suspicion that typically exists between attorneys and public relations professionals. Reber et al. (2001) cited the value of both legal and public relations in addressing any corporate crisis, especially if both are brought in together and early in the crisis. They, too, claim in their Q-methodology and interview study that each side is now beginning to see the value of the other; legal acknowledges the importance of immediate and factual information delivered to the public, and public relations is recognizing the value of legal input into their public communication. Moreover, Reber et al. (2001) noted that nonresponse/silence on the part of an organization points to guilt, whether the organization is guilty of allegations or not.

Reber et al. (2003) presented a case study of just how the legal and public relations functions, when working together, can effectively resolve a crisis. Their study of Norfolk Southern's hostile takeover of Conrail, Inc., demonstrates how, at first glance, this seemingly impossible resolution was, nevertheless, effectively and successfully achieved by both sides, thanks to cooperation and open communication between attorneys and public relations professionals. The success of Norfolk Southern's bid for Conrail is marked by its lack of silence; that is, open and honest communication to all the relevant audiences led to the success of this business negotiation. In contrast, we see in the Stewart case that her nonresponse to critics dominated her crisis strategy, eventually proving to be an unsuccessful choice.

Models for Restoring Image and Managing Crisis Communication

Appreciating that the Stewart crisis represents a significant case for understanding the potential conflicts between public relations communication and legal advice, we turn now to some models of image restoration that allow more detailed and careful analysis of the strategies Stewart attempted to use to repair her own image as well as the image of her company. To Benoit's (1995) model of image restoration strategies we add useful dimensions from Coombs (1995) and Hearit (1995).

According to Benoit (1995), when confronted with the blame of an undesirable action, the actor may choose to deny the act occurred or that she or he was the actor who performed the act. Actors who cannot use simple denial may choose to shift the blame to another plausible actor. Actors may also attempt to evade or reduce responsibility for the act (Benoit, 1995) by using one or more substrategies: provocation (some other act forced the organization to take the offensive act), defeasibility (the act was due to a lack of information or ability), excuse based on accidents (the organization could not have controlled the event), and/or justification based on motives or intentions.

The next strategy in Benoit's (1995) theory of image restoration is reducing offensiveness of the event, which may be done by using the following strategies: bolstering (supporting already-made arguments with more evidence and reasoning), minimization (arguing that the incident is not as bad as it first appears), differentiation (framing the action in a way that compares it to a much worse scenario so that the action in question does not appear as bad), transcendence (placing the situation in a different context to simply change the focus and severity of the situation at hand), attacking the accuser (attempting to reduce the credibility of the source of the charge), and/or compensation (usually by offering reimbursement for losses).

Benoit's (1995) typology also includes corrective action. Using this strategy, the actor may vow to fix the problem by either restoring the situation to the state before the objectionable action and/or promising to "mend one's ways" and make changes to prevent the recurrence of the undesirable act. Of course, to utilize this strategy means accepting responsibility for the action in question. Many times, audiences will be forgiving once ownership of the action has been taken. However, in cases in which assignment and ownership of the action is not enough, actors have one last strategy to use in an attempt to restore a positive image. The last strategy Benoit (1995) mentioned is the act of mortification; using this strategy, the actor fully admits responsibility for the wrongful action and asks for forgiveness.

The work of Coombs (1995) and Hearit (1995) also adds to this model of crisis strategies and informs this case study. Coombs (1995) noted the value of the suffering or victimization strategy: "The idea behind suffering is to win sympathy from publics. . . . Suffering portrays the organization as an unfair victim of some malicious, outside entity" (p. 152). Hearit (1995) additionally discussed the usefulness of three dissociation stances that can be used in the social legitimacy process. The first is an opinion/knowledge dissociation in which, using this strategy, an actor may dispute "the validity of the charges by redefining them as groundless" (p. 7). The second is an individual/group dissociation, in which an organization may acknowledge that wrongdoing has been committed by some of its employees, yet differentiates those individuals from the rest of the organization (p. 8). The third is an act/essence dissociation in which the actors take responsibility for the act but do so while arguing that the act was not representative of the actors' "true nature" (p. 9).

Michel Foucault and Power

The tension between legal and public relations functions and the use of image restoration strategies account for only part of the shortcomings of Stewart's image restoration campaign. In this section we adopt a perspective on power drawn from critical theory to complete our approach to understanding Stewart's image and legal dilemmas. Table 5.1 lays out concepts from Benoit, Coombs, Hearit, and Foucault into a taxonomy for analyzing power in crisis and image communication. Michel Foucault (1965, 1972, 1973, 1980a, 1980b, 1984) was a critical-theory scholar who investigated how power is manifested within a society. Foucault's conceptualization of power within the formation of society provides a dynamic approach that applies equally to image restoration and the legal/public relations dichotomy.

Interestingly, Foucault theorized power relationships throughout his works but resisted using the term "power." Foucault (1980b) himself admitted:

> When I think back now, I ask myself what else it was that I was talking about, in *Madness and Civilization* [1965] or *The Birth of the Clinic* [1973], but power? Yet I am perfectly aware that I scarcely ever used the word and never had such a field of analysis at my disposal. (p. 115)

However, scholars and critics who studied Foucault (e.g., Best & Kellner, 1991; Brown, 2000; Leezenberg, 2004; Sheridan, 1980; Shumway, 1989) have recognized his theorization of power and offered terms for the contrasting levels of power that they find in Foucault's work. Shumway (1989) noted Foucault's concept of "micropower" in *The Birth of the Clinic*

TABLE 5.1. A Taxonomy for Analyzing Power in Crisis and Image Communication.

STRATEGY	DEFINITION
Denial	An actor may choose to deny the act occurred, deny that she or he was the actor who performed the act, or attempt to evade or reduce responsibility for the act by using one or more substrategies: provocation, defeasibility, excuse based on accidents, and/or justification based on motives or intentions.
Offensiveness Reduction	An actor seeks to make an act significantly less offensive through bolstering, minimization, differentiation, transcendence, attacking accuser, and/or compensation.
Corrective Action	An actor may vow to fix the problem by either restoring the situation to the state before the objectionable action and/or promising to "mend one's ways" and make changes to prevent the recurrence of the undesirable act. This strategy requires accepting responsibility for the action in question.
Mortification	An actor fully admits responsibility for the wrongful action and asks for forgiveness.
Suffering/Victimization	An actor tries to win sympathy from publics by portraying he/she/it as an unfair victim of some malicious, outside entity.
Opinion/Knowledge Dissociation	An actor may dispute "the validity of the charges by redefining them as groundless."
Individual/Group Dissociation	An organization may acknowledge that wrongdoing has been committed by some of its employees, yet differentiates those individuals from the rest of the organization.
Act/Essence Dissociation	An actor takes responsibility for the act but does so while arguing that the act was not representative of the actors' "true nature."
Micropolitics of Power	An actor gives respect and allegiance to those in dominant social roles only because social rules and tradition have always dictated it.

Sources: Benoit (1995); Best and Kellner (1991); Brown (2004); Coombs (1995), Hearit (1995)

(1973). Sheridan (1980) offered the term "micro-mechanisms of power," and Leezenberg (2004) utilized the terminology "micro-power" as power from below. Brown (2000) utilized the term "micropolitics," as did Best and Kellner (1991), who claimed "macroforces" (p. 52) and "micropolitics" (p. 56) as levels of power that Foucault sees as "spreading throughout society" (p. 56).

In short, rather than a "power from the top controlling those in a lesser social position" (as most people accept to be true), Foucault claimed that power is found in the relationships between persons or groups. For those located at the social "bottom," their relationships are such that they give power over to those at the top. In an almost unconscious way, people give respect and allegiance to those in dominant social roles only because social rules and tradition have always dictated it. For example, common power relationships found in society include citizens who give power to their leaders, workers who give power to management, patients who give power to their doctors, students who give power to their teachers, and clients who give power to their lawyers.

In this case study of Stewart we identify a micropolitics of power—but with a slight twist. We note that Stewart's nonresponse to her critics at the very onset of her legal and image problems served in effect to give up her power to respond and to tell her story to the people who were criticizing her—to influence her image directly. Stewart had the power to tell her story, but she did not exercise it. In her nonresponse she gave her voice—her micropolitics of power—over instead to the government investigators accusing her of insider trading and to the reporters mediating versions of that story to her key publics.

DATA AND FINDINGS

No doubt the practice of nonresponse or silence as an image restoration strategy is not a new phenomenon in public relations communication. Bringing together Foucault's ideas on the micropolitics of power and the pretrial, legally driven silence strategy employed by Stewart allows an in-depth examination of the concept of *nonresponse*. Our data and findings suggest that, initially, the public figure or "accused" image functions at a "micro" level (i.e., for herself and her company). On the other hand, the government, the media channel, or an investigative reporter who brings initial publicity or accusations to the accused function, initially, at the "macro" level.

This case study suggests that Stewart's nonresponse at the micro level ultimately gave over power to the macro voices (i.e., her accusers and the news media). The communication of nonresponse is not a singular or simple communicative act. Rather, nonresponse functions as a complicated rhetorical process, operates at public (macro) and interpersonal (micro) levels, and, importantly for this study, implies meanings when employed in a public, mass setting. The Stewart crisis demonstrates three crucial implications of the micropolitics of power that essentially served to give up her power to directly communicate personal and corporate images into the hands of others: power handed over to the media, power given to her attorneys, and attempts to disassociate herself from her company, MSO. In the end, this case study demonstrates to public relations professionals the danger and risk of not responding to audiences that question allegations toward the organization. The Stewart case shows the importance of immediate and honest answers to questions the public has of the organization. To not respond inevitably harms the image of a corporation.

Power Handed Over to the Media

Once the initial story of Stewart's crisis came to public light (Pollock, 2002), it took Stewart and her associates months to provide any significant response. In terms of visibility in the mainstream press, Stewart always has enjoyed a positive personal persona through her television show and frequent appearances on late night television and ABC's *Good Morning America*. Therefore, after Stewart's crisis was made public by the media and she refused to answer her critics, people likely began questioning her innocence. Public relations consultant Laura Ries even commented on Stewart's early choice of nonresponse: "Why would you be hiding behind your lawyers unless you did, in fact, have something to hide?" (quoted in Koppel, Chernoff, Lisovicz, Feldman, & Rodgers, 2003). As Ries suggests, this silence could become damaging to both Stewart's credibility and her brand name.

During Stewart's lack of response, former employees, reporters, and even family members began to express their personal disdain for Stewart due to her overbearing, controlling, and, at times, mean personality (Allen, 2003). On May 19, 2003, NBC aired "Martha, Inc.: The Story of Martha Stewart" (Gilbert, 2003; Rosenthal, 2003). This melodramatic, made-for-television movie portrayed Martha as a power-hungry, angry perfectionist who only cared about continuing her successful career, even if it meant severing ties with close friends and family. The movie even played off Stewart's real-life legal troubles by placing her in a prison cell during her ending monologue. These negative portrayals undoubtedly gave the public reasons to doubt Stewart's integrity. Yet it was not until after she was indicted on June 4, 2003, that Stewart or her lawyers made any significant response in the mainstream press.

In response to the indictment, Stewart's team created news releases and a website, http://www.marthatalks.com. Portions of the website, such as the

"Trial Update," served to "correct the errors" presented in the mainstream media. A June 4, 2003 "Press Statement" placed on the website by Stewart's attorneys asserted, "Martha Stewart has done nothing wrong. The government is making her the subject of a criminal test case designed to further expand the already unrecognizable boundaries of the federal securities laws" (Morvillo & Tigue, 2003a). They also asked:

> [Is the government doing] it for publicity purposes because Martha Stewart is a celebrity? Is it because she is a woman who has successfully competed in a man's business world by virtue of her talent, hard work and demanding standards? Is it because the government would like to be able to define securities fraud as whatever it wants it to be? Or is it because the [U.S.] Department of Justice is attempting to divert the public's attention from its failure to charge the politically connected managers of Enron and WorldCom who may have fleeced the public out of billions of dollars? (Morvillo & Tigue, 2003a)

Clearly, Stewart's attorneys used denial of wrongdoing and attacking the accuser strategies to dissociate Stewart from image-damaging actions.

Stewart's attorneys were essentially silent about the details of the crisis; instead, they urged the media to be critical about the allegations in order to avoid presenting false information. Stewart's attorneys stated:

> We urge the media to ask these questions—and to consult with legal experts on the validity and broader implications of these extraordinary charges. We believe such an inquiry will verify that this indictment is unique and goes well beyond any other criminal securities law case. (Morvillo & Tigue, 2003a)

Their call for the media to research these issues was valid, but again it gave power to the media. Instead, the attorneys should have taken the power/voice and conducted their own inquiry, pointing out these injustices to the mainstream media and American public.

Later, Morvillo and Tigue (2003b) used the differentiation strategy to distinguish Stewart's actual actions from much more damaging allegations of insider trading:

> The indictment does NOT allege that Martha Stewart was provided inside information by Sam Waksal about ImClone's application for its cancer drug Erbitux—or about anything else. The indictment does NOT allege that Martha Stewart knew the reason why Waksal placed an order to sell ImClone shares on December 27, 2001—only that he was trying to sell. (n.p.)

These statements were illustrative of the stance Stewart would take when she finally spoke. Yet it was her lawyers who first would position her image as the innocent victim.

On June 5, 2003, in an "Open Letter" that appeared on the website and as a full-page layout in *USA Today*, Stewart used the same strategies her attorneys had (denial, differentiation, and attacking the accuser), but she also added a suffering component. Stewart (2003, n.p.) asserted, "I am confident I will be exonerated of these baseless charges, but a trial unfortunately won't take place for months." Further, Stewart claimed that she would "fight to clear my name." She did not deny the stock sale; she, like her attorneys, chose instead to differentiate her actions from criminal acts by claiming that all her actions were legitimate and lawful.

In short, she did not apologize for her actions. Stewart (2003) reported:

> I simply returned a call from my stockbroker. Based in large part on prior discussions with my broker about price, I authorized a sale of my remaining shares in a biotech company called ImClone. I later denied any wrongdoing in public statements and in voluntary interviews with prosecutors. The government's attempt to criminalize these actions makes no sense to me. (n.p.)

She also argued, "After more than a year, the government has decided to bring charges against me for matters that are personal and entirely unrelated to the business of Martha Stewart Living Omnimedia" (Stewart, 2003, n.p.). Stewart therefore claimed that the focus of this scandal was caused by the government's pursuit and framing of her actions. Clearly, Stewart thus emphasized her role as an innocent victim by attacking her accuser, building on the strategies established by her attorneys.

The victimization strategy detailed in these statements declares Stewart's innocence and provides an excuse for her audience to believe her point of view. Put simply, these statements attempt to reduce offensiveness and tell her audiences that Stewart is innocent of any wrongdoing, insinuating that the government has wrongly accused her. Even with all these responses offered by Stewart and her spokespersons, her lack of response to the actual events and omission of information that the public wanted functioned as a kind of nonresponse to the actual crisis. This silence by omission continued to damage her image as the issue progressed.

Regardless of the arguments made by Stewart and her legal advisors, media sources for the most part continued to present the facts of the story and their "truth" without Stewart's side of the story, much as they had done throughout her period of nonresponse. The facts contained in the media coverage included alleged actions; these facts seemed to have an "already guilty" slant to them. For example, the press mentions "Stewart's sale of stock" multiple times and assumes that this action is truth; for example, "Stewart now faces a trial initiated by her sale of over 2,000 shares of Imclone stock" (Byrnes, 2003, p. 37). The mainstream press was simply "presenting the story," however, they were not presenting the story in a fair or accurate manner that gave justice to the events of the trial. (News coverage of anyone accused of a crime typically includes the word, "alleged" or "allegedly.")

The mainstream press did acknowledge her portrayal of herself as a victim, but instead of offering sympathy, journalists seemed to glory in the downfall of a celebrity with high status. With few exceptions, the critics in the media chose not to include Stewart's statements of denial in their articles. However, Stewart was not even charged with insider trading. Furthermore, when Stewart's acts of denial are mentioned, they are accompanied by words of doubt or judgment. For example, one reporter stated, "Ms. Stewart wants us to believe that she is as innocent as one of her gingerbread men, but too much evidence is against her" (Farrell, 2003, n.p.). Another stated, "She let the door open for skepticism when she didn't say anything. It was probably her biggest mistake" (Puente, 2003, n.p.). Puente (2003) claimed that Stewart was the "maker of her own bed" in the sense that Stewart's troubles had been created by a series of events caused by herself.

In support of Stewart, some critics within the media decried the injustice of the allegations, claiming that she was being made an example of because of her celebrity status and because the government needed a high-profile scapegoat to serve its own ends when attempting to define securities fraud (McClam, 2003a, 2003b; Reynolds, 2003). For example, Reynold's (2003) argued that if the charges about insider trading were dropped, the charges regarding lying about the insider trading should be dropped as well. Clearly, some believed the assertions of Stewart's team.

Even though some media representatives supported Stewart and were persuaded by her arguments, public opinion data indicate that this sentiment was not held by a majority of citizens. To gauge public opinion about Stewart, which was clearly influenced by media coverage of the case, *USA Today* conducted a survey of general consumers. *USA Today*'s poll found that Stewart was ranked as being no more "likable" than boxer Evander Holyfield or actress Pamela Anderson. In the survey of 1,800 consumers, Stewart ranked below more than half of the 1,733 famous people. Although 75% of the participants knew who Stewart was, "she had three times more negative than positive responses" (Puente, 2003, p. D10). We argue that such data indicate that the negative media messages predominated the shaping of audience opinions more than did any messages put out by Stewart or her supporters. Stewart's lack of response to the important issues that people wanted to hear about severely weakened her image.

Stewart's use of a website as the main tool to present her voice also likely played a part in handing over power to the media. An evaluation of using a website to relay information about a crisis must be weighed by comparing the benefits and drawbacks. Stewart's website served as a voice that delivered appreciation to supporters, error corrections, and details about the status of her legal troubles. The website, in theory, was a positive tactic to use.

However, delays in response to her crisis and her unwillingness to speak publicly on the issues people wanted to hear about may have made her story seem a bit fabricated. Stewart's late use of a website (over a year after the initial accusations occurred) and her delaying, nonresponsive strategies hardly helped her win in the court of public opinion. The website was clearly dominated by legal influence and constrained the potential image restoration by an overload of legal jargon. Judging from the website, it appears that the legal counsel was valued more than advice from public relations professionals. Therefore, the use of this medium for response had limitations. Stewart had still not spoken to the public, which for some time was dependent on the media as its sole source of information about Stewart.

Image consultants even reported the website to be "part of a shrewd campaign by the doyenne of home-style perfection to win the battle for public opinion—and influence potential jurors who may one day decide her guilt or innocence" (McClam, 2003a, n.p.). Her website gave Stewart a chance to reach her main audience without the interruptions or editing that would occur in the mainstream media, but her critics' cynical response to her delayed website and refusal to speak publicly nevertheless led to skepticism and negativity toward the Web response. In effect, the media continued to have power over Stewart: she gave up her power to the media by not speaking out and maintaining her silence.

Not surprisingly, Stewart's team worked diligently to counter the negative sentiments that dominated media coverage. For example, in November 2003, her attorneys released a "Memorandum of Law," an official document that pointed out legal problems and arguments regarding Stewart's trial, and an "Executive Summary of Motions," which detailed each charge of the indictment. In the Memorandum of Law Morvillo and Tigue (2003d) argued:

> The government knows Count 9 is problematic. The SEC conducted a parallel investigation but refused to bring a parallel securities fraud charge against Ms. Stewart based on the June Statements. After Ms. Stewart was indicted, commentators rebuked the government for overreaching Count 9 calling the securities-fraud charge "appalling," "troubling and radical," and "preposterous," saying that the government was on a " 'Star Trek' mission to go where no one has gone before," and suggesting that no "sane, fair-minded person" could "truly believe what Martha Stewart did harmed any investor."

In the "Executive Summary of Motions" Morvillo and Tigue (2003c) argued that the most serious charge against Stewart was framed improperly:

> Count Nine, the "securities fraud" charge, seeks to criminalize Ms. Stewart's public declarations that she had not engaged in insider trading in making a personal stock sale. This charge is unprecedented in the seventy-year history of the federal securities laws. It violates the First Amendment, the Due Process Clause, and the securities statute itself.

Stewart also made public appearances where supporters and critics would be able to hear her side of the story. Stewart was on ABC's *20/20* on November 5, 2003, and on CNN's *Larry King Live* December 22 (King, 2003). Not until Stewart's *20/20* interview with Barbara Walters had she actually talked directly to the press. In fact, the only word recorded by Stewart before then was when the judge asked her to comply for a January 2004 trial date, and she replied "Okay" (Walters & Stossel, 2003). Even as a guest on these shows, Stewart stated that she could not comment on the legal issues, a position (advocated by her attorneys) that suggested her guilt. Again, her strategy of nonresponse left her disempowered, remaining at the micro level of power while the media enjoyed power at the macro level. It was too little too late.

After these interviews, some reporters again offered Stewart support, stating that actions of the federal government tend to be covered by leftist reporters who view Stewart as a victimized target to cover up the governmental mistakes of corporate scandals such as Enron and Worldcom. Many of these supporters in the press have been featured on marthatalks.com. For instance, Shargel (2004) charged that, by February 2004, most of the public did not even realize what Stewart was accused of: "It would not surprise me if half of America does not know what is actually bringing Martha to trial. All we are being told is that a famous person is in a scandal" (n.p.). Moreover, despite the fact that over 7.7 million shares of Imclone stock were sold on the same day as Stewart allegedly sold just 3,928 shares, Stewart was still framed as a criminal (Shargel, 2004).

However, these supporting voices could never overtake the negative press against Stewart. Her position as revealed in the press remained at the micropolitics level, given her perceived silence and lack of response. Her attorneys' voice effectively controlled the amount of information she released, thus she never left the microlevel of being the accused public figure. She could never enter the macrolevel where her voice could be heard publicly and where she exercised primary influence over her projected image.

Power Given to Attorneys

Stewart's nonresponse strategy was, most likely, heavily influenced by her legal counsel and did not serve her image restoration campaign. Because Stewart did not deny or accept responsibility for the charges against her for months, publics had reason to believe her silence was a way to buy time in order to effectively hide the truth. In Brummett's (1980) terms, her lack of communication meant mystery, uncertainty, and passivity to her audiences and a relinquishment of power by Stewart.

Without any information from Stewart, this lack effectively served to lend credibility to her accusers. The media led people to believe that the allegations of insider trading were probably true. Further, her main defense statements, which came in the form of simple denial, differentiation, attacking the accuser, and suffering strategies, issued from or were undoubtedly shaped by her attorneys.

The strong statements released by her attorneys, however, came a year after the story broke in June 2002. By this time Stewart's nonresponse had sufficiently lessened her credibility, damaged her personal and professional images, and decreased her power. She had, in effect, given up her power to her attorneys. According to Foucault's micropolitics, Stewart's lack of response functioned at a microlevel and stayed there; she never entered the level of "macropower" where she could control her messages and image restoration strategies. Her initial nonresponse could never overcome the criticism leveled at her.

Some Power to Disassociate from MSO

Stewart's nonresponse not only gave power to the media and her attorneys, but it also seemed to disable her, in the beginning at least, from proactively using dissociation strategies (Hearit, 1995) to effectively distance Stewart the person from Martha Stewart the corporation (MSO). Stewart may have been able to differentiate her individual actions from that of the larger group, but evidence indicates that the public felt her actions were indeed representative of the essence of the organization. The puzzled response of MSO stakeholders to Stewart's nonresponse and the dramatic decline in MSO stock value during the critical periods of this case indicate that key stakeholders saw Stewart's essence and those of MSO as one in the same.

For example, the disclosure of Stewart's personal stock sale severely affected MSO investments. It has been reported that MSO's stock, of which Stewart owns 61%, fell about 40% in 2002 and another 16% June 3 and 4, 2003, following the new media coverage of federal investigations ("Martha Indicted," 2003). As media coverage indicates, the selling of stock that caused Stewart's image crisis saved her $45,000, but her net worth following the crisis fell by at least $300 to $400 million because of declining stock values, legal fees, and lost business opportunities ("Martha Indicted," 2003; Tyre & McGinn, 2003). Even after Stewart created the website, MSO value fell. Between June 6 and June 14, 2003, MSO's stock lost nearly one-third of its value (Arnold, 2003). Further, many consumers reported that they would not support products endorsed or produced by Martha Stewart, and their decisions were arguably tainted by press coverage. Undoubtedly, investors' inability to dissociate Stewart's act from MSO's essence was at least partly to blame for these financial hardships.

However, as Puente (2003) noted, "Then there's the other, maybe larger group of Americans who take a pragmatic approach to Martha: Love her or loathe her, they're still going to buy her towels" (p. 10D). It seems that the longer the crisis lasted, the more members of the public were able to dissociate Martha's acts from MSO's essence. As well, although investors strayed away from MSO's stock while Stewart's trial was pending and the direction of MSO was questionable, many investors were said to have a renewed interest in the company. Some analysts claimed the rally to be "a result of investors believing that closure will soon come in this case and that, regardless of the outcome, the company will thrive once its executives can get back to focusing on the business, not on the trial" (Beck, 2004). Between mid-December and late January 2004, its shares climbed from just over $9 to $13.39—its highest level in 19 months (Beck, 2004).

Perhaps one reason for the recovery might just be that analysts were thankful for closure on the legal allegations so that they could focus once again on MSO, and perhaps her customers just "liked her towels" and bought them. We argue, however, that perhaps Stewart was successful at dissociating herself from MSO during the latter stages of this crisis when she appeared on the talk shows noted earlier. Even though not responding and other rhetorical strategies seemed to have stifled this dissociative move, her eventual solid voice on this issue appears to have had some success in managing her image and taking back her power.

In these interviews, Stewart spoke out, separating her personal feelings from business matters, and she positioned herself as an individual with whom audiences could identify rather than a celebrity who they could easily dislike from afar. The *20/20* interview with Barbara Walters gave the public a look at Stewart's history and background: "Martha Stewart had an all-American upbringing. We visited her hometown in New Jersey where she was an excellent student and a teen model. Early on, she was ambitious but always managed to have time for those she cared about" (Walters & Stossel, 2003, n.p.). This interview encouraged the audience to perceive Stewart as a "real person." For instance, Walters and Stewart drove through Stewart's hometown in New Jersey, and they discussed Stewart's young marriage to her former husband. Stewart's mother was interviewed briefly. The interview also clarified what type of charges were actually being brought against Stewart.

When the topic of her image was introduced, Stewart explained that the jokes made about her on late night television did not bother her. In fact, she noted that television hosts like Jay Leno and David Letterman were ". . . doing their job. . . . I consider them friends actually" (Walters & Stossel, 2003, n.p.). However, Stewart's tone changed when confronted with political cartoons that featured her in striped prison outfits and cooking meals in a prison kitchen. She called the cartoons "unnecessary" and "cruel." She added that they "hurt me. They hurt my family." From a public relations perspective, these responses allowed her audience to see that, even though she was a high-profile celebrity, she could relate to everyone else by having hurt feelings.

Later, Walters (Walters & Stossel, 2003) asked Stewart, "Why do so many people hate you?" In response, Stewart claimed that "it's just a part of being human" and "those who you perceive to hate me, don't know me. I'm not perfect." Stewart also commented on the NBC movie and two unauthorized biographies as being "a far cry from reality." Although her attempts to appear more "human" to her audiences did not help her legal situation, her messages probably gained some public sympathy. Here, the power of talk and honest communication—or responding—help to foster a positive image—a stark contrast to nonresponse that gives up power and angers people.

These guest appearances allowed Stewart finally to be seen in the public eye; however, because of the sensitivity of the trial, she was unable to make comments about legal details of the upcoming trial. In fact, in the *20/20* interview with Barbara Walters (Walters & Stossel, 2003), Stewart shyed away from commenting on the legal situation of Sam Waksal, former CEO of Imclone, by politely saying, "I'm sorry Barbara. You know I can't comment on that." Furthermore, when asked if she was able to say whether or not she was innocent, Stewart hesitantly stated, "I would like to say out loud that I am innocent, and I believe that the trial will prove that." Prosecutors claimed that stating her innocence was a crime because the statements "were false and intended to deceive investors in order to cushion her falling stock price" (Walters & Stossel, 2003). Once again, legal requirements served to silence her voice and disempower her.

It is problematic to claim that her appearances on talk shows and the open letters on her website finally served to give Stewart a voice and move her to a position of control over her image and the disassociation she wanted from MSO. Nevertheless, her stock did recover most of its value after these appearances, a reflection of simple reassurance on the part of investors. Perhaps another factor was Stewart's eventual personal messages, which then made her "real," a "human" and "sensitive" person. In her interviews she recovered some of her voice and consequently moved away from the microlevel of nonresponse and more toward the macrolevel of power and a stronger voice.

CONCLUSION

This study proposes a model for understanding image restoration strategies when nonresponse, in essence, gives up the organization's power in a crisis situation; we term this the *micropolitics of nonresponse.* Using the Martha Stewart case study, we find that bringing together Foucault's micropolitics of power and the image restoration and crisis communication literatures suggests a framework for better understanding rhetorical strategies in campaign communication. More than just nonresponse as a communicative act and image restoration strategies as responses to a crisis, the micropolitics of power explains the strategy of nonresponse and details the process of its uses and consequent effects.

We envision a two-level model of nonresponse and power, the microlevel, which is initially the role of the accused, and the macrolevel, which is initially the role of the accusers. Further, we suggest that, as in the Stewart case, an organizational representative—at the bar of the court of public opinion—who does not respond in a timely manner will remain at the microlevel and give up power to control her/his voice. As suggested by this case, this decision to be nonresponsive (often influenced by the legal department in an organization) effectively gives power over to the accusers. If, however, an accused answers an allegation immediately, with a strong voice and clear position, the accused may move to the macrolevel of empowerment with control over her/his voice.

The vital benefit of the concept of the micropolitics of power is that it captures both power discrepancies and the strategy of nonresponse in a crisis situation. The Stewart case demonstrates that, had Stewart taken the offensive in her defense, openly and honestly answering her critics at the very outset within the legal boundaries she had, she might have mitigated the appearance of guilt and restored her positive image more swiftly. Her reluctance to speak paralyzed her attempts to portray herself as a victim, in essence leaving the public to question why Stewart waited so long to respond if the charges were indeed "baseless." We admit that the importance of an immediate response is recognized by public relations but not necessarily favored by legal advisers. Saying "no comment" in any form may be reasonable legal advice at a *literal* level, but at a *semantic* level, many (especially in the news media) may see it as meaning that there is more to uncover that is not being shown. The Stewart case demonstrates how the lack of cooperation and dialogue between legal counsel and public relations in a crisis interrupts the flow of information, a silent move that ultimately hurts personal and corporation images. We also argue that Stewart might have been able to overcome the negative effects garnered by her nonresponse had she chosen different image restoration strategies such as mortification. Of that, however, we cannot be sure.

We are not arguing that no response is always a bad strategy or that such silence always functions at the microlevel. For Stewart, not answering was elected as a strategy, and it had a negative effect on her image restoration campaign. For other campaign situations, however, silence might be the preferred or desirable strategy that functions at the macrolevel of power; for example, a corporation holding back information until it can be released at a strategic time as a momentous occasion. We suggest that the contribution of Foucault's conception of power is that it incorporates a step-by-step process; identifies a two-site location of power; demonstrates the flow, surrender, and dynamics of power; and, importantly, accommodates rhetorical strategies at both the micro and macro levels, based on the specifics of individual campaign situations.

For the public relations professional, a lesson to take from the Stewart case study is that responding or not responding to audiences during the time of a crisis is indeed a supremely strategic decision. As an advisor to a corporation, a public relations professional must weigh the consequences of not responding to the media, employees, or government investigators. The organization/person, as the accused, must appear honest and open about the crisis situation in order to operate from a "power-full" position. To not answer or not respond can have severe image consequences in some cases, effectively disempowering the organization/person. In particular, when attorneys become involved and resist the need for the organization to respond, the public relations function must step in and plead the importance of some kind of public communication to all relevant and interested audiences.

NOTE

1. Arguably, the personal and professional harm to Martha Stewart's personal and professional images may turn out to be only short term. At this writing, Stewart only recently has concluded her probation after serving jail time.

REFERENCES

Acki, N., & Robertson, T. (2003). Stewart is indicted; steps down charges include conspiracy, fraud. *The Boston Globe,* p. A1.

Allen, C. (2003, May 17). Ready "Martha?" Start talking. *The Washington Times,* p. D01.

Arnold, C. (2003). News roundup. *Marketing News, 37*(14), 3, 26.

Beck, R. (2004, January 31). What's really driving Martha Stewart Living stock up? *The Detroit News*. Retrieved March 5, 2004, from http://www.detnews.com/2004/business/0401/31/business-51140.htm

Benoit, W. L. (1995). *Accounts, excuses, and apologies: A theory of image restoration strategies.* Albany: State University of New York Press.

Best, S., & Kellner, D. (1991). *Postmodern theory.* New York: Guilford.

Brown, A. L. (2000). *On Foucault.* Belmont, CA: Wadsworth.

Brummett, B. (1980). Towards a theory of silence as a political strategy. *Quarterly Journal of Speech, 66*, 289-303.

Byrnes, N. (2003). Propping up the house that Martha built. *Business Week, 3837*, 38.

Cameron, G. T., Cropp, F., & Reber, B. H. (2001). Getting past platitudes: Factors limiting accommodation in public relations. *Journal of Communication Management, 5*, 242-261.

Coombs, W. T. (1995). The development of guidelines for the selection of the "appropriate" crisis-response strategies. *Management Communication Quarterly, 8*, 447-476.

Emling, S. (2003, June 6). Stewart defends her name with ad. *The Austin (TX) American Statesman*, p. C1.

Farrell, G. (2003, June 5). Stewart fights back, says she's innocent. *USA Today*. Retrieved November 5, 2003, from http://www.usatoday.com/money/industries/ retail/2003-06-03-martha-charges_x.htm

Foucault, M. (1965). *Madness and civilization: A history of insanity in the age of reason.* New York: Pantheon Books.

Foucault, M. (1972). *The archeology of knowledge* (A. M. S. Smith, Trans.). New York: Pantheon Books.

Foucault, M. (1973). *The birth of the clinic: An archaeology of medical perception.* New York: Pantheon Books.

Foucault, M. (1980a). *The history of sexuality* (R. Hurley, Trans.). New York: Pantheon Books.

Foucault, M. (1980b). *Power/knowledge.* Brighton, England: Harvester Press.

Foucault, M. (1984). The subject and power. In B. Wallis (Ed.), *Art after modernism: Rethinking representation* (pp. 417-433). New York: The New Museum of Contemporary Art.

Gilbert, M. (2003, May 19). Cliches cause "Martha" biopic to spoil movie: Doesn't deliver the domestic diva's spice. *The Boston Globe*, p. B7.

Griffin, L. M. (1984). When dreams collide: Rhetorical trajectories in the assassination of President Kennedy. *Quarterly Journal of Speech, 70*, 11-131.

Hearit, K. M. (1995). "Mistakes were made": Organizations, apologia, and crises of social legitimacy. *Communication Studies, 46*, 1-17.

King, L. (2003, December 22). Interview with Martha Stewart, Martha Kostyra [Transcript]. *CNN Larry King Live.* Retrieved February 24, 2004, from Academic Universe (Lexis Nexis).

Koppel, A., Chernoff, A., Lisovicz, S., Feldman, C., & Rodgers, C. (2003, June 8). The case against Martha Stewart [Transcript]. *CNN Live Event/Special.* Retrieved November 4, 2003, from Academic Universe (Lexis Nexis).

Leezenberg, M. (2004). Power and political spirituality: Michel Foucault on the Islamic revolution in Iran. In J. Bernover & J. Carrethe (Eds.), *Michel Foucault and theology* (pp. 99-116). Hampshire, England: Ashgate.

Martha indicted: Stewart, broker face charges of securities fraud, obstruction of justice. (2003, June 5). *CNN-Money* [On-line]. Retrieved November 4, 2003, from http://money.cnn.com/2003/06/04/news/companies/martha/?cnn=yes

McClam, E. (2003a, June 3). *Prosecutors seeking criminal charges against Martha Stewart.* The Associated Press. Retrieved February 24, 2004, from Academic Universe (Lexis Nexis).

McClam, E. (2003b, June 9). *Martha's message: 6 million visit Stewart defense web site.* The Associated Press State & Local Wire. Retrieved February 24, 2004, from Academic Universe (Lexis Nexis).

Morvillo, R., & Tigue, J. J. (2003a, June 4). *Press statement.* Retrieved November 12, 2003, from http://www.marthatalks.com/trial_update/011003.html

Morvillo, R., & Tigue, J. J. (2003b, June 10). *Fact sheet.* Retrieved January 14, 2004, from http://www.marthatalks.com/trial_update/011003.html

Morvillo, R., & Tigue, J. J. (2003c, October 6). *Executive summary of motions.* Retrieved February 22, 2004, from http://www.marthatalks.com/trial_update /100603.html

Morvillo, R., & Tigue, J. J. (2003d, November 14). *Memorandum of law.* Retrieved February 22, 2004, from http://www.marthatalks.com/memorandum_of_ law/111403.html

Parkinson, M. G., Ekachai, D., & Hetherington, L. T. (2001). Public relations law. In R. L. Heath (Ed.), *Handbook of public relations* (pp. 247-257). Thousand Oaks, CA: Sage.

Pollock, A. (2002, June 7). Martha Stewart said to sell shares before F.D.A. ruling. *The New York Times,* p. C4.

Puente, M. (2003, June 12). Martha's innocence: Are people buying it? *USA Today,* p. 10D.

Reber, R. H., Cropp, F., & Cameron, G. T. (2001). Mythic battles: Examining the lawyer-public relations counselor dynamic. *Journal of Public Relations Research, 13,* 187-218.

Reber, B. H., Cropp, F., & Cameron, G. T. (2003). Impossible odds: Contributions of legal counsel and public relations practitioners in a hostile bid for Conrail Inc. by Norfolk Southern Corporation. *Journal of Public Relations Research, 15,* 1-25.

Reynolds, A. (2003, June 6). *The sleazy political persecution of Martha.* Retrieved November 15, 2003, from http://www.marthatalks.com/voices/ci_060603.html

Rosenthal, P. (2003, May 19). Serving venom with the dish. *The Chicago Sun-Times,* p. 45.

Shargel, G. (2004, February 8). *Crime's not fit for prime time.* Retrieved February 22, 2004, from http://www.marthatalks.com/voices/nydn_020804.html

Sheridan, A. (1980). *Michel Foucault: The will to truth.* London: Tavistock.

Shumway, D. (1989). *Michel Foucault.* Boston: Twayne.

Stewart, M. (2003, June 5). *An open letter from Martha Stewart.* Retrieved November 14, 2003, from http://www.marthatalks.com/letter/index.html

Tyre, P., & McGinn, D. (2003). A big house for Martha? *Newsweek, 141*(24), 41.

Walters, B., & Stossel, J. (2003, November 7). *20/20* introduction [Transcript]. ABC News: *20/20.* Retrieved February 24, 2004, from Academic Universe (Lexis Nexis)

chapter 6

Restoring Investor Confidence via Model and Antimodel Advocacy by Merrill Lynch

Jeffrey D. Brand

Corporate America in 2002 faced a rash of scandals and damaging revelations that threatened its credibility. The list of corporate scandals and major companies involved was extensive and included many familiar and well-known organizations: Enron, WorldCom, Arthur Anderson, Tyco, Adelphia Communications, Global Crossing, AOL Time Warner, Bristol-Meyers Squibb, Halliburton, Johnson & Johnson, Qwest Communications, Xerox, Boeing, Microsoft, Merrill Lynch, ImClone, and Martha Stewart Omnimedia (Millar, 2003; Nace, 2003; cf. Chapter 6, this volume). The damage caused by these crises was extensive, going beyond the reputations and careers of executives in these companies. They "wiped out whole companies, destroyed pension plans, devastated families and retirees and shook the very foundation of the United States economy" (Millar, 2003, p. 9).

The fear, distrust, and loss of credibility were felt throughout the economy in the United States and abroad. Efforts since 2002 to repair the damage have been extensive. The crises created an exigency that required responses by political and corporate leadership. On July 9, 2002, President George W. Bush responded to this climate of concern with a major policy address. He reaffirmed what many had been arguing about the corporate world: "At this moment, America's greatest economic need is higher ethical standards" (¶3). The federal government held hearings on the issues and passed a series of new regulations designed to improve the credibility of financial disclosures by corporations. One of the more extensive legislative packages was the Sarbanes-Oxley Act of 2002, designed to "alter accounting, board-room and securities industry practices" (Arkin, 2002, p. 3).

To demonstrate commitment to stakeholders, many corporations responded with plans to restore credibility and trust in their financial services. Even those not directly implicated in the scandals needed to promote a positive public image of integrity and credibility. The stock market, for example, because of these scandals and their impact on investments, lost more that $1 trillion in value (Truitt, 2003). Many retirement funds and small investors lost significant value to their portfolios. The New York Stock Exchange, for the first time in its history, published a booklet designed to reassure small investors and the general public about efforts to restore integrity and credibility to the investment market ("*Your Market*," 2002).

In April 2002, New York State Attorney General Eliot Spitzer investigated Merrill Lynch for conflicts of interest in its banking and investment divisions. Based on that investigation the two parties reached an agreement on May 21, 2002, to enact reforms in Merrill Lynch's business practices, issue an apology, and pay $100 million in fines and penalties (Merrill Lynch, 2002a).

The goals for this chapter are twofold. First, this chapter presents an analysis of Merrill Lynch's efforts to respond to this crisis concerning its financial services practices. It needed to enact strategies to help it restore credibility and legitimacy. Merrill Lynch was not alone on Wall Street; many organizations faced critical scrutiny over their business practices. Yet Merrill Lynch was one of the first to settle with the New York State Attorney General, so its early effort to present a crisis public relations response is worthy of analysis.

A second goal is to reveal how Merrill Lynch's response demonstrates one type of power possessed by public relations professionals. During a crisis, public relations practitioners have a variety of choices to make in framing a response. An important objective is to shape the direction of the crisis in ways more favorable to the organization. In their study of the nuclear power industry's response to the Three Mile Island accident, Dionisopoulos and Crable (1988) identified one aspect of public relations power: "definitional hegemony." This involves "establishing new frames of reference for interpreting 'relevant' information and thus, influencing the discussion in ways designed to have policy impact" (p. 136). They believe that one potentially important strategy by public relations professionals is the "attempt to secure a desired outcome by aiming their messages toward leading and dominating the terminological parameters of emergent issues" (p. 143).

PUBLIC RELATIONS POWER AND MANAGING MESSAGES DURING A CRISIS

The ability to control the discourse surrounding an organizational crisis is a valuable form of power. Elwood (1995) defined one type of power as "terminological control," which is a means to "influence the way people think about those issues and the ethical choices involved with them" (p. 260). By recognizing this form of power as an important feature of the rhetorical process, we can better understand "the influence that symbol makers like public relations practitioners have in a culture through word and image" (Mickey, 2003, p. 19).

This view is representative of contemporary research that now views organizational crises as opportunities as well as obstacles. A crisis is no longer considered the death knell for organizations. Effective public relations can help turn a crisis into something that can actually help an organization. Alsop (2004) explained that "most companies manage to emerge intact from crises," and "most adroit companies actually burnish their reputations" (p. 219). By viewing crises in this way, it is possible to view them as a means for organizations "to transform and restructure in ways leading to growth and renewal" (Seeger & Ulmer, 2002, p. 137).

To exercise this power, organizations need to create a response that is capable of changing the focus of the crisis from a negative association to one that is more positive. One type of discourse that reflects this strategy is a "discourse of renewal" (Seeger, Sellnow, & Ulmer, 2003, p. 152). Renewal can be a powerful resource when an organization can frame a crisis in a way that develops a positive view of itself. The crisis becomes an important opportunity for the organization to present itself in a way that is more in line with the values of society. An organization, then, has the potential to better fulfill the public's expectations of an organization's social responsibility. By pursuing this strategy, "crises have the potential to transform companies into more responsive, efficient, and effective competitors matched more appropriately to their environment" (p. 266).

Merrill Lynch used this crisis of conflicts of interest in its banking and investment divisions to not only restore a measure of credibility for its organization, but it also employed symbolic resources to manage the conditions and definition of the discourse surrounding its business and the industry as a whole. This case study illustrates the exercise of power by public relations campaigns to manage crisis and public debate. The key to this power exercise is practitioners' use of model and antimodel argumentation strategies, which is the focus of this chapter.

Corporate Responses to Reputation Crises

Corporate America has a long history of dealing with attacks to its image due to actions within and beyond its control. Crisis communication is an established professional and academic research focus, and scholars in public relations and other disciplinary perspectives have studied the strategies available to these organizations. Typical of this research are studies of corporate *apologia*, directed toward an understanding of how to answer charges of wrongdoing. Ware and Linkugel's (1973) work on political *apologia* identified strategies appropriate for apologetic discourse surrounding accusations toward individuals faced with attacks on their credibility. That research has been expanded to apply it to "rhetoric which is corporate rather than individual centered" (Schultz & Seeger, 1991, p. 53).

Benoit (1995) identified five image restoration strategies for organizations faced with threats to their reputations: denial, evading responsibility, reducing offensiveness of the event, corrective action, and mortification (for the last of these, cf. Burke, 1961/1970). These strategies have been the subject of a variety of studies designed to explore their effectiveness. The strategy of corrective action is the one most vital to this study of Merrill Lynch's efforts to restore its reputation. Benoit and Czerwinski (1997) explained that corrective action is useful because, "unlike compensation, which seeks to pay for a problem, corrective action seeks to prevent or correct it" (p. 45).

Corrective action has been identified as particularly useful because it can go beyond the moment and suggests long-term solutions to a crisis and the hope that it will not be repeated (Benoit & Brinson, 1994; Hearit, 1995; Sellnow, 1993). This approach would seem valuable in crisis situations that involve a set of corporate practices and values. The 2002 scandals mentioned at the beginning of this chapter demonstrated an ongoing pattern of negative behaviors that had created the crises. An organization searching for a way to restore its reputation needed to address the causes of these scandals and recommend effective solutions. Benoit and Drew (1997) evaluated the appropriateness and effectiveness of different image repair strategies. Their study concluded that corrective action was "perceived as more effective and appropriate than most image restoration options" (p. 159). There are different ways to justify and explain corrective action taken by an organization, and this study evaluates the strategy behind the discourse surrounding Merrill Lynch's corrective action efforts.

Contemporary corporate crises suggest that, more and more, corporations are being held responsible for their commitment to goals beyond profit making. Seeger (1997) explained that corporations must support "important social goals and values" and help solve "social problems that affect both society and the organization" (p. 119). These expectations are covered by a variety of umbrella terms, including *corporate virtue*, *social responsibility*, and *corporate citizenship* (Alsop, 2004). The controversies faced by companies in 2002 are complicated by these expectations because they place additional burdens on corporate behavior and discourse. It is not enough to say that a company has done nothing illegal. Its actions are evaluated on other criteria, including ethics and corporate values. These expectations mean that public relations on behalf of corporations must include messages that reflect these larger expectations.

There can be advantages to having these additional expectations from stakeholders. Organizations that can successfully represent themselves as ethical and with a concern for other values can use such discourse to their advantage. Bostdorff and Vibbert (1994) explained that advocating values serves three functions for organizations: "(1) It enhances the organization's image; (2) It deflects criticism of the organization and/or its policies, products, and services; (3) It establishes value premises that can be used in later discourse" (p. 146). During a time of crisis, values advocacy would appear to be a useful resource. This approach could assist in the organization's rebuilding of its image and help it to move beyond the current crisis.

The crises of 2002 suggest that an appropriate public relations response would include messages designed to promote corrective action on the part of organizations accused of wrongdoing in combination with a recommitment to the values expected by the public of an ethical, socially responsible organization. This combination of expectations may be accomplished by a rhetoric of corporate responsibility. Heath (1997) explained that values of "corporate responsibility are the product of advocacy" (p. 127). The choices made concerning corporate values and corrective action during a crisis must be justified and argued before stakeholders if they are to achieve legitimacy with those audiences.

One strategy to use when engaging in values advocacy is to employ model and antimodel arguments in structuring a response. Sellnow and Brand (2001) evaluated the response by Nike CEO Phil Knight to offer corrective action to counter criticism of Nike's manufacturing processes. Sweatshop protests, boycotts, and negative publicity about Nike's use of labor and its environment policies had damaged the organization's credibility and profitability. Within the organization's changes in policies were efforts to reform the athletic shoe industry as a whole and a commitment to establish new standards for conducting business. Sellnow and Brand's study identified possible advantages to using model and antimodel arguments, both to assist in restoration of Nike's reputation and deflect criticism directed toward its specific behavior. They concluded their study with the observation that Knight's "arguments have given Nike the opportunity to refocus the debate and the time needed to regain credibility" (p. 293).

MODEL AND ANTIMODEL ARGUMENTS

Perelman and Olbrechts-Tyteca (1969) provided an extensive analysis of argument schemes that may be used to influence audiences. These schemes reflect "culturally-held beliefs about the ways we form new beliefs from already accepted premises" (Warnick & Kline, 1992, p. 3). The "power of corporate communications" lies in the ability "not only to reflect the society of which they are part, they also help create and recreate it" (Cheney & Dionisopoulos, 1989, p. 144). For the purposes of this study, Perelman and Olbrechts-Tyteca's (1969) argument scheme identified as model and antimodel argument is an instructive place to begin to understand the argumentation strategies available to corporate rhetors faced with a crisis and endeavoring to restore credibility through corrective action efforts.

Perelman and Olbrechts-Tyteca (1969) identified discourse that resorts "to the particular case" as arguments that establish the structure of reality (p. 350). This discourse becomes an example of model and antimodel argumentation when "particular behavior may serve, not only to establish or illustrate a general rule, but also to incite to an action inspired by it" (p. 362). Warnick and Kline (1992) expanded on Perelman and Olbrechts-Tyteca's definition: "Argument from model and antimodel presents a person or group as a model to be imitated or avoided" (p. 9). In a crisis such as the one Merrill Lynch faced, an organization might resort to model argumentation to help it restore credibility. Sellnow and Brand (2001) explained that an "organization can regain its model status by shunning unacceptable practices. As such, an organization can reemerge as a model by stressing its unwillingness to conform to standards that are not acceptable" (p. 283).

The model and antimodel argumentation scheme functions by use of a rhetorical process known as *dissociation*, "whereby a unitary idea is bifurcated into two rival ideas" (Hearit, 1995, p. 121). For the crisis communicator, this means that it may be possible to "separate the juxtaposition of the organization with wrongdoing and thus diffuse the degree of guilt and reduce organizational culpability" (Hearit, 1995, p. 121). Faced with a challenge to its image, a corporation might seek corrective action that responds to the specific allegations and appeals to a form of model argument. This new advocacy might serve as a strategy to help overcome the damage to its reputation. In the economic climate of 2002, an appeal to model and antimodel behavior that responds to issues of corporate responsibility would be a valuable one. This strategy might also help the organization to reinforce the positive image of renewal as part of its discourse in response to a crisis situation.

MERRILL LYNCH'S REPONSES TO THE CHARGES

On April 8, 2002, New York State Attorney General Eliot Spitzer announced an investigation into charges of conflicts of interest on the part of Merrill Lynch. The investigation discovered e-mail messages within the organization that revealed "analysts privately disparaging companies while publicly recommending their stocks" (Office of New York State Attorney, 2002a). The smoking gun represented by the e-mail messages helped the New York State Attorney General to pressure Merrill Lynch into a settlement. It also threatened Merrill Lynch's reputation sufficiently that it needed to seek ways to restore confidence in its stock analyst and investment banking divisions.

Merrill Lynch was actually faced with three crises in 2002. The conflict of interest charges were the most serious charges faced by the company. The company was also involved in Enron Corporation's collapse for its help in setting up deals that Enron used to hide its poor financial condition. On top of these incidents, charges against Martha Stewart for insider trading (cf. Chapter 5, this volume) involved a Merrill Lynch broker and his assistant. The company's credibility and reputation took a powerful hit, according to its own internal research division. Before the accusations against Merrill Lynch by the New York State Attorney General, internal research revealed that, among its client investors, 64% thought that the company had "high integrity." By the fall of 2002, only 39% of its client investors thought that company had high integrity, a drop of 25%. Only 16% of nonclient investors thought the company deserved high marks for integrity after the scandal broke (Alsop, 2004). The confluence of these crises is credited with creating a financial loss of "more than $20 billion in market capitalization due in large part to the reputation damage" (Alsop, 2004, p. 212).

Settlement Terms and Effects on Public Relations Messages

On May 21, 2002, Merrill Lynch and the New York State Attorney General's office announced a settlement of the case (Office of New York State Attorney, 2002b). The agreement consisted of three parts: an apology, a fine of $100 million, and a set of reforms to Merrill Lynch's business practices. All three parts of the settlement deserve evaluation. The apology and fine were not remarkable as argumentation strategies. The reform package, however, reflects the strategy of model and antimodel argumentation and therefore receives most of the evaluation in this chapter.

The company apologized, but it did not admit to doing anything wrong or illegal. Merrill Lynch explained that the "settlement represents neither evidence nor admission of wrongdoing or liability" (Merrill Lynch, 2002a, p. 1). The apology focused on the e-mail messages that helped spark the controversy, a kind of mortification for the inappropriate behavior of Merrill Lynch employees. David Komansky, chairman and CEO at Merrill Lynch, explained, "We were embarrassed by them. Some of the e-mails were inappropriate. We felt an apology was in order" (Marchini, 2002, p. 2).

Merrill Lynch's reluctance to issue a more extensive apology was understandable. It was subject to significant civil suits by investors who felt analysts misled them. The wording of the apology allowed the company "to sound apologetic while being careful not to assume any culpability for its actions" (Hearit & Brown, 2004, p. 463). As an apology, it was perfectly appropriate in light of the company's efforts to limit its legal liability. As litigation public relations, the apology fulfilled its role as a statement. The apology alone would not, however, be a sufficient response by a company seeking to restore lost credibility and clients in light of the scandal's severity. The other two parts of the settlement agreement also have roles to play in the process of restoring credibility.

The $100 million in fines was certainly a substantial penalty, but it was not considered restitution for people who might have been misled by the company. The money was paid as fines to the State of New York and other states joining the settlement. Some of the money went into a victims' compensation fund, but it was far less than the value of claims against the company by angry investors. The fines appear to an outsider to represent a significant penalty and, therefore, serve as a way to create the appearance that the company is serious about its contrition on the issue of the e-mails. But, as one reporter explained, "according to its most recent annual financial report, $100 million is less than one-third of what the firm paid for office supplies and postage last year" (Morgenson, 2002a, p. C1). Symbolically, the fine communicated that Merrill Lynch agreed to a significant settlement. It helps Merrill Lynch's reputation more than it damaged its bottom line.

Hearit and Brown's (2004) essay on the Merrill Lynch settlement argues that, because of liability concerns, corporations are not going to make a strong apology statement. They claim that it is in the compensation, by paying a fine or making restitution, that the "acknowledgement of wrongdoing lies," not the apology statement (p. 465). By making a weak apology, the company protected itself from liability issues and used a fine or penalty to communicate its assumption of some guilt or responsibility. Hearit and Brown (2004) were critical of Merrill Lynch's settlement because it did not offer a strong apology and did nothing to compensate the victims of its corporate policies.

There is a third part of the settlement agreement that Hearit and Brown's (2004) essay does not address: the proposed changes in Merrill Lynch's organizational structure and how it would conduct its investment business. Hearit and Brown argued, "Merrill Lynch showed little regard for the process of correction" (p. 464). But the third part of the settlement agreement does address the issue of correction and reputation management. In their essay, Hearit and Brown (2004) did not look at how this part of the settlement functions. An analysis of the third element of the settlement reveals that it is a form of corrective action, articulated in the language of a model and antimodel argument. It is a significant part of the whole public relations effort by Merrill Lynch to get through the crisis and reestablish its legitimacy in the investment industry. This part of the settlement represents an example of public relations' power to influence perceptions of a crisis. It contributes to the process of restoring credibility to the organization and reflects the discourse of renewal that allows the organization to move past the immediate crisis and advance its image.

The proposal to alter Merrill Lynch's business practices was the most heavily publicized part of the settlement agreement by both Merrill Lynch and its chief critic, New York State Attorney General Eliot Spitzer. This part of the settlement also continued to be, for the next year, a point of reference and evidence of reform by both Merrill Lynch and the investment industry. As an example of corrective action, it fulfilled the expectations one should have of an effort to argue that the mistakes that created the original crisis would not recur (Benoit, 1995).

In a paid advertisement that ran in major financial and general newspapers in the United States and Europe the day after the settlement, Merrill Lynch (2002b) explained that it had "set new standards for independence, objectivity and excellence in securities research" (p. 1). In its press release, David H. Komansky, chairman and CEO, and Stan O'Neal, president and COO of Merrill Lynch, claimed: "Our objective from the start has been to reinforce investor confidence in the way securities analysts conduct their research and make investment recommendations" (Merrill Lynch, 2002a, p. 2).

The new standard Merrill Lynch promoted was an effective way to deflect criticism of the company and offer corrective action designed to restore investor confidence. The success of this strategy can be seen by the publicity it generated for both Merrill Lynch and the Attorney General's office. Merrill Lynch announced the new standards in press releases and paid advertisements designed to promote its changes in business practices. The advertisements ran in major national financial newspapers and in papers in major U.S. cities. A nearly identical advertisement appeared abroad. In its apology statement, Merrill Lynch argued: "Through the adoption of new policies, intensified oversight, and strengthened enforcement of existing ones, we pledge to provide investors with research that sets a new industry standard for independence" (Merrill Lynch, 2002a, p. 2). This same message was reflected in its advertising campaign, which announced, "Today, our clients benefit from a new standard of research excellence and a Merrill Lynch more committed than ever to earning their trust" (Merrill Lynch, 2002b, p. 1).

By publicizing its agreement in this way, Merrill Lynch adopted model arguments to redefine this crisis and its outcome. Perelman and Olbrechts-Tyteca (1969) explained that a model argument "shows what behavior to follow, and also serves as a guarantee for an adopted behavior" (p. 364). By setting itself up as a new industry standard for behavior, Merrill Lynch's business practices were elevated from questionable to exceptional. This corrective action strategy helped it to eliminate the fear that inappropriate behaviors might return and made it a model corporate citizen with newly established corporate practices and values that exceeded the industry's norm. This move set Merrill Lynch on the road toward a restoration of its reputation with clients and other stakeholders.

Merrill Lynch's use of antimodel argumentation is more subtle and implied in its discourse about new standards of excellence. Nowhere in its advertising or press releases, which announced the new standards, is there any explicit reference to the scandal that led to these changes. By proposing a model argument in favor of organizational changes, Merrill Lynch is implying its intention "to emulate the one or to shun the other" (Perelman & Olbrechts-Tyteca, 1969, p. 368). The antimodel is represented by its past behaviors and in its commitment not to repeat them. Stakeholders familiar with Merrill Lynch already know about its past problems and the accusations against it. There is no need to explicitly refer to its antimodel performance in the past when promoting new model behaviors in the future.

Merrill Lynch is also using an implied antimodel argument by claiming that it represents a new standard for the industry. By announcing reforms that go beyond its competitors, it became a model for credible investment activity; its competitors, as part of the old way of practicing business, implicitly became the antimodel because defining any idea implies the existence of its opposite (Burke, 1966). The "strategy of suing one bad actor in an industry and then pressuring the whole industry into agreeing to wholesale reform" (Walha & Filusch, 2005, p. 1114) was part of the strategy employed by Eliot Spitzer, the New York State Attorney General. Merrill Lynch looks better if it follows the prescribed path created by this strategy, especially if it is the first in the industry to take these steps. Other firms would be encouraged to follow its lead, but only the leader gets credit for its innovation. By taking the initiative, Merrill Lynch obtained the most benefit from its settlement with Spitzer, one which its competitors could not receive. Merrill

Lynch was placed in a position of power and influence. It led its competitors with a message that established the standards to be used to evaluate itself.

As Attorney General of New York, Eliot Spitzer was on a campaign to clean up and regulate many of the industries on Wall Street. In reaching this agreement with Merrill Lynch, Spitzer also promoted it as a new standard or model of corporate behavior and represented it as a viable solution to reform the entire industry: "Mr. Spitzer said the settlement should be used as a 'template' for other brokerages to make necessary changes" (Goff, 2002). Spitzer also was up for reelection. As of September 2005, he was considered a candidate for state governor. Spitzer was making model arguments by representing this agreement as a model capable of transforming an entire industry and its practices.

Spitzer's own campaign to reform Wall Street practices helped Merrill Lynch because it placed it out of his crosshairs: The company already settled with him, and Spitzer's action gave Merrill Lynch the upper hand because it now represented a model to which others in the industry should aspire. Speaking to Bill Moyers on *NOW*, Spitzer explained, "We need the other companies to step up to the standard that Merrill Lynch has adopted today. We need the other regulators, the S.E.C., the N.A.S.D., to adopt more rigorous standards of conduct, hopefully that will happen" (Moyers, 2002). Spitzer was out to use this case to promote industry-wide reform efforts and respond to investor concerns. "Real reform is the key to restoring investor confidence" (Office of New York State Attorney, 2002c, p. 1).

Spitzer's campaign for reforms also presents the other side of the model argument—the antimodel. According to Perelman and Olbrechts-Tyteca (1969), "whereas reference to a model makes it possible to encourage a particular kind of behavior, reference to an antimodel or foil serves to deter people from it" (p. 366). Spitzer's goal to reform the standards for the entire industry received a boost from the Merrill Lynch agreement: "Mr. Spitzer said he wants the SEC to accept the reforms as industry standards" (Goff, 2002). Merrill Lynch's competitors and other regulatory agencies serve as antimodels because they operate under old standards that represent a conflict of interest and endanger investors. By establishing these sides to the issue, Merrill Lynch's reputation was enhanced, not damaged, by making changes in its business practices.

Benefits of the Model/Antimodel Argument Strategy

The strategy in this settlement agreement placed Merrill Lynch in a powerful position, removing the negative emphasis and news the scandal had originally generated. Discussion and news about Merrill Lynch shifted in the media away from fraud to industry reforms. The impressive thing about this strategy is that Eliot Spitzer, who was at one time aggressively attacking

Merrill Lynch as representative of Wall Street fraud, was now publicly praising and advocating Merrill Lynch's program of reforms as a new model for the industry. By changing the focus and language of the issue, Merrill Lynch effectively silenced one of its most influential critics and transformed him into a spokesperson for its business practices.

Reactions by other members of the investment community also helped Merrill Lynch by positively responding to this model argument and adopting the new proposed standards for investment banking and stock analysts in their own organizations. Salomon Smith Barney announced plans to alter its research unit after seeing the model offered by Merrill Lynch. Solomon's chief executive said that the Merrill settlement "set a new industry standard necessary to maintain investor confidence and provide a useful template for the rest of the industry to follow" (Chaffin & Boroff, 2002, p. 11). Spitzer hailed the action as one of the goals behind the Merrill Lynch agreement: "To see the substantial changes in compensation that we crafted for Merrill now be adopted by another major investment house is an affirmation that this can work" (Morgenson, 2002b, p. C1). Goldman Sachs also announced changes to its research division at the same time as the Solomon decision (Morgenson, 2002b).

Unlike the Nike case in which industry-wide behavior was not readily changed to emulate the model offered by Phil Knight in his speech, the Merrill Lynch agreement has been treated as a model for reform. Corporations that have adopted some of these changes have pushed Merrill Lynch's reputation higher, helping it overcome the original complaints that led to the agreement in the first place. In April 2003, Eliot Spitzer and William Donaldson, Chairman of the Securities and Exchange Commission, announced a "global settlement" with 10 investment firms to address the same kinds of accusations originally leveled against Merrill Lynch. The $1.4 billion settlement included structural changes to the investment industry that were first modeled in the Merrill Lynch settlement (Office of New York Attorney, 2003). These efforts helped to vindicate Merrill Lynch's original settlement and efforts to become an industry leader. With the global settlement announcement, Stanley O'Neal, Merrill Lynch's chief executive, announced at the company's annual meeting that the "process of rebuilding investor confidence is well underway" (Morton, 2003, p. FP1).

There are indications that the global settlement that followed the framework established in the original Merrill Lynch settlement was successful in improving investor confidence. Stock shares of the firms involved in the global settlement were up 6% five months after the first announcement of the agreement, even with an average overall drop in the Dow Jones Industrial Average of 2.4% over the same period of time (Morton, 2003). Merrill Lynch also began to receive additional good news over a year after the original settlement. The courts rejected or dismissed at least four initial class-action lawsuits filed against Merrill Lynch for misleading investors (Chaffin & Silverman, 2003). The litigation public relations campaign by Merrill Lynch appears to have been successful, and Merrill Lynch has weathered some of its threatened legal problems. By mid-2003, Merrill Lynch had posted strong second-quarter earnings, and its own research unit reported a 65% favorability rating for the company by nonclient investors (Alsop, 2004).

The settlement model that State Attorney General Eliot Spitzer agreed to with Merrill Lynch in 2002 continues to be used to investigate and change Wall Street. The trio of apology, fine, and structural changes has been applied to other financial industries and organizations. In January 2005, Marsh & McLennan Companies (2005) agreed to a similar type of settlement as part of an investigation of the insurance industry. This format continues to be applied to corporations facing accusations of wrongdoing and, as such, offers them a way out, just as Merrill Lynch was able to accomplish. Spitzer admits that the goal of his investigations has never been to destroy companies, which would be too harmful to the market, small investors, and capital formation. His goal was to "change the rules of the game" and to "create a system of structural reform" that would benefit investors and punish companies who cheat (Federal News Service, 2003). Organizations that respond to accusations with an appropriate model and antimodel strategy can overcome crises and find the way back to restoration of their reputation and credibility.

CONCLUSION

Public relations efforts by organizations facing a crisis are opportunities to reveal some of the power of public relations to influence audiences. Crisis may provide "an important opportunity to transform and restructure the ways leading to growth and renewal" (Seeger & Ulmer, 2002, p. 137). One method for expressing the power of public relations is to use it as a means of "terminological control; to control the terms about a particular issue is to influence the way people think" (Elwood, 1995, p. 260). The application of model and antimodel argumentation has the power to reframe the crisis into terms more favorable to the image restoration campaign for an organization or even an industry.

Most corporations belong to a larger community of similar businesses, all competing for customers and clients. As in the Nike case, this study "suggests that the value of model and antimodel arguments that propose industry-wide corrective action is based on their capacity to enable an organization to frame the debate surrounding the crisis" (Sellnow & Brand, 2001, p. 290). With its suggestions for reform, Merrill Lynch took control of the charges against itself and used its own model behavior to direct public attention to its reforms, not its past actions. Without having to give ground on possible legal action by clients through an extensive apology, Merrill protected its reputation with other clients and future business opportunities.

Merrill Lynch successfully used model argumentation in crafting its corrective action response to claims of dubious business behaviors. Going beyond an apology and fine, the model argument created conditions for the restoration of Merrill Lynch's public image. Despite the effort of political leaders to ensure the integrity of the market, CEOs "understand something that politicians won't admit, which is that only business is truly capable of restoring confidence in business" ("The November Markets," 2002).

The publicity that must occur when an organization is accused of wrongdoing does not have to always damage its reputation. By capitalizing on this publicity, the organization can use the opportunity to promote future actions (Crable & Vibbert, 1985; Johnson & Sellnow, 1995; Sellnow & Brand, 2001). The advantage that Merrill had with publicity about its situation is that some of its competitors and attackers joined its efforts at industry-wide reform. This cooperation demonstrates the effectiveness of the model arguments because they could actually be followed and implemented by other companies. This scenario makes such reform efforts more genuine and less likely to be viewed as an attempt to avoid taking blame and placing it on the industry. As Sellnow and Brand (2001) explained, "Ethical organizations responding to crises would restructure the reality of their industry with the primary intent to correct its flaws" (p. 292).

This study reveals some of the strategic importance to organizations of using model arguments with corrective action when responding to a crisis. This argument form makes it possible to direct the debate past the immediate issue to one of future actions. It brings a whole industry into an issue, softening the critique of the specific organization and broadening the issue to include other companies. This argument type can also lead to positive evaluations of corrective action because it can be adopted by other organizations, lending them greater credibility and force.

The current public scrutiny of corporate behavior indicates that challenges to the reputation of corporations are far from over. The insertion of political and legal remedies is expanding the role of the public in private corporate activities. The choice of model and antimodel arguments to respond to these attacks is appropriate and may be applied even more often in the future. Understanding how such a strategy influences public debate and perceptions of industries is vital to adopting a critical perspective on this public relations approach. Effective public relations strategies have the power to influence the public perception of an organization. They have the power to control the way a crisis is defined, described, and resolved in the public mind.

REFERENCES

Alsop, R. J. (2004). *The 18 immutable laws of corporate reputation: Creating, protecting, and repairing your most valuable asset.* New York: Wall Street Journal Books.

Arkin, S. S. (2002). Business crime corporate responsibility legislation: Conflicts, uncertainties. *New York Law Journal, 228,* 3.

Benoit, W. L. (1995). *Accounts, excuses, and apologies: A theory of image restoration strategies.* Albany: State University of New York Press.

Benoit, W. L., & Brinson, S. L. (1994). AT&T: "Apologies are not enough." *Communication Quarterly, 42,* 38-57.

Benoit, W. L., & Czerwinski, A. (1997). A critical analysis of US Air's image repair discourse. *Business Communication Quarterly, 60*(3), 38-57.

Benoit, W. L., & Drew, S. (1997). Appropriateness and effectiveness of image repair strategies. *Communication Reports, 10,* 153-161.

Bostdorff, D., & Vibbert, S. L. (1994). Values advocacy: Enhancing organizational images, deflecting public criticism, and grounding future arguments. *Public Relations Review, 20,* 141-158.

Burke, K. (1966). *Language as symbolic action: Essays on life, literature, and method.* Berkeley: University of California Press.

Burke, K. (1970). *The rhetoric of religion: Studies in logology.* Berkeley: University of California Press. (Original work published 1961)

Bush, G. W. (2002, July 9). *President announces tough new enforcement initiatives for reform: Remarks by the President on corporate responsibility* [Public address at the Regent Wall Street Hotel, New York City]. Retrieved October 3, 2005, from http://www.whitehouse.gov/news/releases/2002/07/20020709-4.html

Chaffin, J., & Boroff, P. (2002, May 23). Solomon agrees to new standards for analysts. *The Financial Post,* p. 11.

Chaffin, J., & Silverman, G. (2003, July 3). Merrill wins third legal victory: Judge finds no evidence firm caused investors to lose money. *The Financial Times,* p. 21.

Cheney, G., & Dionisopoulos, G. N. (1989). Public relations? No, relations with publics: A rhetorical-organizational approach to contemporary corporate communications. In C. H. Botan & J. V. Hazelton (Eds.), *Public relations theory* (pp. 135-157). Hillsdale, NJ: Erlbaum.

Crable, R. E., & Vibbert, S. L. (1985). Managing issues and influencing public policy. *Public Relations Review, 11,* 3-15.

Dionisopoulos, G. N., & Crable, R. E. (1988). Definitional hegemony as a public relations strategy: The rhetoric of the nuclear power industry after Three Mile Island. *Central States Speech Journal, 39,* 134-145.

Elwood, W. N. (1995). Public relations and the ethics of the moment. In W. N. Elwood (Ed.), *Public relations inquiry as rhetorical criticism* (pp. 255-275). Westport, CT: Praeger.

Federal News Service. (2003, April 28). Press conference with William H. Donaldson, Chairman, Securities and Exchange Commission; and New York Attorney General Eliot Spitzer [Transcript]. Retrieved May 1, 2003, from Academic Universe (Lexis Nexis).

Goff, S. (2002, May 21). *Merrill to pay $100 million to settle state charges of misleading investors.* Dow Jones Newswires; 609-520-7835. Retrieved May 23, 2002, from http://www.quicken.com/investments/news_center/article/printer.dcg?story=/news/stories/dj/20020521/on20020521000426.htm

Hearit, K. M. (1995). From "we didn't do it" to "it's not our fault": The use of *apologia* in public relations crises. In W. N. Elwood (Ed.), *Public relations inquiry as rhetorical criticism: Case studies of corporate discourse and social influence* (pp. 117-131). Westport, CT: Praeger.

Hearit, K. M., & Brown, J. (2004). Merrill Lynch: Corporate *apologia* and business fraud. *Public Relations Review, 30*, 459-466.

Heath, R. L. (1997). *Strategic issues management: Organizations and public policy challenges.* Thousand Oaks: Sage.

Johnson, D., & Sellnow, T.L. (1995). Deliberative rhetoric as a step in organizational crisis management: Exxon as a case study. *Communication Reports, 8*, 54-60.

Marchini, D. (2002, May 21) Press conference: Merrill Lynch stresses tradition of rigorous research, renewed investors' confidence. *Halftime Report.* Cable News Network Financial. Transcript # 052101cb.130. Retrieved on May 24, 2002, from Academic Universe (Lexis Nexis).

Marsh & McLennan Companies. (2005, January 31). *MMC reaches settlement agreement with New York State Attorney General and Superintendent of New York State Insurance Department* [News release]. Retrieved July 7, 2005, from http://www.mmc.com

Merrill Lynch. (2002a, May 21). *Merrill Lynch announces agreement with New York State Attorney General* [News release]. Retrieved May 23, 2002, from http://www.ml.com/about/press_release/05212002-1_ag_agreement-pr.htm

Merrill Lynch. (2002b, May 22). *A new standard for investment research* [Advertisement]. Retrieved May 23, 2002, from http://www.ml.com/media 522.htm

Mickey, T. J. (2003). *Deconstructing public relations: Public relations criticism.* Mahwah, NJ: Erlbaum.

Millar, D. (2003). *Annual ICM crisis report. News coverage of business crises during 2002.* Louisville, KY: The Institute for Crisis Management. Retrieved July 13, 2005, from http://www.crisisexperts.com/pub.htm

Morgenson, G. (2002a, May 22). Settlement is a good deal for Merrill. How about investors? *The New York Times*, p. C1.

Morgenson, G. (2002b, May 23). Salomon to alter research unit along lines of Merrill settlement. *The New York Times*, p. C1.

Morton, P. (2003, April 29). Wall Street cleans house: US $1.4 billion settlement will dramatically change how brokers supervise and compensate analysts. *Financial Post*, p. FP1.

Moyers, B. (2002, June 21). *NOW* [Broadcast transcript]. Washington, DC: Public Broadcasting System. Retrieved September 15, 2002, from http://www.pbs.org /now/.html

Nace, T. (2003). *Gangs of America: The rise of corporate power and the disabling of democracy.* San Francisco: Berrett-Koehler.

The November markets. (2002, July 10). *The Wall Street Journal*, p. A14.

Office of New York State Attorney General Eliot Spitzer. (2002a, April 8). *Merrill Lynch stock rating system found biased by undisclosed conflicts of interest* [News release]. Retrieved September 15, 2002, from http://www.oag.state. ny.us/press /2002/apr/apr08b_02.html

Office of New York State Attorney General Eliot Spitzer. (2002b, May 21). Agreement between the Attorney General of the State of New York and Merrill Lynch, Pierce, Fenner & Smith, Inc. [Legal document].

Office of New York State Attorney General Eliot Spitzer. (2002c, May 21). *Spitzer, Merrill Lynch reach unprecedented agreement to reform investment practices* [News release]. Retrieved September 15, 2002, from http://www.oag.state. ny.us/press/2002/may/may21a_02.html

Office of New York State Attorney General Eliot Spitzer. (2003, April 28). *Conflict probes resolved at Citigroup and Morgan-Stanley* [News release]. Retrieved May 1, 2003, from http://www.oag.state.ny.us/press/2003/apr/apr28a_03.html

Perelman, C., & Olbrechts-Tyteca, L. (1969). *The new rhetoric: A treatise on argumentation* (J. Wilkinson & P. Weaver, Trans.). Notre Dame, IN: University of Notre Dame Press.

Schultz, P. D., & Seeger, M. W. (1991). Corporate centered apologia: Iacocca in defense of Chrysler. *Speaker and Gavel, 28*, 50-60.

Seeger, M. W. (1997). *Ethics and organizational communication*. Cresskill, NJ: Hampton Press.

Seeger, M. W., Sellnow, T. L., & Ulmer, R. R. (2003). *Communication and organizational crisis*. Westport, CT: Praeger.

Seeger, M. W., & Ulmer, R. R. (2002). A post-crisis discourse of renewal: The cases of Malden Mills and Cole Hardwoods. *Journal of Applied Communication Research, 30*, 126-142.

Sellnow, T. L. (1993). Scientific argument in organizational crisis communication: The case of Exxon. *Argumentation & Advocacy, 30*, 28-41.

Sellnow, T. L., & Brand, J. D. (2001). Establishing the structure of reality for an industry: Model and anti-model arguments as advocacy in Nike's crisis communication. *Journal of Applied Communication Research, 29*, 278-295.

Truitt, R. H. (2003). Public relations in post-bubble America. *Public Relations Quarterly, 48*(1), 45-48.

Walha, K., & Filusch, E. E. (2005). Eliot Spitzer: A crusader against corporate malfeasance or a politically ambitious spotlight hound? A case study of Eliot Spitzer and Marsh & McLennan. *Georgetown Journal of Legal Ethics, 18*, 1111-1131.

Ware, B. L., & Linkugel, W. A. (1973). They spoke in defense of themselves: On the generic criticism of apologia. *Quarterly Journal of Speech, 59*, 273-283.

Warnick, B., & Kline, S. L. (1992). The new rhetoric's argument schemes: A rhetorical view of practical reasoning. *Argumentation & Advocacy, 29*, 1-15.

Your market. (2002). New York: New York Stock Exchange.

Managing Power with Publics

chapter 7

Issue Management and Policy Justification in Malaysia

Maureen Taylor

Michael L. Kent

Issue management scholarship examines organizations as they participate in the public policy process. Research that analyzes the ways in which organizations attempt to define issues, legitimate positions, and lobby for favored policies shows that many organizations take an active role in attempting to shape public policy. Strategic issue management has become an accepted and valued way that individual corporations can use communication to exercise power over the public policy process and achieve particular organizational goals (Grunig & Repper, 1992; Heath, 1988; Taylor, Vasquez, & Doorley, 2003). However, as Ewing (1990) argued, the practice of issue management needs to move from the micro realm of single issues to a more macro realm of social issues and policy management. This chapter takes a macro look at issue management and focuses on the offices of government which, like corporate and nonprofit organizations, have the desire and resources to influence public policy perceptions. (The issue management literature tends to focus on government as a target public, not as a source of issue advocacy.)

The offices of government (local, state, and national figures, both appointed and elected) have environmental needs similar to other types of organizations. Moreover, government officials have agendas and visions about how they want to shape their environments. They also possess the resources required to affect change. Although resources vary on an organization-by-organization basis, government officials at all levels generally have more access to financial resources, the media, public opinion leaders, and political action groups than do regular citizens and most organizations. Indeed, the very close relationship between government officials and the resources available to them to affect change make the discussion of government officers as organizational rhetors in the public policy process a timely endeavor.

This chapter illustrates how governmental officials use strategic communication to legitimate stands on public policy issues. Government rhetors, because of their role as decision makers and influencers over the public policy process, have power that even the leaders of multinational organizations often do not have. This chapter first reviews the issue management literature to show how government has traditionally been viewed as an audience for corporate communications. This view of government as merely a public to be influenced misses the fact that government officials are often the creators of strategic communication to various publics and agents of change themselves. To highlight how government rhetors influence public policy and engage in issue management, this chapter examines four different strategies governments use to define and legitimate their own goals in the court of public opinion: a priori solutions, bifurcation, casuistic stretching, and issue masking. The chapter concludes with a case study showing how political leaders use issue communication to shape public policy and gain public acceptance, and even praise, for controversial policy decisions.

GOVERNMENT ISSUE COMMUNICATION

Government, as both a source and a receiver of persuasive communication, has always been included in discussions of the public relations process (Cutlip, 1995). However, many scholars have treated noncorporate communicators (government rhetors, nonprofit organizations, etc.) as somehow different from corporate communicators (cf. J. Grunig, 2001; L. Grunig, 1992; Olson, 1971). Consider, for example, how scholars have treated activists and government communicators. As L. Grunig (1992) suggested, "Activism, indeed, represents a major problem for organizations. Hostilities between organizations and pressure groups are commonplace and often lead to a marshaling of public opinion against the organization that may, in turn, result in government regulation" (p. 522). Activists and government regulators are described as essentially "hostile" to for-profit organizations.

The argument that for-profit organizations possess some special status as communicators is interesting in light of the fact that there are so many nonprofit and government communicators (churches; hospitals; school boards; local, state, and national government representatives; the Humane Society; etc.). From an organizational communication standpoint, nonprofit organizations and government offices are organizations and thus engage in persuasive communication. Government officials and activist communicators must use the broadcast media or other communication channels to get their messages out to stakeholders, as do corporate communicators. Mission/vision statements guide corporate, governmental, and activist communicators alike. Government officials and activists function within hierarchical structures and must adhere to organizational rules and norms just like corporate communicators. They too are constrained by public approval/disapproval. Indeed, in all ways, except for earning a profit, the communication options available to activist, governmental, and for-profit communicators are nearly identical. Beyond these obvious structural similarities, however, governmental policymakers and activist groups actually believe that their organizations have the best interests of the general public at heart.

Indeed, L. Grunig's (1992) suggestion that activist groups are inherently harmful to organizations—because they force organizations to expend resources responding to the interests of a minority of citizens—really misses the mark. As a citizen, I might believe that Merck is only interested in selling more drugs. I might look to the FDA (or some vocal activist group) for regulation of the pharmaceutical industry and protection of my health. Merck, on the other hand, might legitimately see activist groups and the FDA as nuisances for forcing them to expend resources on issue management. How you see an issue depends on where you stand, and it has little to do with whether activists or government communicators are different from corporate communicators. L. Grunig (1992) is correct when she noted, "Without a thorough understanding of adversarial groups, the organization may be at their mercy" (p. 507; cf. J. Grunig, 2001, p. 18). Although L. Grunig was talking about activists, regulators, and the like here, her admonition applies just as accurately to government persuaders. Without a thorough understanding of constituencies (publics/stakeholders), government communication efforts may be headed for failure as well.[1]

Issue Management Literature

Research on issues management can be found in a wide variety of disciplines. Scholars from such fields as political science, futurism, business management, public policy, communication, public relations, strategic planning, management information systems, and business ethics have advanced the concept of *issues management*. Mintzberg (1983), a business management professor, viewed government as one of the most important external publics with which an organization must communicate. Mintzberg argued that organizations must always give special consideration to government officials because "they represent the ultimate legislative authority of the society . . . [and] establish the rules—the laws and regulations—within which every organization must function" (p. 44). The management literature clearly identifies government as a public to be researched, monitored, and managed (Mintzberg, 1983). However, the management literature, like much of the public relations scholarship, ignores the fact that government actors (appointed and elected) have agendas and make efforts of their own to manage issues.

The inclusion of government itself in the issue management process is not a new or surprising development. Jones and Chase (1979) are credited with the systematic approach that explained how organizations can legitimize and validate organizational positions on relevant public policy issues. As part of this process, government officials are considered one of the three major targets (along with business and citizens) of communication for strategic management. Jones and Chase (1979) encouraged organizations to "increase efforts to anticipate social change and respond to reasonable public expectations" (p. 11) rather than wait for others to set the public agenda. In Jones and Chase's initial conceptualization of issue management, issues precede government policies and organizations should "react" to events and be ready to proactively guide issues in the direction of favorable outcome. However, no mention of government representatives as organizational communicators who might also attempt to manage issues is found in their groundbreaking essay.

Crable and Vibbert (1985) extended Jones and Chase's (1979) model of issue management and created the "catalytic issue management" model. Crable and Vibbert claimed that organizations could actually create issues and then proactively guide an issue "through its life cycle so that it is resolved in directions favorable to the organization" (pp. 11-12). In this model, organizations may first desire a specific policy and then find or create an issue that calls for (or demands) a predetermined policy. However, Crable and Vibbert (1985) admitted that business, citizens, and government are not coequal publics for organizations; rather, "public policy rests where it has for more than two hundred years—in the halls of government" (p. 4). What Crable and Vibbert failed to mention, however, is that government actors may also catalytically define and guide issues through this public opinion process. Indeed, politicians have been influencing public policy longer than individuals and organizations have. Crable and Vibbert conceded that even in the lower levels of state and local government, the need for government support for organizational decisions is clear. The offices of government are viewed as a public to be acted on, rather than as agents of change. As noted previously, however, by stepping back from their analysis which focuses on corporations' issue management communication, the efforts of government actors to enact public policy supportive of initiatives is qualitatively the same as an organization exercising its muscle to shape a public policy that serves the organization's ends.

A variety of scholars have expanded on Jones and Chase's (1979) and Crable and Vibbert's (1985) models of issue management to identify theoretical underpinnings (Heath, 1988) for various reasons: to test the value of environmental scanning (Lauzen, 1997), test the relationship between issue management and technology (Ramsey, 1993), clarify the cyclical development of issues and organizational response (Hainsworth, 1990), update its current status as a field of study (Gaunt & Ollenburger, 1995; Heath & Cousino, 1990), and place issue management into an international perspective for multinational corporations (Wilson, 1990). These efforts, however, view issue management from the perspective of the corporation. Obviously, where one stands when defining issue management matters. From a pedagogical perspective, the focus of previous scholarship on for-profit organizations is not problematic because organizational communicators need to understand how to influence public policy and manage organizational issues. However, equally important to understanding how to influence government policy is understanding the power that government leaders and bureaucrats are themselves trying to exert when they identify, frame, and enact public policy. Controlling the public agenda is the first step toward controlling policy. This is as true for Time Warner as it is for a Texas politician.

Government as a Source of Strategic Communication

Only a handful of articles exist that discuss government as an organizational rhetor. Nelson (1994) noted that the use of communication for persuasion "is an increasing component of both private and government communication" (p. 225). Ponder (1990) observed that "press offices, under one title or another, have spread throughout the American federal, state, and local governments in the twentieth century" (p. 94) and government has relied on these press offices in shaping supportive public opinion. Lee (2005) recently provided a historical account of how the Office of Government Reports (OGR) was created, institutionalized, and eventually challenged. Indeed, although the Gillette Amendment makes it illegal for the U.S. government to employ public relations practitioners to persuade its citizens, the law is effectively skirted by the use of public information officers and press secretaries. These officials shape public opinion. Public relations efforts by government have a historical place in the public relations literature, and work by scholars like Primlott (1951), Pearson (1990), and Cutlip (1995) have examined the relationship between democracy and public relations.

So what strategies do governments use when they communicate their agendas to various publics? There are many. On the most basic level, politicians and government officials use the same persuasive strategies that every student of public speaking learns. The four particular strategies discussed in this chapter, however, are far more sophisticated: a priori solutions, casuistic stretching, bifurcation, and issue masking.

ISSUE MANAGEMENT STRATEGIES

To understand how issue management communication is used by governmental rhetors we focus on several rhetorical strategies. In everyday parlance, especially in the mass media, the term "rhetoric" is often used pejoratively. As our online dictionary defines it, rhetoric is comprised of "complex or elaborate language that only succeeds in sounding pretentious" (Encarta, 1999). Unfortunately, the mass media approach to defining rhetoric really misses the point. Rhetoric is not empty or pretentious language; it is language that moves people. It persuades and thus allows organizational rhetors to influence. Pretentious language is just that: pretentious, pompous, poorly crafted. But when a nation's leaders draw on enthymemes like "family," "evil doers," or the "war on terror," they do not bore but excite. The strategies that follow are rhetorical in the technical sense of the word. A priori solutions, casuistic stretching, bifurcation, and issue masking are strategic, careful, compelling rhetorical tools that allow organizational rhetors to influence public discussions and policies.

A Priori Solutions

One strategy for issue definition and policy management is found in the work of political theorist Murray Edelman. Edelman (1988) addressed the situation of issue definition and policy development in his examination of the construction of social realities and the links between problems and solutions. Edelman claimed, "The striking characteristic of the link between political problems and solutions in everyday life is that the solution typically comes first, chronologically and psychologically" (pp. 21-22). Edelman contended that "those who favor a particular course of governmental action are likely to cast about for a widely feared problem to which to attach to it in order to maximize its support" (p. 22). For Edelman, solutions can be created by government officials a priori (or before the fact) and then offered when a convenient problem appears.

An excellent example of using a priori solutions can be found in the rhetoric of President Lyndon Johnson's three speeches associated with the Gulf of Tonkin resolution, the presidential act that committed the United States to deeper involvement in Vietnam. Cherwitz (1978) argued that Johnson's messages actually created an international crisis, although his rhetoric used the attack on destroyers *Maddox* and *Turner Joy* as a pretext for the resolution. Johnson used vivid, descriptive language to dramatize the event that ostensibly prompted the resolution:

> In all three speeches he used the words "hostile" and "deliberate" repeatedly. For example, in his address to the nation Johnson spoke of "repeated attacks" by "hostile vessels" using "torpedoes." This attack, declared the President was an "act of aggression." (1978, p. 98, source citations omitted)

As Cherwitz (1980) later noted, Johnson had become convinced of the need to intervene in Vietnam early in 1964, prepared plans to do so, but did not announce an escalation of U.S. involvement until August 1964 once the events in the Gulf of Tonkin gave him the pretext to do so. The administration used events prompted by our own military's spy missions as a justification or excuse to pursue a desired policy. The solution had been developed before the fact—a priori—before the alleged triggering event took place.

Casuistic Stretching

A second way that organizations can rhetorically define problems and solutions is through casuistic stretching. *Casuistry* refers to subtle or meticulous reasoning based on interpretations of primary texts. Such argument is typically used by theologians, logicians, critics, and lawyers. Any person or organization is capable of "stretching" a concept in order to redefine—and sometimes control—public dialogue. As Kenneth Burke (1937/1961) explained, casuistic stretching is the practice of "introducing new principles while theoretically remaining faithful to old principles" (p. 229). In other words, casuistic stretching is a rhetorical device used to incorporate a new concept into an already accepted definition or policy. Casuistic stretching creates a new dimension of social understanding when it links terms together to create new concepts. A governmental rhetor can use casuistic stretching to extend public understanding of, and add new meanings to, definitions and policy decisions.

One of the best examples of casuistic stretching was President Ronald Reagan's effort to justify cuts to a number of social programs in the nation's "social safety net." As Zarefsky, Miller-Tutzauer, and Tutzauer (1984) explained:

> Reagan did not specify who were the "truly needy" or what characteristics distinguished true from only apparent need. This omission might have been a wise move, since those with a vested interest in any program would perceive that program as addressed to true need. Thinking it therefore immune from cuts, its supporters might be less inclined to attack the general strategy of cuts, so long as the ox to be gored belonged to someone else. (p. 114)

By modifying the concepts of a "social safety net" and the concept of citizens who are "truly needy" to a "safety net for the truly needy," Reagan was able to substantially decrease funding for the nation's social support programs for disadvantaged children, the elderly, social security recipients, and others (Zarefsky et al., p. 116). By stretching/combining the definition of "needy" to "truly needy," Reagan was able to control the terms of the debate and how the media would cover the issue. Reagan convinced most public health professionals, teachers, and aid workers (until it was too late) that *their* programs were safe. He "stretched" the concept and minimized opposition to his desired policy.

Bifurcation

Bifurcation, also called *false dichotomy* or *polarization*, is a third way in which a governmental rhetor might persuade others. Strictly speaking, *bifurcation* is a logical fallacy in which a persuader outlines an argument in such a way as to suggest that there is only one of two possibilities—typically diametrically opposed options. Undoubtedly everyone has heard the expression "you are either with us or against us." Such a polar argument is the essence of bifurcation. Bifurcation is used everyday, consciously and unconsciously, by people from all walks of life. More typically, however, bifurcation is used when an individual is trying to persuade another. Bifurcation is also closely linked to Burke's (1966) notion of identification through antithesis, in which symbols are used to induce an audience to align themselves with a speaker based on what that source opposes (e.g., all Americans might be said to be against terrorism after September 11, 2001).

Bifurcation appears to be an argument fallacy that Richard Nixon employed throughout his political career (King & Anderson, 1971). Examples from three of his landmark speeches demonstrate how this strategy is used politically to rally support and quash dissent. In 1952, in a speech deemed by many to have saved his early political career, Nixon delivered the "Checkers" speech to defend his place on the Republican ticket as Dwight Eisenhower's running mate. As part of his defense against that he had used money from a secret campaign "slush" fund, Nixon not only argued his innocence but indirectly linked the Democratic Party and its presidential nominee with Communism and the rich. One memorable bifurcation is his characterization of his opponent's wife being able to own mink while his own wife, of course, had "a respectable Republican cloth coat" (Hart, 1990, p. 117, citation omitted).

Years later, at the beginning of his presidency, Nixon would again use bifurcation to crystallize public opinion in his favor. Rather than bring troops home from Vietnam during his first year in office, Nixon used his November 3, 1969, message to the nation as an appeal to "decent people" who "pay their taxes" and "care" (King & Anderson, 1971, p. 245). He rhetorically pitted this "great silent majority of Americans" (p. 247) against peace groups, people he painted as "a vocal minority" who were part of a "drug culture," promoted a "new morality," and threatened to make the majority of Americans fearful of becoming "a nation of outsiders" (p. 248). Clearly, bifurcations such as these can be used to rally support and quash dissent.

Issue Masking

A final way in which a governmental rhetor may create links between problems and solutions is through the strategy of issue masking. Issue masking occurs when a rhetor constructs an issue that is accepted "naively at face value" by the audience (Bennett, Harris, Laskey, Levitch, & Monrad, 1976, p. 110). However, the function of a masking issue is really to influence the audience's perceptions of another issue that may be more central to the rhetor's situation (Bennett et al., p. 110).

Bennett et al. (1976) suggested that there are different types of images (or public perceptions) in the construction of political issues that create a continuum, ranging from deep to surface images. The surface images provide the "face value" meaning, whereas the deep images provide the rhetorical warrants to resolve another issue(s). For instance, Bennett et al. (1976) showed how President Ford employed both surface and deep images in respect to the amnesty issue. On the surface, the president advocated amnesty for conscientious objectors to the war in Vietnam as an act of national reconciliation and forgiveness. However, the amnesty issue operated on a much deeper level because it provided the rhetorical premises for the Ford administration to later pardon Richard Nixon for his involvement in Watergate. In other words, a surface masking issue paves the way for a later or perhaps alternative deeper issue resolution. On the surface, Vietnam conscientious objectors and former President Nixon have little common. However, the concept of amnesty transcends this surface issue and creates a justification for the pardoning of Nixon on a deeper level—that of reconciliation or redemption. In debate this concept is known as a warrant, or support for actions or arguments to come in the future.

These four rhetorical strategies—a priori solutions, bifurcation, casuistic stretching, and issues masking—are ways that government rhetors can participate in the issue management process.[2] However, they are not unique to democratic political institutions, as the case study that follows shows.

A CASE STUDY OF GOVERNMENT ISSUE AND POLICY COMMUNICATION

In our analysis of the persuasive tactics of the Malaysian ruling party, we demonstrate how each persuasive strategy functions to support governmental persuasive goals and bolster the power base of leaders and public officials. This case study illustrates how specific rhetorical tactics are used to perpetuate governmental agendas and manage public policy issues.

The Malaysian ruling party, the United Malays National Organization, used issues communication to define a problem to the nation's citizens and legitimate a policy solution to a controversial issue. Although, as noted previously, little scholarly attention has focused on government officials as agents of change, several scholars have pointed out (tangentially) how important government leaders and officials are to corporate rhetors—because they shape public policy and have the power to control how rewards and punishments are administered.

Background

Malaysia, Singapore, Sabah, and Sarawak merged in 1963 to create the Independent Federation of Malaya. Chinese citizens in Singapore left the federation in 1965 when they felt threatened by Malay dominance of the political system. Even today, ethnic, religious, and economic inequalities continue to divide Malaysian society. The many inequalities contribute to racial tensions between the indigenous Malays who make up 55% of the population, ethnic Chinese who make up 34% of the nation, and Indians who make up 10% of the national population. Most of the tension in Malaysia, however, occurs between Malays and Chinese. Malays are the largest ethnic group, yet fall behind the Chinese in economic development. Ethnic Malays traditionally work in the government or civil service sector, but, after 25 years of government incentive programs, they have had minimal success entering into the private sector.

Ethnic Chinese are the second largest ethnic group within Malaysia. Chinese have lived in Malaysia since British rule began in the 1820s and consider themselves part of Malaysian society (Koon, 1988). The Chinese dominate the business sector of the economy but traditionally have had minimal political power. Government efforts over the last 25 years to provide political opportunities have increased Chinese participation in government; however, Chinese youth continue to gravitate toward the private sector, where as Malay youth continue to seek opportunity in government posts. Uneasy relations continue today. An understanding of contemporary ethnic tensions can be gained by an explanation of the riots of 1969.

The Malaysian government's efforts to ensure peace ended when racial tension intensified between Malays and Chinese in May 1969. At the root of tensions were the successful election results of the ethnic Chinese political party, the Democratic Action Party (DAP). The DAP surprised the ruling Alliance coalition (headed by the United Malays National Organization) and won a large number of political seats in the Parliament (Koon, 1988). Riots occurred in the capital of Kuala Lumpur as the DAP held what was perceived by Malays as "victory processions . . . considered to be provocative, arrogant, and abusive" (Ongkili, 1985, p. 203). Malays who feared that the Chinese would take over the nation reacted violently to the election celebration. The 1969 riots resulted in the death of hundreds of people and facilitated the implementation of the Internal Security Act (ISA). The ISA was a form of martial law that abridged all political rights and emerged as a tool that the Malaysian government could use when it felt threatened by domestic or international events.

In October 1987, the government once again employed the ISA to end political dissent when an issue surrounding the Chinese language gained national attention. The trouble started when the Malaysian government, pressured by ethnic Malay teachers and professional groups, passed a resolution requiring all administrators in Chinese secondary schools to speak the Malay national language as a prerequisite for promotion. Language in multiracial states is often a sensitive subject and many times becomes a rallying point for ethnic conflict (Horowitz, 1985). As *The New York Times* reported:

> Relations have been steadily deteriorating for a year or two as programs intended to enhance the lives of Malays begin to have some negative effects on other communities. But the immediate crisis was provoked by a Government decision to assign administrators who are not fluent in Mandarin to Chinese language schools. (Crossette, 1987, p. 8)

However, the Chinese language issue and the subsequent tension between the Chinese and Malay communities may have been merely a symptom of another power struggle. In 1990, the government planned to review the Fifth Malaysian Plan (1986-1990). This plan attempted to redistribute business ownership from the Chinese community and opportunity and economic power to the Malay community. One analysis noted that the Chinese language issue was merely a dress rehearsal for the public upheaval that would occur once the Fifth Malaysian Plan ended and a new strategy would be implemented to further erode the Chinese economic power base in the nation (FBIS, October 20, 1987, p. 20). When students in Chinese-dominated areas continued to boycott schools, Malaysians of all races feared escalation. The government of Prime Minister Mahathir bin Mohammed blamed the press for heightening racial tensions, and, when the prime minister addressed the issue for the first time on October 21, he "advised all quarters, especially newspapers, to refrain from making and publishing provocative statements to ensure peace and stability in the country" (FBIS, October 21, 1987, p. 18). Public debate, however, continued in the newspapers and within the local mixed-race communities.

Method

The time period studied in this analysis covers one month preceding and following the 1987 ISA policy decision (October-November 1987). A rhetorical analysis of public communication by the Mahathir government during these 2 months allows an examination of the ways in which the government and opposition attempted to define the issue and solution to both national and international publics. Two issues management perspectives provide the foundation for this case study about the enactment of government power through rhetorical strategies.

The findings presented in this case study are based upon the textual analysis of two sources. First, to see how the Malaysian government was explaining the ISA to local publics, documents from the Foreign Broadcast Information Service (FBIS, 1987) provide English translations of news stories published in Malaysian newspapers from Malay and Chinese media sources. Second, to better understand how the Malaysian government attempted to communicate its controversial policy decision to international audiences, *The New York Times* and the *London Times* serve as additional sources. This sample includes daily articles, editorials, interviews, and communications from both the Malaysian government and its opposition.

Finding and Defining the Issue

Chinese political groups defined the language issue not only as the beginning of Malaysian government efforts to "change the character of Chinese language schools" but also an attempt to take ethnic identity away from the Chinese community (FBIS, October 15, 1987, p. 22). Chinese groups called for a student boycott of the schools, and the "issue united 6 million

Chinese" (FBIS, 1987, p. 20). Chinese leaders in the coalition government claimed that the language issue was "taking the country to the edge of a racial volcano" (FBIS, October 21, 1987, p.18). The Chinese language issue served as one of many catalysts that strained Chinese and Malay relations. Furthermore, Chinese and Malay political groups planned "large rallies" (FBIS, October 28, 1987, p. 11) later that month to show support for their respective positions on the issue and lobby for other important ethnic issues or policies to resolve such issues.

Both the Malay and Chinese ethnic groups defined the issue as central to their own survival. For instance, the youth wing of the United Malays National Organization urged the government not to compromise its stand on the issue and pledged "to defend Malay honor and . . . birthright to rule" (FBIS, October 20, 1987, p. 20). Malay youths planned a "mammoth rally" to "urge the government to stand firm," saying that "Chinese politicians should not interfere with a purely administrative matter" (p. 20). Another Malay organization, the Peninsular Malaysian Malay Teachers Union, supported the youth rally "as an effort to unite and determine the future direction of the Malays," and the organization gave its full support to "returning to the original struggle to maintain the status of Malays in the country" (FBIS, October 19, 1987, p. 21).

The Chinese defined the language issue as an attempt by the Malay-dominated bureaucracy to eliminate Chinese culture. Conversely, Malay groups defined the language issue as part of the nation-building process to have all Malaysian citizens speak the same language. Most importantly, the Malaysian government legitimized the issue by addressing it in national speeches with urgent language. It had the power to define the issue and the solution.

Defining the Policy

The government offered the ISA as a policy solution to the perceived threat of ethnic conflict. Mahathir defined the policy as an extension of government responsibility for "national peace and security" (FBIS, October 28, 1987, p. 22). The prime minister placed the ISA in the context of his 6-year rule of liberalism, which he claimed had been abused by various factions in the Malaysian population. Prime Minister Mahathir described his responsibility for safeguarding the nation from "irresponsible people," "irresponsible attitudes," and "irresponsible actions."

The government used the 1987 ISA to detain 106 people, although "most were released by fall of 1988, and by January 1989 only two remained imprisoned. In 1989 a national human rights commission was established to investigate human rights abuses resulting from the ISA" (Freedom House, 1990, p. 166). Amnesty International (2003) appealed to the Malaysian government on behalf of the detainees, but applications for writs of habeas corpus were rejected by the Kuala Lumpur High Court in November 1987. Throughout the definition of the policy solution, Prime Minister Mahathir named national development as the major reason for the ISA. The prime minister claimed that the country's peace and stability must be cherished and that "Malaysia's development and economic well-being of its citizens' (sic) depend on peace and stability" (FBIS, October 28, 1987, p. 22). Mahathir offered the ISA as a way to prevent the world recession from promoting "an unstable political situation and racial disturbances" because the "country [could not] afford racial disturbances" (pp. 21-22).

Leading government officials, empowered to deliver the talking points of the government, addressed the issue of economics in their promotion of the ISA as part of the nation-building process. Foreign Minister Dato' Haji Abu Hassan bub Haji Omar claimed that the ISA "maintained national security" and provided for "the sake of tourists and investors" (FBIS, October 30, 1987, p. 15). The information minister, Datuk Mohamed Rahmat, reiterated this claim. He defended the actions as a step by the government to "maintain peace and harmony among the races, to ensure the success of its development programs, and a brighter future" (p. 15). Rahmat ended a national press conference on the ISA with the claim that "all quarters must place national interest above everything else" (p. 15).

Linkage of National Unity with National Security

The Malaysian government maintained a united effort to frame the ISA as an extension of its existing nation-building programs and not as a political act to suppress the opposition. Several high-ranking national figures addressed the ISA and supported the action as a beneficial policy for the nation. Prime Minister Mahathir told a group of the nation's newspaper editors that "they would have to understand that liberalism would have to take a back seat to development" (Watts, 1987c, p. 1). However, Mahathir promised that more "discussions [would] be held among community leaders to formulate a program to foster national unity" (FBIS, November 6, 1987). The national chief of police reiterated the claim that the ISA was a policy of nation-building when he said that the ISA was "issued only for the sake of maintaining peace and security in Malaysia" (FBIS, October 29, 1987, p. 21)—in order not to appear racially biased the government arrested several leaders of the ruling party. The police chief attempted to define the ISA as a measure of nation-building when he said, "Looking at it from any angle, the most important issue which must be given attention is national security and stability. National security and stability cannot exist without the stern enforcement of regulations" (FBIS, p. 21).

The deputy prime minister, Ghafar Baba, supported the argument that the government would not "use the ISA to victimize anyone" and claimed instead that "national security was the main priority" (FBIS, November 9, 1987). Furthermore, Trade Minister Rafidah Aziz attempted to reassure international interests that the Malaysian government was continuing its economic and national development and that action "under the ISA to maintain political and economic stability in the country has further enhanced the confidence of foreign investors" (FBIS, November 2, 1987, p. 33). Minister Aziz bolstered the government's decision to enact the ISA by claiming that "investors are now confident that the Malaysian government [would] not hesitate to act against extremists who threaten the nation's stability" (FBIS, November 1, 1987, p. 33).

The government enacted its power by censoring all national media representatives who disagreed with the policy. In addition to the newspaper closings, the police invoked the ISA to arrest the managing director of Malaysia's third largest independent television station (Watts, 1987a). The strategy of high-ranking official support for the ISA, plus the censoring and intimidation of media outlets, allowed the government to define the ISA as one more part of the overall nation-building process. These nation-building programs promised economic and political rewards to those who followed the party line. Therefore, there was little incentive for Malaysian citizens to disagree with the motives of the ISA.

Reports also showed that opposition leaders within the coalition government openly supported the ISA. For example, S. Samy Vello, president of the Malaysian Indian Congress (MIC) said, "every right thinking Malaysian must support the government's action undertaken to maintain peace and harmony in the nation" (FBIS, October 29, 1987, p. 23). Likewise, Pan-Malaysian Islamic Party leader Yusuf Rawa viewed the ISA as "specifically used to maintain security" (p. 23). Finally, even the secretariat of the Malaysian Chinese Association (MCA), who opposed the Chinese language legislation, claimed that his party supported "the efforts of the Prime Minister in maintaining solidarity and national stability" (p. 23).

Additionally, editorials that appeared both on television and in the press agreed that the ISA "certainly had a calming effect" (FBIS, October 30, 1987, p. 16) and that "the immediate shock of the 89 arrests so far had begun to give way to a thankfulness" (FBIS, November 3, 1987, p. 32). The government employed its strategy of linking national unity to national security to persuade the Malaysian people to accept its definition of the situation and its subsequent policy solution.

Linkage between Riots of 1969 and the Chinese Language Issue

A second strategy linked the Chinese language issue to the race riots of 1969 and further attempted to persuade audiences that the government acted in the national interest and in accord with its previous nation-building promises. The rhetoric of "nation building," not the "language issue," was really the use of bifurcation. Symbolically, the "language issue," rioting, and other ideas associated with racial division were all cast in a negative light. Using this strategy, leaders, in the name of nation-building, did not have to justify what they were doing.

Implementation of the ISA followed a week of public insecurity about ethnic conflict after unsubstantiated rumors circulated about ethnic violence in other parts of the nation. Reports claimed that Prime Minister Mahathir's "statement came as nervous citizens began stocking up food or arranged to leave town in anticipation of trouble" (Pillai, 1987, p. 11). On October 28, 1987, Mahathir addressed the Lower House of the Parliament and defined the situation in the nation as a crisis reaching a "dangerous level" and claimed "if such a situation is allowed to go unchecked, it will bring about the destruction of all that we have built together" (FBIS, October 28, 1987, p. 18). Mahathir claimed the potential of ethnic crisis prompted action because the "government cannot wait for riots to break out before they take action"; therefore we must "safeguard the country from the dangerous calamity that we may face" (p. 18). To further compare the Chinese language issue with the race riots of 1969, Mahathir admonished that "we still remember the May 1969 incident and surely there is none among us who would want to cause such a riot" (p. 18). Therefore, he argued that "the crackdown began to avoid an outbreak of racial clashes" and claimed that "if we did not take precautionary measures, here are signs of recurring incidents like those of 1969" (FBIS, November 13, 1987, p. 26; November 18, 1987, p. 34).

The Information Minister, Datuk Mohamed Rahmat, attempted to place the ISA into the existing nation-building framework when he reminded both national and international audiences that nation-building is a priority for the government. Rahmat informed newspaper, radio, and television stations that "all programs that could arouse racial sentiments should be replaced with those promoting solidarity and interracial understanding" (FBIS, November 2, 1987, p. 33). Similarly, Mahathir's assistant deputy, Ghafar Baba, commented that the government closed the newspapers because "we do not issue publishing permits for the newspapers to create tension in the country" (FBIS, November 12, 1987, p. 12).

Rhetorically, the Malaysian government consistently defined the Chinese language issue as a crisis. The government selected the situation as an urgent and important matter for action and simultaneously deflected attention away from the stagnant economy and other problems facing the nation. Nation-building was presented positively with the promotion of racial harmony and solidarity. Besides ensuring national stability, the policy also served the political functions of intimidation and, ultimately, silencing the opposition.

DISCUSSION: ISSUE MANAGEMENT BY THE MAHATHIR GOVERNMENT

Several lessons about issue management and the application of political power in public relations become clear through this analysis. International governments, like organizations, sometimes promote crises and then advocate their policies to resolve the constructed problems. This examination shows that the Malaysian government catalytically managed (Crable & Vibbert, 1985) the policy of the ISA—it defined the terms of the debate and polarized the choices for all ethnic groups. The a priori selection of the Chinese language issue as an important situation, defining the issue as a crisis, and identifying the ISA as a policy solution allowed the government to achieve several short- and long-term goals. Prime Minister Mahathir not only defined the Chinese language issue as a crisis but also responded to the perceived crisis with a policy that maximized his government's power while it simultaneously minimized the power of his enemies—the press, Chinese politicians, and even dissenters within his own political party (Watts, 1987c).

Crisis promotion can serve an issue masking function with different dividends for the rhetor (Bennett et al., 1976). In Malaysia, the government reaped three benefits. First, it silenced press outlets openly critical of the government. The government described the ISA as a measure to "safeguard democracy in the country" and "reduce ethnic tensions between Malays and ethnic Chinese" ("Malaysia to Issue," 1987, p. A5). The government silenced three national newspapers publishing in the three popular languages that had criticized and questioned the government's actions leading up to the ISA. The only newspapers sold during the implementation of the ISA supported the government program and offered enthusiastic editorials and commentaries in favor of the act. National editorials, entitled "All for the Better" and "National Security Overrides Liberalism," epitomize the way in which progovernment newspapers justified the ISA as part of the nation-building process.

Second, using the ISA, the government intimidated opposition politicians. Opposition groups called the prime minister's actions a reaction not to the rising tensions in the nation but to his failed economic policies. Opponents criticized his vision for Malaysian "industrialization and a gleaming capital full of the chrome and smoked glass symbols of success" (Watts, 1987b, p. 12)—at the price of real national development and unity. One Chinese opposition leader said, "With one fell swoop he has switched attention from all these problems [the crumbling economy] to the ISA detainments. Now everybody is concentrating on the ISA and ignoring the real problems" (p. 12).

Third, the government reassured international investors that it would protect their interests and provide a stable place for their investments. In other words, the Malaysian government restored its public image as a profitable and safe place for foreign investment. Mahathir framed the ISA as the result of a "misuse of liberalism" and attempted to shift the blame to opposition groups that "forced the government to act this way" (Watts, 1987d, p. 8). He claimed that "if people insist upon misusing the liberal attitudes of the government and threatening the country with instability, then it's very difficult for us to be as liberal as before" (p. 8). Some analysts believed that it was not the racial tensions that prompted the ISA but the tensions between Mahathir and his own party, the UMNO, that prompted arrests of national politicians. The "Father of Malaysia," Tunku Rahman, claimed that "it's not a question of Chinese against the government but his own party, the UMNO, who are against him" (Watts, 1987e, p. 11). Here we see bifurcation—"us against them," "our policy or chaos"; obviously there were other issues and possibilities that were not raised by government officials. The outcome of the ISA had national as well as political party implications. It solidified the Prime Minister's power at all levels of government.

This study shows that governments can act as issue managers when they employ rhetorical tactics to support issues and policies. By developing a masking issue through the use of casuistic stretching, the government carefully defined the goals of the ISA policy so that it appeared compatible with the traditional definition of national unity. This study also has implications for public relations scholars, students, and practitioners. It shows how commonly used concepts such as "national unity" and "national security" can be used in a variety of ways to accomplish personal and political goals. By tracing how the government stretched these concepts, we can see the true power of language to shape opinion and policy.

Moreover, there is an international dimension to this study. The Mahathir government attempted to persuade both national and international audiences that the policy benefited responsible citizens and international investors. The announcement of the ISA could have resulted in massive civil demonstrations by Malaysians of all ethnic groups if they viewed the act as a violation of their human rights. However, the government carefully framed the issue to portray the ISA as a protection against the people's loss of rights by the activities of extremists. Indeed, "many ordinary Malaysians greeted the Prime Minister's moves with relief" (Watts, 1987e, p. 11)—just as many citizens of the United States embraced the USA Patriot Act after September 11. The definition of the situation as a crisis and the subsequent definition of the ISA as an extension of the nation-building efforts to promote ethnic harmony convinced the Malaysian population that the ISA was not martial law. By casuistically stretching the definition of national unity to include national security and reminding Malaysians of all races of the ethnic riots in 1969, the government remained in power, minimized or eliminated opposition, and reassured the nation as well as international investors that it placed "national interest above all else" (FBIS, October 29, 1987, p. 21). The government enjoyed several dividends from the ISA policy; therefore, the action could also be viewed as the Mahathir government catalytically managing an issue by placing its interests "above all else."

Overseas, the ISA masked the larger and more central issue of the Mahathir government—its survival as the ruling party. Bennett et al. (1976) claimed that "'masking issues' may be designed specifically to affect the resolution of other issues in a political situation" (p. 110). Masking issues by their very nature often serve more than one issue, and a close look at the Mahathir government's discourse supporting the ISA as a part of the nation-building process illustrates the link between the constructed crisis of national unity and the solution of the ISA for more than one issue—language dominance, political control, and international financial concerns.

According to Freedom House (1988), the British rulers of Malaya first instituted the Internal Security Act (ISA) in 1960 during the Communist insurgencies. The ISA was an attempt to control internal subversion during colonial rule. The Malaysian government overturned the act and rarely employed its provisions until 1987. The Malaysian government carefully cultivated an image of national unity for both domestic and international audiences to promote social and economic development. However, the ways in which the Malaysian government defined the issue of national unity changed after the Internal Security Act of 1987. More specifically, the government utilized the issue of national unity to mask other issues while it terministically "stretched" its original definition to justify the actions taken under the ISA.

Public relations practitioners, scholars, and students can benefit from understanding how this can happen. Casuistic stretching allowed the government to incorporate a new policy into its nation-building programs as a solution to problems of national unity. The use of national unity as a "masking issue" also created the impression the government was fighting a threat to national unity, when actually it was fighting the political opposition.

In political discourse, Edelman (1988) warned that sometimes the solution is decided on first, and a convenient problem is then identified to justify the desired policy solution. The Internal Security Act in Malaysia exemplifies this type of a priori issue definition and policy development. Additionally, by limiting the terms of debate to polarized options (bifurcation), the government was able to control what was said and the way the issue was discussed. During a time of political crisis, the Malaysian national government used all four of the rhetorical strategies to legitimate its position on a controversial issue.

This chapter has illustrated how government enacts and protects its power through common rhetorical strategies. The Malaysian officials employed aspects of issues communication to achieve their goals.

Rhetorically, the Malaysian government also proved to be quite savvy in its use of language. It benefited from the Chinese language issue. It allowed Mahathir to consolidate power within the UMNO, intimidated oppositional leaders in the other political parties, and reassured international investors that Malaysia was indeed a safe place. By controlling the media agenda and providing frames for the problem and the solution, Mahathir showed the enormous power of government communication. Malaysia, however, is not the only nation that has government rhetors willing and capable of enacting such power. Citizens across the world need to be more critical of governmental communication and question the implementation of political policies. Only then will citizens be able to see whose interests are served by policy decisions suggested by corporate or governmental leaders.

NOTES

1. Some might ask, "What distinguishes governmental issue management efforts from propaganda?" Quite simply, the means of communication and the intent. Propaganda typically involves attempts to generate conditioned reflexes that replace reasoned actions, employing controlled use of the media and unethical rhetorical techniques (appeals to authority, bandwagon appeals, fear, glittering generalities, name-calling, "plain folks" appeals, testimonials, transfer, slippery-slope arguments). Every nation, whether democratic or dictatorial, takes advantage of the media to get their arguments out to the public. Some control over the channels of the media is exercised in every country to a varying degree. Persuasion becomes propaganda, however, when citizens are systematically deprived of competing messages, fed lies and deception, and not given the opportunity to voice competing positions or seek alternative solutions to problems. For excellent treatments of the subject of propaganda, see Ellul (1965/1973), Jowett and O'Donnell (1999), and Sproule (1994, 1997).
2. All persuasion depends on several factors: the goals of the persuader, the time frame available in which to present one's case, the channels available, the education and willingness of the audience to attend to the message, the cultural background of the listener/reader, and so on. All four strategies discussed have the potential for abuse by institutional persuaders. Like all persuasion, these strategies are not inherently ethical or unethical. How the strategies are employed depends on the motives of the persuader. All of the four strategies discussed here correspond to various forms of logical fallacies. Indeed, any rhetorical tactic designed to mislead or distract a listener might be called a logical fallacy. A priori solution is a form of the post hoc, ergo propter hoc fallacy, bifurcation is essentially the false dichotomy, casuistic stretching is a form of equivocation, and masking issues could be called a form of the non causa, pro causa fallacy. A logical fallacy is an error in reasoning, sometimes unintentional, but, equally often, intentional.

REFERENCES

Amnesty International (2003). *Malaysia: The Internal Security Act (ISA)*. Retrieved September 28, 2005, from <http://web.amnesty.org/library/Index/ENGASA 280062003?open&of=ENG-2AS>

Bennett, W. L., Harris, P. D., Laskey, J. K., Levitch, A. H., & Monrad, S. E. (1976). Deep and surface images in the construction of political issues: The case of amnesty. *Quarterly Journal of Speech, 62*, 109-126.

Burke, K. (1961). *Attitudes toward history*. Berkeley: University of California Press. (Original work published 1937)

Burke, K. (1966). *Language as symbolic action: Essays in life, literature, and method*. Berkeley: University of California Press.

Cherwitz, R. A. (1978). Lyndon Johnson and the "crisis" of Tonkin Gulf: A President's justification of war. *Western Journal of Speech Communication, 42*, 93-104.

Cherwitz, R. A. (1980). Masking inconsistency: The Tonkin Gulf crisis. *Communication Quarterly, 28*(2), 27-37.

Crable, R. E., & Vibbert, S. L. (1985). Managing issues and influencing public policy. *Public Relations Review, 11*, 3-15.

Crossette, B. (1987, October 29). Malaysia shuts down 3 newspapers. *The New York Times*, p. A8.

Cutlip, S. M. (1995). *Public relations history: From 17th to the 20th century: The antecedents*. Hillsdale, NJ: Erlbaum.

Edelman, M. (1988). *Constructing the political spectacle*. Chicago: University of Chicago Press.

Ellul, J. (1973). *Propaganda: The formation of men's attitudes* (K. Kellen & J. Lerner, Trans.). New York: Vintage Books. (Original work published 1965)

Encarta. (1999). *World English dictionary* (Microsoft Word). Redmond, WA: Microsoft Corporation.

Ewing, R. P. (1990). Moving from micro to macro issues management. *Public Relations Review, 16*, 19-24.

Foreign Broadcast Information Reports (FBIS). (1987). *Asia and Pacific* [Microfiche]. New Canaan, CT: NewsBank/Readex. Available online from http://www.newsbank.com/

Freedom House. (1990). *Freedom review*. New York: Author.

Gaunt, P., & Ollenburger, J. (1995). Issues management revisited: A tool that deserves another look. *Public Relations Review, 21*, 199-210.

Grunig, J. E. (2001). Two-way symmetrical public relations: Past, present, and future. In R. L. Heath (Ed.), *Handbook of public relations* (pp. 11-30). Thousand Oaks, CA: Sage.

Grunig, J. E., & Repper, F. C. (1992). Strategic management, public and issues. In J. E. Grunig (Ed.), *Excellence in public relations and communication management* (pp. 117-158). Hillsdale, NJ: Erlbaum.

Grunig, L. A. (1992). Activism: How it limits the effectiveness of organizations and how excellent public relations departments respond. In J. E. Grunig (Ed.), *Excellence in public relations and communication management* (pp. 503-530). Hillsdale, NJ: Erlbaum.

Hainsworth, B. E. (1990). The distribution of advantages and disadvantages. *Public Relations Review, 16*, 83-89.

Hart, R. P. (1990). *Modern rhetorical criticism.* Glenview, IL: Scott, Foresman.

Heath, R. L. (1988). *Strategic issues management: How organizations influence and respond to public interests and policies.* San Francisco: Jossey-Bass.

Heath, R. L., & Cousino, K. R. (1990). Issue management: End of the first decade progress report. *Public Relations Review, 16*, 6-18.

Horowitz, D. L. (1985). *Ethnic groups in conflict.* Berkeley: University of California Press.

Jones, B. L., & Chase, W. H. (1979). Managing public policy issues. *Public Relations Review, 5*, 3-23.

Jowett, G. S., & O'Donnell, V. (1992). *Propaganda and persuasion* (2nd ed.). Newbury Park, CA: Sage.

King, A. A., & Anderson, F. D. (1971). Nixon, Agnew, and the "silent majority": A case study in the rhetoric of polarization. *Western Speech, 35*, 243-255.

Koon, H. P. (1988). *Chinese politics in Malaysia: A history of the Malaysian Chinese Association.* Singapore: Oxford University Press.

Lauzen, M. M. (1997). Understanding the relation between public relations and issue management. *Journal of Public Relations Research, 9*, 65-82.

Lee, M. (2005). *The first presidential communications agency: FDR's Office of Government Reports.* Albany: SUNY Press.

Malaysia to issue new press curbs. (1987, November 28). *The New York Times,* p. A5.

Mintzberg, H. (1983). *Power in and around organizations.* Englewood Cliffs, NJ: Prentice-Hall.

Nelson, R. A. (1994). Issues communication and advocacy: Contemporary ethical challenges. *Public Relations Review, 20*, 225-231.

Olson, M. (1971). *The logic of collective action: Public goods and the theory of groups.* Cambridge, MA: Harvard University Press.

Ongkili, J. P. (1985). *Nation-building in Malaysia.* New York: Oxford University Press.

Pearson, R. (1990). Perspectives on public relations history. *Public Relations Review, 16*, 27-38.

Pillai, M. G. G. (1987, October 29). 63 held in Malaysia security crackdown. *The* (London) *Times*, p. 11.

Primlott, J. A. R. (1951). *Public relations and American democracy.* Princeton, NJ: Princeton University Press.

Ponder, S. (1990). Progressive drive to shape public opinion, 1898-1913. *Public Relations Review, 16*, 94-105.

Ramsey, S. A. (1993). Issues management and the use of technologies in public relations. *Public Relations Review, 19*, 261-276.

Sproule, J. M. (1994). *Channels of propaganda.* Bloomington, IN: ERIC/Edinfo Press.

Sproule, J. M. (1997). *Propaganda and democracy: The American experience of media and mass persuasion.* New York: Cambridge University Press.

Taylor, M., Vazquez, G. M., & Doorley, J. (2003). Merck and AIDS activists: Engagement as a framework for extending issues management. *Public Relations Review, 29*, 257-270.

Watts, D. (1987a, November 2). TV chief and two Christians seized: Tensions in Malaysia. *The* (London) *Times*, p. 11.

Watts, D. (1987b, November 4). Malaysia elite rest uneasy up at the club. *The* (London) *Times*, p. 12.

Watts, D. (1987c, November 6). Mahathir battling to weather storm: Tension in Malaysia. *The* (London) *Times*, p. 12.

Watts, D. (1987d, November 7). Mahathir takes a hard line on "misuse" of liberalism. *The* (London) *Times*, p. 8.

Watts, D. (1987e, November 10). "Police state" seen by veteran leader: Malaysian clampdown. *The* (London) *Times*, p. 11.

Wilson, L. J. (1990). Corporate issues management: An international view. *Public Relations Review, 16*, 40-51.

Zarefsky, D., Miller-Tutzauer, C., & Tutzauer, F. (1984). Reagan's safety net for the truly needy: The rhetorical uses of definition. *Central States Speech Journal, 35*, 113-119.

chapter 8

Internet Activism and Institutional Image Management*

Jeffrey L. Courtright

As foretold by gurus in the profession, new technologies have changed the face of public relations practice. Although not a complete substitute for older technologies, the Internet, Intranets, e-mail, and, to a growing extent, blogs have become part and parcel of how organizations communicate. What is less clear is to what extent the Internet, in particular, provides advantages to organizations and their publics, often creating disparities in power and influence.

This chapter focuses on two entities that deserve greater study to understand the power struggles that Internet communication (and communication practices in general) brings to public relations, particularly to nonprofit (specifically, religious) organizations and individual critics of such organizations. In particular, I focus on the Church of Scientology International, arguably one of the most successful religious institutions, economically

*An earlier version of this chapter was presented at the 66th annual meeting of the Central States Communication Association, Chicago, IL, with John C. Bristol as co-author. The author wishes to thank Mr. Bristol for the original online search results that form the primary data for this study.

speaking, and a handful of Internet critics of the Church (also referred to hereafter as CSI). The Church limited its campaign against these cyberactivists (and, at times, their Internet providers) to the courts, which handed down some of the first rulings regarding copyright infringement of an organization's intellectual property on the Internet.

The Church won its cases or settled them out of court. Based on the news coverage these cases received in media outlets, the everyday citizen therefore might assume that CSI merely had much greater power than the activists. Such a conclusion would be based on what I call an "armchair definition" of power. There is much more to power than an organization drawing on its considerable monies to fight its critics. For the purposes of this chapter, power is not merely the ability to muster resources in order to communicate (cf. Ihlen, 2002b). Power also entails the ability to control and influence the production of messages and their meanings. For example, it is not enough to have access to the Internet; activists must create a symbolic "space" for themselves from which to critique organizations and successfully bring about organizational change. This is a tall order because organizations, through internal and external communication, already have established for themselves a sizable symbolic space from which to communicate, exercise power and influence, and acquire further control over meanings associated with their organizational images.

From this perspective of power, I argue that the promise of the Internet as a rhetorical tool for activists to gain legitimacy and influence institutional social responsibility is not as great as corporate public relations professionals might fear or academics and activist organizations might hope. This is because the organization can manage the space in which it addresses its "cybercritics," if you will. I present two arguments to support my contention: (a) the Internet is as much a site of corporate domination as it is a forum in which all computer-literate participants may have a voice; and (b) organizational power is exercised as much by silence in public spheres as by the use of public argument in them. The so-called "Scientology versus the Internet" (2005) case thus provides lessons regarding the roles of rhetoric, voice, and symbolic power in the public relations activities of organizations and activists alike. Before I go into my core argument, I cover the prevailing perspectives on cyberspace's value to society, which are at the heart of corporate communications in the case.

THE PROMISE AND THE REALITY OF CYBERSPACE

Burgeoning new technologies certainly have benefited organizations and their publics, yet a review of writings in the field suggests that the Internet itself is far from a panacea to communication problems with stakeholders:

> Unfortunately, for those of us in the information business, the Web's utility and value have been overrepresented. Communication professionals have been sold a bill of goods. The situation we currently face is one where web presence is seen as inherently valuable, and where content takes a back seat. (Kent, 1998/1999, p. 31)

Although the Internet surely offers opportunities for corporate transparency and public access, that potential has yet to be realized. This is true both for corporations and institutions as well as for favorable publics and activist critics.

The Promise for Organizations

In the early 1980s, public relations professionals already were predicting the importance of new technologies to the practice (e.g., Lesly, n.d.). By the 1990s, many recognized its numerous advantages for public relations: client recruitment, services and training; issues and audience research; monitoring the competition (Bobbitt, 1995); and, of course, the possibilities for reaching publics (Marken, 1995, 1998). Throughout the decade, though, the Public Relations Society of America's principal publications, *Public Relations Journal,* and its successor, the *Public Relations Strategist*, remained generally cautious. As Wiesendanger (1993) observed early on, "What will *you* do with the new technological tools for message delivery? Certainly, knowing they exist is the first step. The hard part is folding them into the everyday practice of public relations in a way that makes sense" (p. 14; cf. Hauss, 1995; Paster, 1995). Still, there remained the temptation as we approached the 21st century to treat the Internet as something public relations could not possibly do without, with little to no regard for its possible drawbacks (e.g., FitzGerald & Spagnolia, 1999; "The Future of Public Relations," 1999).

The few extant studies of practitioner perceptions of new technologies as communication tools indicate that public relations professionals are sensitive to these drawbacks. Johnson (1997) reported that a purposive sample (17 practitioners in a southeastern urban area of the United States) were selective in their use of new technologies for a variety of reasons: whether publics were comfortable with the new media, if they had access to it, and how to cut through the clutter of messages vying for attention. Interestingly, Johnson suggested that tactically oriented practitioners, rather than those with greater managerial (decision-making) responsibilities, tended to be more audience-focused. Although most respondents were concerned with the perceived need to adopt new technologies—and the steep curve for learning them—the pressure to adopt them was balanced by concerns for the lack of time and resources available to make their use efficient and productive. Focusing primarily on 13 practitioners in organizations with a working website, Hill and White (2000) found the same perceptions. They also found the perception of having a website to be part of the organization's image to appear professional and competitive (cf. Springston, 2001).

Still, these and other studies emphasize the potential benefits the Internet can accrue to public relations efforts. New technologies should be used strategically, like those used often in media relations as part of the media mix (Hill & White, 2000; Johnson, 1997). Hill and White's (2000) respondents believed that a website could reach new audiences for an organization and help strengthen existing relationships (as long as the website was not seen as a substitute for face-to-face interaction). Moreover, although Heath (1998) contended that the Internet provided a promising opportunity for issue management, Esrock and Leichty (1998) found that few of the Fortune 500 companies were using their webpages to gauge public opinion on public issues or advocate particular policy positions on them. Still, 82% of those companies addressed at least one corporate social responsibility topic on their websites, and more than half highlighted involvement in a given public sphere (e.g., community, environment, education). Although few corporations were found to highlight such efforts with convenient links from their home pages, it was clear that the Internet was becoming accepted as a medium appropriate for image-building but less so for corporate advocacy (Esrock & Leichty, 1998).

Given Heath's (1998) arguments, ideally the Internet should provide the opportunity for two-way, symmetrical communication:

> In this era of cyberspace, the Internet and Web have come to be a powerful arena for such [public policy] discussions which do not allow media reporters, editors, and news directors—or government officials—to be the final power in determining whether issue discussants can have their voices heard. . . . Any organization—no matter how financially limited—can sustain its messages over time and reach people around the world. The electronic playing field helps to democratize public policy debate—a crucial contribution to the issues management process. (pp. 275-276; cf. Kent & Taylor, 1998; Marken, 1998)

Interestingly, notice where Heath places the seat of power—in the ability of the organization to control its own destiny (usually a far from symmetrical outcome; cf. Roper, 2005). Ideally, critical theorists argue that cyberspace, like any other public space, should be a "place" where all citizens are engaged in free, public discussions of any and all matters vital to the health of society (Dahlgren, 2000; Weaver, 2001). This perspective places Internet-based communications in the realm of symmetrical outcomes.

Instead, cyberspace has become dominated more by for-profit interests than marked by open, public dialogue. At best, the electronic public square is populated by virtual communities rather than one global village (Weaver,

2001); these "communities" are dwarfed by the dominance of major media/communication conglomerates that focus our online attention in ways that privilege the corporate sector (Dahlberg, 2005). These conglomerates do so through the search engines they own. As noted earlier, the majority of corporate home pages focus on publics as consumers (Scammell, 2000), relegating value statements, community relations efforts, and stakeholder feedback mechanisms to links, which (based on the research experiences of approximately 150 public relations students of mine in the last few years alone) often are hard to find (cf. Esrock & Leichty, 1998). As Purves (1998) aptly states, "The shift from the McLuhanesque global village appears to be toward global villages or the shopping mall" (p. 143; cf. Deetz, 1992).

Influencing Organizations in Cyberspace

There is another side to the argument, of course. The Internet does indeed provide opportunities for stakeholders, who "can now communicate with each other about an organization in a very public way" (Merwe, van der Pitt, & Abratt, 2005, p. 39), and such networking between stakeholders increases their potential to influence organizations (e.g., Manheim, 2001; Rubach, 1999). This is true of activists, although activist organizations have not taken advantage of the potential for dialogue the Internet might afford (Taylor, Kent, & White, 2001), and have not done so any more than other types of organizations. What *has* contributed to the use of the Internet by activists has been the user-friendly design of initial websites for their organizations (Taylor, Kent & White, 2001) and the success of online activist efforts in recent years.

In general, organizations today ignore what's being said about them on the Internet at their peril. There are at least five reasons for this.

First, consumers quickly can crystallize an issue and make it difficult for an organization to get its side of the story believed. Such was the case for Intel and its updated version of the Pentium chip (Hearit, 1999). After discovery by a university professor and publicity from a trade publication, computer mavens learned quickly through online newsgroups that a technical flaw made the chip imperfect; granted, it was an imperfection that would rarely if ever affect the everyday consumer, but it was an imperfection nonetheless. Instead of solving the problem, Intel's lack of attention to what a specialized newsgroup could do to its image created a major product recall problem and image crisis.

Second, consumers themselves can quickly harness the Internet and create an activist organization online. Ford Motor Company resisted a recall of over 8.7 million vehicles to replace faulty ignition switches. After a Georgia couple's 1985 Ford Ranger suddenly caught fire in their driveway, they formed the Association of Flaming Fords website (Coombs, 1998). The website encouraged other owners of the "flaming Fords" to contact their dealers for assistance. The site also garnered news attention from major broadcast networks. The recall ended up costing Ford an estimated $200 to $300 million.

Third, activist activity on the Internet can harm an organization's reputation—especially if the organization makes a tactical public relations error in response. In 1994, McDonald's chose to sue two environmentalists in Great Britain who had distributed leaflets accusing the restaurant chain of having an unhealthy menu, paying low wages, and perpetrating other "evil" business practices (Kernisky & Kernisky, 1998, citing Keiler & Middleberg, 1997). The trial was one of the longest libel trials in British history, but it also gave activist groups ample time to paint McDonald's as a bully, a Goliath to the two activists' David. McDonald's won the lawsuit, but lost in the court of public opinion with the resulting negative press and lasting public memory.

Fourth, barring any legal impediments, activists can induce organizational change through online intervention in an issue's life cycle. Bullert (2000) reported that activists' protests against the use of sweatshops by Nike received about three articles per year until 1996, when a variety of stakeholders, nongovernment organizations, media, and celebrities came together through e-mail and the Internet to bring greater pressure on Nike to change its labor policies in Asia. Similarly, Chiapas guerillas' use of the Internet to attract an international community of supporters was helpful in drawing attention to an uprising in southern Mexico, adding to pressure that eventually resulted in successful peace talks after 2 years of fighting (Froehling, 1997; Knudson, 1998).

Finally, activists also may build and sustain an issue's salience, along with their organizations and working relationships, through persistent online efforts in coordination with other media channels. For example, activists in the United Kingdom have continued to draw attention to radio and television programming and policies that favor market-driven broadcasting (Kovacs, 2003). Groups used the Internet as well as other communication channels to facilitate coalitions and sustain (and expand) public policy concerns such as digital access, ownership consolidation, access for the disabled, and public service broadcasting.

Limitations to Cyberactivism

Given these advantages,[1] what prevents online activism from being even more successful? There are at least four reasons. First, activists face the same problems with new technologies as organizations do—getting noticed in the hyperabundance of sources available (cf. Levine, 2002). Second, not all stakeholders get an equal hearing, especially activists, who often are not treated as desirable stakeholders. Third, the activists may be discounted by most people as self-appointed, self-important cranks who rant about a topic, especially if that topic is not on the public agenda in some recognizable form or, most important, not viewed as locally important to individual citizens. Fourth, organizations themselves can coopt the Internet, even creating fake blogs to stimulate buzz (Nishi, 2004). Much like employees who may not trust management, people in chat rooms will guard their comments or go elsewhere if they perceive that communication openness has been violated or is not valued or rewarded. Indeed, Altheide (2004) argued that participants' awareness of Internet surveillance in any form can serve to stifle freedom of expression. (For discussions of how organizations can use the Internet ethically, see Holtz, 1999.)

Clearly there are power issues at stake as organizations and activists negotiate their roles and seek to affect the potential influence of the other. (This is true not only in cyberspace, but it is also true in other public spheres.) The promise of symmetrical communication, of dialogue between organizations and their publics on the Internet, can only be fulfilled when organizations put the importance of power subordinate to transparency. The tendency not to do so invites frustration from consumers and other publics who, in turn, may take their case directly to cyberspace. Whether as individuals or as organized publics, the resulting criticism when placed on the Web can propel a complaint into an issue and generate greater media attention. To fight criticism on the Internet may come at a cost of image if not profit. To better appreciate the case of Scientology's efforts to curtail activist criticism on the Internet, what is needed is a rhetorical perspective that addresses the issue of power in public relations.

ORGANIZATIONAL SPACE AND CYBERSPACE ACTIVISM

If we treat any and all messages produced by an organization as an expression of *who* the organization is (i.e., its *persona*; cf. McMillan, 1987), the Internet becomes a site of potential struggle when individuals and groups other than that organization employ the organization's words to express themselves or critique the organization. As illustrated in crisis situations in which an organization refuses to acknowledge that a problem exists (e.g., Ihlen, 2002a), an organization quickly can become the victim of its own words being used against itself, resulting in a loss of public confidence or, worse, long-term loss of credibility (e.g., Kernisky & Kernisky, 1998). Any Internet audience member may produce messages as well as receive them;

and, even if not challenged legally, at what point do those symbols no longer serve their function in the organization's ongoing narrative? Significant for public relations practitioners, according to Fisher (1987), all communication may be reduced to stories. The interactive nature of the Internet merely heightens our awareness of the issue of control over those narratives (Cover, 2004), for publicity efforts always have given away parts of the organization's story in hope of favorable news coverage.

Most important for this chapter is Fisher's (1987) notion that all communication is some form of narrative. As noted earlier, traditional public relations models privilege rational, reasoned decision making (i.e., traditional argument supported by evidence) in a day when such logic no longer necessarily governs corporate communication (e.g., advertising; cf. Simons, 2001). Yet one of public relations' chief activities is telling the organization's side of the story. If all messages are essentially narrative, then the metaphorical ownership of all texts and their uses in social interaction is key to understanding the messages of organizations, media, and publics alike. Textual ownership is central to the work of de Certeau (1980/1984, 1980/1990), as is explained in this section with a look at the Church of Scientology International (CSI) and its critics on the Internet.

Certeau and the "Propre"

Certeau (1980/1984, 1980/1990) argues that the uses of language develop different logics, different ways of doing (*arts de faire*), in relation to the circumstances in which they arise. Games, accounts, legends, and other linguistic practices develop particular norms within every society. For example, standard practices in public relations might include the company backgrounder as an expression of what the organization stands for, where it's been, and where it's going. Therefore, central to the understanding of public relations as a rhetorical practice through Certeau are two principles: the *propre* (in this case, the rhetoric produced by an organization for its own purposes) and its resulting *trajectoire* (a trajectory, the direction and shape of its symbolic existence determined by its communication). Also figuring in this discussion are two subordinate terms, *la perruque* (the wig) and *poaching*.

According to Certeau (1980/1990), all social systems use language to create a proper place, or *propre*, from which to organize all other symbolic and physical action. This *propre* not only makes up a "space" for an organization, for example, but also serves "as a base from which relations with an *exteriority* composed of targets or threats (customers or competitors, enemies, . . . etc.) can be managed" (1980/1984, p. 36). This *propre* is not merely a physical space, but is created symbolically and made up of *usages propres* (what I call "proper usages"), the primary messages and texts by which all other messages (i.e., *usages faibles*; what I call "weak usages") may be understood.[2] Proper usages are those controlled by the source, and they become standard assumptions regarding an organization, what it stands for, who its stakeholders are, and so on. The ways that we talk about an organization or social system recognizes its legitimacy to be defined in certain ways. The *propre,* therefore, constitutes a place of power and establishes proper ways of doing things as well. Weak usages are messages created by others who would use the *propre* for their own purposes, even though they may not have as much legitimacy, if any, to do so.

Applied to public relations, Certeau's terminology can be understood this way: Messages fundamental to what an organization is (its history, mission statement, etc.) serve as proper usages, the basis for subsequent messages. In the case of CSI, the sacred writings of L. Ron Hubbard (e.g., *Dianetics* [Hubbard, 1950/1992]; Hubbard, 1965), other publications (e.g., CSI, n.d., 1978, 1994, 1998; *L. Ron Hubbard*, 1999), its training practices, its websites and pages associated with the Church (e.g., CSI, 2003-2005c), its offices (e.g., CSI, 2003-2005a), and affiliated organizations (e.g., CSI, 1999-2004, 2002-2004, 2003, 2003-2005a, 2003-2005b) would serve as proper usages. Other usages build on CSI's *propre* and would include any publicity texts produced by CSI staffers (e.g., news releases [CSI, 2003-2005d]; its *Freedom* magazine contents [e.g., Thorpe, 1996]) and advocacy advertising (e.g., *Freedom* Magazine, n.d.; cf. Courtright, 1995). Although these messages and/or texts do not necessarily connect with one another in the way an argumentative position relates to its evidence, proper usages form an indeterminate pattern—a direction in which the organization's discourse is headed—what Certeau calls its "trajectory" (a *trajectoire* based on "*lignes d'erre*"; Certeau, 1980/1990, citing Deligny, 1970). At the very least, the trajectory's pattern can be discerned after the fact (cf., Weick, 1979). This *propre*, along with employees' weak usages allowed by the organization (e.g., personal innovations that are informally allowed as well as those that become formalized as standard operating procedures, managerial practices, new product developments, etc.), can be seen like traces of writing on a page or a series of points in space: a "walking rhetoric" (Certeau, 1980/1984, p. 100).

Certeau (1980/1984) used an analogy to pedestrian travel to explain how proper and weak usages are employed. For example, a court proceeding serves as an "operation marking out boundaries" (p. 122), and therefore constitutes part of the government's "proper place" in which the organization and others may operate. For example, Food and Drug Administration (FDA) statutes provide guidelines for all pharmaceuticals, yet herbal supplements do not enjoy the same legitimacy as vitamin supplements from the major drug companies. All health supplement companies must act and communicate within the *propre* articulated by the FDA as a federal oversight agency. The *propre* thus serves "as the basis for generating relations with . . .

competitors, adversaries, 'clienteles,' 'targets,' or 'objects' of research" (p. xix, parentheses omitted). Informally, however, people operating with the system use bits and pieces of the *propre* and combine their own messages with them in the form of weak usages. Put in terms of public relations theory, weak usages belong to those who are not part of the dominant coalition in the organization: "The place of a[n *usage faible*] belongs to the other [those outside the power of the *propre*]" (Certeau, 1980/1984, p. xix). Weak usages are "determined by the *absence of power* just as a [proper usage] is organized by the postulation of power" (p. 38).

I read Certeau's view of power to be consistent with the explanation offered in the first pages of this chapter; for example, we enact the power of relationships through communication; therefore, "knowing someone who knows someone" is not just a networked connection, but it is rather a fully communication-based phenomenon that we exercise as a *source* of power. For example, opinion leaders are very important in community relations (Burke, 1999). Although they may have their own proper sphere of influence they have built up over time (their *propre*), the personal relationships they build within the organization may be articulated as a means of acquiring influence. They may have their own personal power, but they depend on power communicated and sustained through the organization's *propre* to capitalize on their network of relationships. The strength of networking can only be understood for that specific situation in relation to the organization's *propre*. An employee also may take advantage of a philanthropic matching program to make his or her personal donation go farther economically, but the availability of matching dollars has been determined by the organization's messages (i.e., guidelines) regarding which charities qualify for the program—the *proper usages* for donations articulated through those points in the organization's *propre*.

This concept of weak usages, thus, takes three forms. First, members of the organization have uses for the organization's proper usages, adding their own purposes to them. If this is done without incurring organizational disapproval, such usages work in a way similar to those in which specialized servants served the nobility. For example, a wig maker would provide the master with a new creation and yet embellish it with his or her own artistic expression, pleasing him- or herself while pleasing the master; hence Certeau's term, *la perruque* (the wig) for this combination of proper and weak usages. Given Certeau's example of the wig, it should be noted that *la perruque* could be any instance of persons affiliated with an organization when they engage in symbolic action, not just message production. For CSI, examples would include celebrity comments to the media and others regarding public issues and their relationship to the Church or their personal beliefs (e.g., actor John Travolta, musician Isaac Hayes, and jazz artist Chick Corea testifying before Congress regarding religious discrimination in

Europe [United States, 1997]); or Tom Cruise being interviewed on NBC's *Today Show*, when he repeated his belief that pharmaceuticals were inappropriate for the treatment of postpartum depression [MSNBC.com, 2005]).

Activist Weak Usages and "Poaching"

Two kinds of commentary by organizational outsiders join *la perruque* as weak usages. The first of these stitches together arguments, stories, and other rhetorical resources to allow the disenfranchised their own "space" from which to speak. The second, as is demonstrated in this section, is a parallel to the insider's practice of *la perruque*. Weak uses unassociated with the organization's *propre* per se may take their style and form from a variety of sources, pieced together like a quilt (hence Certeau's [1980/1984] term *bricolage* [p. 29]). As Certeau put it, these weak usages "seize on the wing the possibilities that offer themselves at any given moment" (p. 37).

The weak usages of CSI's cybercritics can be characterized as a combination of traditional argument and elements of atrocity tales common to critics of cults. According to Bromley, Shupe, and Ventimiglia (1979), U.S. news media coverage of new religious movements (NRMs) as cults often are framed as accounts of atrocities, rationalizing them as "evil" to legitimize sanctions against them. Such narratives feature moral outrage and specific ways in which the group has violated social norms and values. Scientology's online critics employ atrocity tales in the same way to provoke moral outrage regarding the Church's actions toward new and former members.

Two examples suffice to illustrate the values that cybercritics claim Scientology has violated. One critic, Xenu (n.d.a), who continues to host a site called "Operation Clambake," explains the Church's practices with initiates:

> Scientology appeals to people by offering them a grand game; a unique and comprehensive self-improvement system; a solution for almost every problem (many people come to Scientology when their lives are in crisis); and a welcoming group focused on major societal issues such as drug abuse, mental health, education, spirituality and morality. After joining the Church of Scientology, one meets with increasing demands for money, time and recruiting others. (Xenu, n.d.b)

The story goes on to tell of further psychological and economic harm to which CSI subjects its members.

Perhaps the most repeated atrocity tale on anti-Scientology websites is the *cause célèbre* of Lisa McPherson's death in Clearwater, Florida, in 1995 ("Lisa McPherson," n.d.). One website puts her story, laced with irony, in the first person:

> On November 18, 1995, I had a minor car accident. When the paramedics arrived, I took off my clothes and ran to them asking for help. They took me to the local hospital's psychiatric ward. When the Church found out where I was, they sent people who talked me into signing out and leaving with them. I went to the Fort Harrison Hotel.
>
> I was at the Fort Harrison, in Scientology custody, for 17 days. During that time, according to their own records, I claimed I was L. Ron Hubbard, refused to eat, did not sleep, drank my own urine, and displayed other signs of psychosis, as well as obvious signs of deteriorating health. ("Scientology Kills," n.d.)

Such atrocity tales create a strong emotional appeal by demonstrating how the alleged cult violates physical, psychological, legal, and other social norms—generally, violations of human rights (FACTNet, n.d.).

Scientology cybercritics' most logical arguments refute the Church's factual and doctrinal claims. To debunk Scientology, this requires that they intrude on CSI's *propre*. Subversive uses of an organization's proper usages constitute the *poaching* (*braconnage*) of the organization's *propre* (Certeau, 1980/1984, 1980/1990). Those who employ these usages for their own purposes combine them with their own weak usages because they lack the power of those who define the organization through their discourse and actions; that is, in terms of the public relations literature, the "dominant coalition" (Grunig, 1990, pp. 120-121; cf. Berger, 2005). Like members of the organization, activists develop their own uses for its symbolic territory. Unlike the employee who buys into the dominant culture and values of the organization, however (cf. Conrad, 1990), outsiders often adopt those usages for ends not intended by the organization. For example, Jenkins (1988) documents how *Star Trek* fans adapt the series' characters to express themselves, with unconventional results. Activists do the same with the rhetoric of organizations they wish to attack.

Scientology most certainly has had its detractors (e.g., Garrison, 1974), among them former members (e.g., Atack, 1990) and even the founder's son (Corydon & Hubbard, 1987). Although many studies of the Church have been academic in grounding (e.g., Berger, 1989; Wallis, 1976), some critics, to the extent that they borrow and reinterpret CSI's own rhetoric, can be said to be *poaching* the Church's *propre*. For example, Atack (1990) describes in detail the series of drills and training courses he underwent as a Scientologist for over 10 years. Others (e.g., Miller, 1987) systematically have investigated and refuted CSI's continuing claims that L. Ron Hubbard was a well-traveled explorer and World War II hero prior to his writing of *Dianetics*.

Internet attack sites typically display similar message content. How activists *poached* L. Ron Hubbard's writings became the focus of several court cases involving CSI and its critics from 1995 to 1999, due to questions of copyright infringement. On the alt.scientology.org newsgroup, former Scientologist Dennis Erlich began in August 1994 to post "portions of church publications and documents" ("Internet Providers Cleared," 1995; "Scientology Suit Takes," 1995; cf. "alt.religion.scientology," n.d., 2005). In August 1995, Arnaldo Lerma also provided on the same newsgroup information on Scientology's seventh level of spirituality, "'confidential and unpublished' teachings that the Church provides to its members only through one-on-one counseling" (Nguyen, 1995, p. B06; cf. Allen, 1995b). Around the same period, two Colorado men, the owners of FACTNet.com, a Web bulletin board with information on about 300 cults at the time, also posted CSI secret texts, allegedly containing information about "secret rituals in which [church] officials claim they are aliens from outer space whose purpose is to take over the Earth" (Allen, 1995b, p. 4A). Two less-publicized cases involved Californians Grady Ward and Keith Henson for similar publication of Scientology "Advanced Technology" levels (Gaura, 1998; cf. Wasserman, 1995).[3]

The Church of Scientology's response to these possible infringements was not characteristic of its counterattacks to criticism in the 1990s (cf., e.g., Courtright, 1995; *Freedom Magazine*, n.d.). Rather than full-page advocacy advertisements designed to draw attention to the issue, the Church attempted to extend its rights and *propre* through the American judicial system and strategic use of limited media coverage. (Such extension also could add legitimacy in the larger society beyond the Church, if and only if the case prevailed in court.)

Scientology's Poaching of Legal and Media Propre

The Church utilized its institutional organ, *Freedom* magazine, a natural part of its *propre*, to advocate its position on policies regarding Internet protection of copyright and trademarks (e.g., Thorpe, 1996); however, it confined the bulk of its efforts to the state and federal court systems and statements to the media surrounding any legal action. In doing so, CSI articulated a rhetorical trajectory that legitimized its legal standing as a copyright holder, seized opportunities to obtain media coverage, and defined its critics and its relationship to them. The lawsuits clarified the Church's copyright protection on the Internet but did not increase Scientology's symbolic power over its critics' symbolic action on the Web to any great degree.

Although extensive financial resources of the Church allowed it to pursue litigation against cyberactivists, what is most striking when viewed via the concepts of Certeau is its poaching of the *propres* of the courts and the media. It had not been that long, after all, since CSI had regained its tax-exempt status as a religious institution under the Internal Revenue Code

("Scientologists Granted Tax Exemption," 1993).[4] The Church, through its Religious Technology Center (RTC) publishing arm, went well beyond the assertion that its sacred texts enjoyed complete copyright protection. In 11 cases, Scientology interpreted (poached) statutes and legal precedent in attempts to seize and retain critics' software pending the outcome of trial proceedings (e.g., *RTC v. F.A.C.T.Net,* 1995a, 1995b; cf. Abbott, 1995a), enjoin website and newsgroup site providers to censor and/or ban Scientology critics who use their services (e.g., *RTC v. NETCOM,* 1995; cf. "Internet Providers Cleared," 1995; Wasserman, 1995), and apply constitutional principles such as the free exercise of religion (e.g., *RTC v. Lerma,* 1995b).

Based on Certeau's definition of poaching, the standard public relations practices of producing news releases and issuing verbal statements to the press would be considered poaching of the *propre* of a given media outlet—intruding its message into each outlet's message *trajectory*. As such, the Church of Scientology employed letters to the editor from official spokespeople (Goodman, 1995) and church members (Harrison, 1995) and press statements during the first copyright cases it pursued. A few of the latter were couched in purely legal terms by CSI's lawyer for the Religious Technology Center, Helen Kobrin. For example, "If these documents left the church, it's because someone stole them. Mr. Lerma posted materials to the Internet which are copyrighted, unpublished, confidential material, and he had no permission to do that" (Allen, 1995a, p. A12); "The Internet is part of this universe and country, and you can't just take copyright laws and say they don't apply" ("Scientology Wins," 1996, p. A-17).

For the most part, however, the Church's press statements employed intense language to frame its relationship to its critics, the courts, and the media; for example, the critics had engaged in "copyright terrorism" ("Marshals Seize Computer Files," 1995, p. A22; Nguyen, 1995, p. B06). Another Scientology lawyer, Earle Cooley, claimed that cyberactivist Larry Wollersheim "for 15 years has been obsessed with the destruction of the Church of Scientology" (Pankratz, 1995, p. A01). As Kobrin summed up the situation in a public letter during the first court case, "We are trying to deal with an anarchy created by some net users who callously trample on the intellectual property rights of organizations" ("CyberSurfing," 1995, p. C07).

Equally withering was the Church's attitude toward the courts when rulings favored its critics. In its actions against FACTNet, Church officials refused to return specific computer files in equipment CSI had seized from the defendants—allegedly the files contained the copyrighted material in question (Fong, 1995; *RTC v. FACTnet,* 1995b)—claiming First Amendment rights of the free exercise of religion. As Denver's *Rocky Mountain News* reported, "That includes keeping the beliefs secret. . . . 'That religious tenet is firm and immutable,' the church said in court documents. 'The materials cannot be surrendered to apostates'" (Abbott, 1995c, p. 4A). In some cases, Scientology's criticism of court rulings engaged in hyperbole:

> What the appeals court judges failed to see is that Judge Kane's decision is fraught with prejudice. . . . We're now in the same disadvantaged position as the blacks of the South were until Martin Luther King and other honest individuals ended the injustice. (Abbott, 1995b, p. 16A)

The Church's efforts to protect its sacred texts went so far as to include attempts to prevent the media themselves from including any quotation of them in reporting the lawsuits. The *Washington Post* maintained that it did not violate copyrights or trade secrets, yet CSI sued the newspaper for damages. In addressing the case, CSI lawyer Earle Cooley said, "I don't deny this is a newsworthy article, but thousands of articles are written about Coca-Cola, and they don't print the formula for Coca-Cola" (Hall, 1995a, p. A18). The suit was later dismissed and the Church ordered to pay all attorney costs (Hall, 1995b).

Although I have cited only the court cases and media coverage in major and regional newspapers, it is important to recognize two important results of the Church's handling of the issue of intellectual property on the Internet. First, the Church did maintain and extend copyright protection to warn cyberactivists that Scientology could successfully prosecute illegal posting of CSI material on the Internet. After winning its second case, the Church announced, "After a ruling like this, if a person has any brains, they will think twice about (posting church writings on the Internet)" ["Sect Wins Copyright Suit," 1996]. Second, from an issue management perspective, CSI legitimized the cybercritics through its statements to the media from 1995 to 1997, including television and radio coverage beyond the cases themselves.

During progress of its litigation against Dennis Erlich (*RTC v. NETCOM*, 1995, 1997), Larry Wollersheim (*RTC v. FACTNet,* 1995a, 1995b; *RTC v. Wollersheim,* 1996), and Arnaldo Lerma (*RTC v. Lerma*, 1995a, 1995b, 1996), the Church of Scientology and its representatives spoke to the press multiple times. This choice, however, raised the visibility of these cases and gave the defendants opportunities to be covered and sometimes quoted in over 60 articles in national and regional newspapers in 1995 and 1996. This figure does not include legal and computer trade publications, which also covered these cases. (My count comes from a series of searches on Academic Universe [Lexis-Nexis]).

Moreover, although a cause-and-effect relationship cannot be established, it is interesting that these early cases received national and regional broadcast news coverage—at least 25 different media outlets over a 3-year period, including CNN (e.g., Holliman, 1995) and ABC's *World News Tonight* (e.g., Crier, 1995). Granted, some of these news stories did not feature the activists alone; for example, the Church's media relations officer, Lisa Goodman, was heard on an *All Things Considered* story on National Public Radio (Charles, 1995). One copyright defendant, Keith Henson, whose case (*RTC v. Henson,* 1997/2000) received little newspaper coverage—and no Scientology press statements—appeared on the public television program *The Computer Chronicles* (1997) in a 10-minute segment. More important, Erlich, Wollersheim, and Lerma also appeared later on major television network news segments focusing on Scientology (*Fox News Live*, 2000; *20/20 Sunday*, 1998). This suggests that their further media visibility is linked to the visibility they received when the Church chose to speak to the press during their respective court cases.

COPYRIGHT, VOICE, AND POWER

Although legal scholars have studied the Church of Scientology's cases as important steps in the application of copyright law to cyberspace, few have questioned the Church's economic power to muzzle its critics. This study of those cases and their news coverage suggests that, although CSI asserted and won some recognition of copyright protection for its material online, the Church may have won the battle but lost the war. Scientology not only is very limited in its ability to curtail cyberactivism against it, but it may have learned an important lesson in using the courts as a means to fight what little legal standing it has to do so. Activist websites and newsgroups continue to question the legitimacy of this new religion, and sometimes it is better to allow them to exist than to legitimize the critics by taking them to court. Still, the Church and its *propre* are quite secure in the age of the Internet, given the multiple messages and sources Scientology has at its disposal. In this final section, I examine some implications for public relations practice that "Scientology versus the Internet" suggests regarding copyright law, activists' voice and legitimacy, and the "proper usages" of an organization's *propre.*

Copyright Law and the Web

Perhaps it was only natural that Scientology would attempt to secure its *propre* in the form of intellectual property on the Internet. Cyberspace laws established internationally are easily circumvented (Drucker & Gumpert,

1999), for each nation regulates the Internet in its own way (May, Chen, & Wen, 2004). In the 1990s, application of copyright and statutes established for previous communication channels were insufficient to cover the ambiguities of digital forms—the nature of the beast simply did not fit the language of the law. So the question of who really owns electronically distributed material was up in the air (Gailey, 1996). At the time, Scientology's efforts to fight its Internet critics prompted many to suggest that an update of copyright and communications statutes was needed urgently (e.g., "Speech in Electronic Space," 1995).

The result was the Digital Millennium Copyright Act (1999). The act has preserved the rights of "fair use" and "fair comment" for educational and other purposes, but prohibits the type of wholesale dumping of copyrighted material onto the Internet of the kind perpetrated by Arnaldo Lerma (Hall, 1996). Less clear has been the responsibility of Web providers as hosts for websites and newsgroups (Lee, 2001), as in the case of Dennis Erlich. Even though the judge in the case had not found NETCOM guilty of contributing to copyright infringement in providing Erlich access to an electronic bulletin board, NETCOM eventually settled with CSI out of court (Pimentel, 1996). What this means for public relations is that, with the exception of clear copyright infringement, by and large the Internet is a space where free speech reigns—and, using Certeau's terminology, where activists and other publics may *poach* an organization's *propre* as long as they do not violate the law.

Voice and Legitimacy

As a result, criticism of Scientology is alive and flourishing in cyberspace. Because CSI was unsuccessful in getting the courts to declare its training information to be "trade secrets," information about Church practices is readily available online. Even activists who were on the Internet in the 1990s and sharing details of Scientology's "Advanced Technology" such as "OT III" and new versions of it (e.g., "NOTs on the net," n.d.; Touretzky, 1997a, 1997b), are there today, some with the same content as before (Touretzky, n.d.a, n.d.b, n.d.c, n.d.d). Moreover, those subject to lawsuits a decade ago are on the Web, still criticizing the Church (e.g., Lerma, 2005). New sites about Scientology also exist, some as rogue sites (e.g., "Scientology lies," 2005; cf. Hallahan, 2004) and some as parts of larger sites regarding various NRMs (e.g., Rick A. Ross Institute, 1996-2000). Other sites such as "Operation Clambake"—the virtual home of "Xenu"—have moved to new Web addresses (Heldal-Lund, n.d.) to continue their efforts and provide links to other cyberactivists. The site that started it all, the "alt.religion.scientology" (2005) newsgroup itself, continues, now housed on Google (2005).

Monitoring an organization's critics on the Internet, let alone litigating them, thus constitutes a huge undertaking, depending on the size of the target. Information that is in the public domain can be posted, quoted, or linked by anyone. For example, Ron Newman (1996, 1997a, 1997b, 1997c) placed transcripts and other information regarding the Scientology cases against Grady Ward, Keith Henson, and Arnie Lerma on his website and continues to add to his criticism of the Church, at least in cyberspace. He and Marina Chong (1995) linked to one another through newsgroups and website links and continue to do so. Mitra and Watts' (2002) call for further study of the eloquence of representation on the Web merits reemphasis here—the "voices" with which people and institutions present themselves in cyberspace may be a critical factor in communication on the Internet. As has been shown, legitimizing that voice in other channels may extend the influence of cyberactivists beyond the Internet.

Until I found the amount of news coverage Scientology's critics gained as a result of the lawsuits, I had suspected that all the power—in that "armchair" definition of the word—lay with the Church. As Ihlen (2002b) argued, "the question of deep pockets is too easily dismissed" (p. 261). Given the fact that the Church itself provided a space beyond cyberspace for its Internet critics, I would suggest that the activist's voice can be confined to limited public spheres, assuming Certeau's sense of power associated with any *propre*. The question remains as to whether activism on the Internet has limitations or differences in the ways legitimation processes work, especially when compared to agitation as defined in the social movement literature (e.g., Bowers, Ochs, & Jensen, 1993). With one rare exception, a planned public protest by cyberactivists such as Arnie Lerma and Dennis Erlich in front of Scientology's Clearwater, Florida, religious retreat in March 1996 (Wallsten, 1996), the Church's cybercritics gained a hearing in print and broadcast media only insofar as the Church exercised its voice to the press. After that, I consider the door to have been opened to further news exposure. Only in the case of Grady Ward (*RTC v. Ward*, 1999, 2002) did the Church issue no statements at all, with a result of no regional or national news coverage. Organizations need not legitimize activists as publics; if they are ignored, they are not treated as legitimate stakeholders (cf. Phillips, 2003), for legitimacy is "the right to be heard and be taken seriously" (Simons, 2001, p. 218).

Expansion of the Organization's Propre

Without doubt, the rhetorical resources at Scientology's disposal—its publications, affiliate organizations around the globe, increasing celebrity presence, and so on—far outweigh any real damage that cybercritics have managed to inflict. At the expense of giving a handful of activists a voice beyond the Web, the Church clarified its legal rights on the Internet. It expanded its *propre* through use of the courts and the media—both important venues in its own quest for legitimation as a religious institution. Certeau's notion of the *propre* as defined by its trajectory suggests that rhetoric is a symbolic resource that not only addresses matters of the legal rights of intellectual property (i.e., patents, copyrights, and trademarks), but it also includes the articulation of relationships to publics and other organizations. An organization's *propre* is an "establishment of a place of power" (Certeau, 1980/1984, p. 38) and can be used carefully to manage public spheres in such a way that the corporate right to speak (*Central Hudson Gas & Electric v. Public Service Commission,* 1980) and *not* to speak (*Pacific Gas & Electric v. Public Utilities Commission*, 1986) in the United States. Likewise, stakeholders are given—or denied—a voice.

In terms of cyberspace as a public sphere, I would suggest that activists need not be seen as "virtual barbarians at the gate" (Grady & Gimple, 1998, p. 23). With careful management, Kent and Taylor (1998) argue that the Internet can be a place to nurture dialogue with stakeholders. In contrast, the Church of Scientology's efforts suggest that activists will hold forth on the Web, despite organizational efforts to curb the power of their voice. There is, however, an important piece of the Church's *propre* that deserves further study in this regard—the organization's own voice on the Internet as a counterbalance to criticism in cyberspace. The sophistication afforded by its vast resources, economic and symbolic, as Frobish (2000) reported, allows CSI to construct "an image of goodwill built upon a communal portrait of peace and well-being," a direct contrast to its offline (and online) credibility problems. Rather than attack one's detractors, to turn a phrase, the best defense is a good, ethical offense—a rhetorical trajectory that legitimizes an organization's *persona* and voice without denying a voice to others.

Such would be my hope as practitioners and scholars take up the work of Certeau and apply it to further public relations phenomena. The power inherent in an organization's *propre* makes the role of public relations in extending the rhetorical trajectory of any organization that much more important. From this perspective, public relations' responsibility to management and publics takes on even greater significance. Public relations is formative to the creation and maintenance of an organization's *proper usages*. Management also must be encouraged to recognize the power of giving publics *voice* to their *weak usages*. Communicating fairly with publics will allow an organization's image to be more consistent across its symbolic trajectory, inviting publics to participate in its *propre*—to *poach* its symbols—decreasing threats to the organization and securing goodwill with publics so that their support can be counted on when substantial perils to the organization arise.

NOTES

1. A website also initially may provide an important identity function for activist organizations (cf. Henderson, 2005), especially extending the reach of existing organizations (cf. Holtz, 1999). Altering perceptions of self is an important rhetorical function for any social movement, creating a sense of identity for members as well as the group (Stewart, Smith, & Denton, 1994).
2. Readers familiar with the work of Certeau (1980/1990) should forgive me for the retranslation of his basic concepts, *stratégies* and *tactiques* (pp. 50ff.). His choice of terminology is unfortunate for those in public relations because we already have disagreements as to what constitute *strategies* and *tactics* in our literature and practice (cf., e.g., Cutlip, Center, & Broom, 2000; Wilcox, Cameron, Ault, & Agee, 2003). To minimize confusion, I have chosen phrases consistent with the French and English versions of Certeau's work. Readers who consult the latter (Certeau, 1980/1984) will notice some of the liberties I have taken in quoting his text and should be forewarned that his discussion of strategies and tactics must be understood with his intent, not with preconceived definitions drawn from the public relations literature and personal experience.
3. Some material posted on the Internet went beyond Scientology training material and included Hubbard's organizational policies, both official and unofficial. The latter often are criticized and quoted in exposés (e.g., Atack, 1990; Corydon & Hubbard, 1987). For a sample listing of documents in question in some of these cases, see Exhibit A at the end of *Religious Technology Center v. NETCOM* (1997).
4. Interestingly, the very reason CSI's tax exemption had been revoked was due to the Internal Revenue Service's determination in the 1960s that monies paid by church members for programs such as the Advanced Technology levels were not donations, but payment for services rendered and, therefore, taxable income. These services were based on some of the same secret writings released on the Internet by the Church's critics (cf., e.g., Touretzky, n.d.b).

REFERENCES

Abbott, K. (1995a, August 23). Dispute with church brings raids: Documents, computer gear seized from men using Internet against Church of Scientology. *Rocky Mountain News* (Denver, CO), p. 4A.

Abbott, K. (1995b, September 15). Scientologists lose appeal of computer case. *Rocky Mountain News* (Denver, CO), p. 16A.

Abbott, K. (1995c, September 27). Scientology church, duo battle again: Hearing is planned for Friday on disputed computer materials. *Rocky Mountain News* (Denver, CO), p. 4A.

Allen, M. (1995a, August 14). Dissidents use computer network to rile Scientology. *The New York Times*, p. A12.

Allen, M. (1995b, August 20). Internet gospel; Scientology's expensive wisdom now comes free. *The New York Times,* sec. 4, p. 2.

Altheide, D. L. (2004). The control narrative of the Internet. *Symbolic Action, 27,* 223-245.

Alt.religion.scientology. (2005, July 12). [Home page]. Retrieved July 25, 2005, from http://en. wikipedia.org/wiki/Alt.religion.scientology

alt.religion.scientology. (n.d.). [Home page]. Retrieved July 1, 2005, from http://www.modemac. com/cgi-bin/cos.pl/alt.religion.scientology

Atack, J. (1990). *A piece of blue sky: Scientology, Dianetics and L. Ron Hubbard exposed.* New York: Lyle Stuart.

Berger, A. I. (1989). Towards a science of the nuclear mind: Science-fiction origins of Dianetics. *Science-Fiction Studies, 16,* 123-144.

Berger, B. K. (2005). Power over, power with, and power to relations: Critical reflections on public relations, the dominant coalition, and activism. *Journal of Public Relations Research, 17,* 5-28.

Bobbitt, R. (1995). An Internet primer for public relations. *Public Relations Quarterly, 40*(3), 27-32.

Bowers, J. W., Ochs, D. J., & Jensen, R. J. (1993). *The rhetoric of agitation and control.* Long Grove, IL: Waveland Press.

Bromley, D. G., Shupe, A. D., Jr., & Ventimiglia, J. C. (1979). Atrocity tales, the Unification Church, and the social construction of evil. *Journal of Communication, 29*(3), 42-53.

Bullert, B. J. (2000). Progressive public relations, sweatshops, and the net. *Political Communication, 17,* 403-407.

Burke, E. M. (1999). *Corporate community relations: The principle of the neighbor of choice.* Westport, CT: Praeger.

Central Hudson Gas & Electric Corp. v. Public Service Commission of New York. 47 U.S. 557 (1980).

Certeau, M. de. (1984). *The practice of everyday life* (S. Rendall, Trans.). Berkeley: University of California Press. (Original work published 1980)

Certeau, M. de. (1990). *L'invention du quotidien: 1. Arts de faire.* [The invention of the everyday: 1. Ways of making]. Paris, France: Gallimard. (Original work published 1980)

Charles, D. (1995, June 13). Scientologists sue to stop criticism on Internet. In *All Things Considered* [Transcript #1877-13]. Washington, DC: National Public Radio. Retrieved October 22, 2005, from Academic Universe (Lexis-Nexis).

Chong, M. (1995, December 18). *A.R.S. web page summary.* Retrieved March 2, 1998, from http://home.pacific.net.sg/~marina/welcome.htm

Church of Scientology International. (1978). *What is Scientology?* Los Angeles: Church of Scientology of California.

Church of Scientology International. (1994). *A description of the scientology religion.* Los Angeles: Bridge.

Church of Scientology International. (1998). *Theology & practice of a contemporary religion: Scientology.* Los Angeles: Bridge.

Church of Scientology International. (1999-2004). *Church of Scientology Human Rights Office—Germany: Religious freedom.* Retrieved August 18, 2005, from http://www.humanrights-germany.org/

Church of Scientology International. (2002-2004). *Church of Scientology International Human Rights Department.* Retrieved August 18, 2005, from http://www.scientology.org/humanrights/

Church of Scientology International. (2003). *Worldwide activities.* Retrieved March 15, 2004, from http://www.scientology.org/html/en_US/world/index.html

Church of Scientology International. (2003-2005a). *Church of Scientology International European Public Affairs and Human Rights Office.* Retrieved August 18, 2005, from http://www.scientology-europe.org/

Church of Scientology International. (2003-2005b). *Narconon: Drug rehabilitation and drug education.* Retrieved August 18, 2005, from http://www.scientology.org/en_US/world/betterment/narconon/index.html

Church of Scientology International. (2003-2005c). *Scientology—Church of Scientology official site.* Retrieved July 1, 2005, from http://www.scientology.org/

Church of Scientology International. (2003-2005d). *Scientology newsroom.* Retrieved July 1, 2005, from http://www.scientology.org/html/en_US/news-media/index.html

Church of Scientology International. (n.d.). *The Church of Scientology: 40th anniversary.* Los Angeles: Author.

Conrad, C. (1990). *Strategic organizational communication: An integrated perspective* (2nd ed.). Fort Worth, TX: Holt, Rinehart and Winston.

Coombs, W. T. (1998). The Internet as potential equalizer: New leverage for confronting social irresponsibility. *Public Relations Review, 24,* 289-304.

Corydon, B., & Hubbard, L. R., Jr. (1987). *L. Ron Hubbard: Messiah or madman?* Secaucus, NJ: Lyle Stuart.

Courtright, J. L. (1995). "I am a Scientologist": The image management of identity. In W. N. Elwood (Ed.), *Public relations inquiry as rhetorical criticism: Studies of corporate discourse in public relations campaigns* (pp. 69-84). Westport, CT: Praeger.

Cover, R. (2004). Interactivity: Reconceiving the audience in the struggle for textual "control" of narrative and distribution. *Australian Journal of Communication, 31*(1), 107-120.

Crier, C. (1995, August 28). *World News Tonight* [Transcript]. New York: ABC News. Retrieved October 22, 2005, from Academic Universe (Lexis-Nexis).

Cutlip, S. M., Center, A. H., & Broom, G. H. (2000). *Effective public relations* (8th ed.). Upper Saddle River, NJ: Prentice-Hall.

CyberSurfing; Scientology deplores net losses. (1995, February 2). *The Washington Post,* p. C07

Dahlberg, L. (2005). The corporate colonization of online attention and the marginalization of critical communication. *Journal of Communication Inquiry, 29,* 160-180.

Dahlgren, P. (2000). The Internet and the democratization of civic culture. *Political Communication, 17,* 335-340.

Deetz, S. A. (1992). *Democracy in an age of corporate colonization: Developments in communication and the politics of everyday life.* Albany: State University of New York Press.

Deligny, F. (1970). *Les vagabonds efficace* [The effective vagrants]. Paris, France: Maspero.

Digital Millennium Copyright Act, 17 U.S.C. § 512 (Supp. 1999).

Drucker, S. J., & Gumpert, G. (1999). Legal geography: The borders of cyberlaw: Introduction. In S. J. Drucker & G. Gumpert (Eds.), *Real law @ virtual space: Regulation in cyberspace* (pp. 1-27). Cresskill, NJ: Hampton Press.

Esrock, S. L., & Leichty, G. B. (1998). Social responsibility and corporate web pages: Self-presentation or agenda-setting? *Public Relations Review, 24,* 305-319.

FACTNet. (n.d.). *Scientology's human rights abuses and victims stories.* Retrieved October 22, 2005, from http://www.factnet.org/Scientology/dianetics_abuse.html

Fisher, W. R. (1987). *Human communication as narration: Toward a philosophy of reason, value, and action.* Columbia: University of South Carolina Press.

FitzGerald, S. S., & Spagnolia, N. (1999). Four predictions for PR practitioners in the new millennium. *Public Relations Quarterly, 44*(3), 12-14.

Fong, T. (1995, September 26). Scientologists deleted data before returning computers. *Rocky Mountain News* (Denver, CO), p. 20A.

Fox News Live. (2000, May 31). [Transcript]. New York: Fox News Channel. Retrieved October 22, 2005, from Academic Universe (Lexis-Nexis).

Freedom Magazine. (n.d.). *The rise of hatred & violence in Germany.* Los Angeles: Freedom.

Frobish, T. S. (2000). Altar rhetoric and online performance: Scientology, *ethos,* and the World Wide Web. *American Communication Journal, 4,* Article 1. Retrieved August 19, 2005, from http://www.acjournal.org/holdings/vol4/iss1/articles/frobish.htm

Froehling, O. (1997). The cyberspace "war of ink and Internet" in Chiapas, Mexico. *Geographical Review, 87,* 291-307.

The future of public relations is on the Internet [interview]. (1999). *Public Relations Strategist, 5*(1), 6-10.

Gailey, E. A. (1996). Who owns digital rights? Examining the scope of copyright protection for electronically distributed works. *Communications and the Law, 18,* 3-28.

Garrison, O. V. (1974). *The hidden story of Scientology.* Secaucus, NJ: Citadel Press.

Gaura, M. A. (1998, September 19). Church of Scientology wins $3 million ruling. *The San Francisco Chronicle,* p. A23.

Goodman, L. (1995, September 16). Scientology suit [Editorial]. *The* [Memphis, TN] *Commercial Appeal,* p. 9A.

Google, Inc. (2005). *Google groups: alt.religion.scientology.* Retrieved July 1, 2005, from http://groups-beta.google.com/group/alt.religion.scientology?hl=en&lr=&safe=off

Grady, D., & Gimple, J. (1998). Virtual barbarians at the gate. *Public Relations Strategist, 4*(3), 23-27.

Grunig, L. A. (1990). Power in the PR workplace. In L. A. Grunig & J. E. Grunig (Eds.), *Public relations research annual* (Vol. 2, pp. 115-155). Hillsdale, NJ: Erlbaum.

Hall, C. W. (1995a, August 31). Court lets *Post* keep Scientology texts. *The Washington Post,* p. A18.

Hall, C. W. (1995b, November 29). Scientology suit against *Post* dismissed; U.S. judge orders plaintiff to pay attorney fees in secrecy case. *The Washington Post,* p. D03.

Hall, C. W. (1996, January 20). Church of Scientology wins cyberspace copyright fight; dumping of texts onto Internet ruled illegal. *The Washington Post*, p. B01.

Hallahan, K. (2004). Protecting an organization's digital public relations assets. *Public Relations Review, 30*, 255-268.

Harrison, L. (1995, September 1). Scientologists are not the bad guys here [Editorial]. *Rocky Mountain News* (Denver, CO), p. 74A.

Hauss, D. (1995). Technology forecast: The age of instant information is here. *Public Relations Journal, 51*(4), 16-19.

Hearit, K. M. (1999). When the organization's image becomes the issue: The corporate *apologia* of the Intel Corporation in defense of its Pentium chip. *Public Relations Review, 25*, 291-308.

Heath, R. L. (1998). New communication technologies: An issues management point of view. *Public Relations Review, 24*, 273-288.

Heldal-Lund, A. (n.d.). *Operation clambake: The fight against the Church of Scientology on the net.* Retrieved July 1, 2005, from http://www.xenu.net/index.html

Henderson, A. (2005). Activism in "paradise": Identity management in a public relations campaign against genetic engineering. *Journal of Public Relations Research, 17*, 117-137.

Hill, L. N., & White, C. (2000). Public relations practitioners' perception of the World Wide Web as a communications tool. *Public Relations Review, 26*, 31-51.

Holliman, J. (1995, August). Church of Scientology seizes apostate's computer files [Transcript #1265-3]. Atlanta, GA: Cable News Network. Retrieved October 22, 2005, from Academic Universe (Lexis-Nexis).

Holtz, S. (1999). *Public relations on the Net: Winning strategies to inform and influence the media, the investment community, the government, the public, and more!* New York: AMACOM.

Hubbard, L. R. (1965). *Scientology: A new slant on life.* Los Angeles: Church of Scientology of California.

Hubbard, L. R. (1992). *Dianetics: The modern science of mental health.* Los Angeles: Bridge. (Original work published 1950)

Ihlen, Ø. (2002a). Defending the Mercedes A-Class: Combining and changing crisis-response strategies. *Journal of Public Relations Research, 14*, 185-206.

Ihlen, Ø. (2002b). Rhetoric and resources: Notes for a new approach to public relations and issues management. *Journal of Public Affairs, 2*, 259-269.

Internet providers cleared in Church of Scientology suit. (1995, February 23). *The Houston* (TX) *Chronicle.* Retrieved October 15, 2005, from Academic Universe (Lexis-Nexis).

Jenkins, H., III. (1988). *Star Trek* rerun, reread, rewritten: Fan writing as textual poaching. *Critical Studies in Mass Communication, 5*, 85-107.

Johnson, M. A. (1997). Public relations and technology: Practitioner perspectives. *Journal of Public Relations Research, 9*, 213-236.

Keiler, E., & Middleberg, D. (1997). Tales from the dark side of cyberspace. *Chief Executive, 123*(5), 46-50.

Kent, M. L. (1998/1999). Does your website attract or repel customers? Three tests of website effectiveness. *Public Relations Quarterly, 43*(4), 31-33.

Kent, M. L., & Taylor, M. (1998). Building dialogic relationships through the World Wide Web. *Public Relations Review, 24*, 321-334.

Kernisky, I. F., & Kernisky, D. A. (1998, April). *Trouble under the golden arches: Signifiers gone astray.* Paper presented at the annual meeting of the Central States Communication Association, Chicago, IL.

Knudson, J. W. (1998). Rebellion in Chiapas: Insurrection by Internet and public relations. *Media, Culture & Society, 20,* 507-518.

Kovacs, R. (2003). The broadcasting public sphere: Enduring issues, enduring relationships, enduring activists. *Journal of Communication Management, 7,* 209-238.

L. Ron Hubbard, the photographer: Writing with light. (1999). Los Angeles: L. Ron Hubbard Library.

Lee, Y.-C. (2001). A step toward balance? Third-party liability in the Digital Millennium Copyright Act. *Communications and the Law, 23,* 1-27.

Lerma, A. (2005, July 24). *Exposing the CON: World's largest news archives of 53 years of Scientology Dianetics and L. Ron Hubbard.* Retrieved July 25, 2005, from http://www.lermanet.com/scientologynews/index.html

Lesly, P. (n.d.). The future of public relations. In *Vernon C. Schranz distinguished lectureship in public relations: 25th anniversary* (pp. 21-26). Muncie, IN: Department of Journalism, Ball State University.

Levine, M. (2002). *Guerilla P.R. wired: Waging a successful publicity campaign online, offline, and everywhere in between.* New York: McGraw-Hill.

Lisa McPherson: The Clearwater Police Department files. Retrieved October 22, 2005, from http://www.lisafiles.com/

Manheim, J. B. (2001). *The death of a thousand cuts: Corporate campaigns and the attack on the corporation.* Mahwah, NJ: Erlbaum.

Marken, G. A. (1995). Getting the most from your presence in cyberspace. *Public Relations Quarterly, 40*(3), 36-37.

Marken, G. A. (1998). The Internet and the Web: The two-way public relations highway. *Public Relations Quarterly, 43*(1), 31-33.

Marshals seize computer files of man sued by Scientologists. (1995, August 13). *The New York Times,* p. A22.

May, B. E., Chen, J.-C. V., & Wen, K.-W. (2004). The differences of regulatory models and Internet regulation in the European Union and the United States. *Information & Communications Technology Law, 13,* 259-272.

McMillan, J. J. (1987). In search of the organizational persona: A rationale for studying organizations rhetorically. In L. Thayer (Ed.), *Organization/communication: Emerging perspectives II* (pp. 21-45). Norwood, NJ: Ablex.

Merwe, R. van der Pitt, L. F., & Abratt, R. (2005). Stakeholder strength: PR survival strategies in the Internet age. *Public Relations Quarterly, 50*(1), 39-48.

Miller, R. (1987). *Bare-faced messiah: The true story of L. Ron Hubbard.* London, England: Penguin Books.

Mitra, A., & Watts, E. (2002). Theorizing cyberspace: The idea of voice applied to Internet discourse. *New Media & Society, 4,* 479-498.

MSNBC.com. (2005, June 25). *"I'm passionate about life": Actor Tom Cruise talks with 'Today' host Matt Lauer about his new love, new movie and his recent controversial comments.* Retrieved July 1, 2005, from http://www.msnbc.msn.com/id/8343367/

Newman, R. (1996, July 24). *The Church of Scientology v. Grady Ward.* Retrieved March 2, 1998, from http://www.xs4all.nl/~kspaink/cos/rnewman/grady/home.html

Newman, R. (1997a, March 24). *The Church of Scientology v. Keith Henson.* Retrieved March 2, 1998, from http://www.xs4all.nl/~kspaink/cos/rnewman/henson/home.html

Newman, R. (1997b, March 23). *The Church of Scientology vs. Arnie Lerma, Digital Gateway Systems, and the* Washington Post. Retrieved March 2, 1998, from http://www.xs4all.nl/~kspaink/cos/rnewman/lerma/home.html

Nishi, D. (2004, October 4). Fake blogs, true buzz. *Chicago Tribune,* sec. 2, p. 3.

Nguyen, L. (1995, August 13). Va. man's computer seized in Internet lawsuit; Church of Scientology claims postings infringed on copyrights. *The Washington Post,* p. B06.

NOTs on the Net. (n.d.). Retrieved March 2, 1998, from http://www.Tiac.net/users/modemac/nots

Pacific Gas & Electric Co. v. Public Utilities Commission of California et al. 475 U.S. 1 (1986).

Pankratz, H. (1995, September 9). Data feud reaches U.S. court Scientologists; critics argue over seized files. *The Denver* (CO) *Post,* p. A01.

Paster, H. (1995). The new public relations manifesto. *Public Relations Strategist, 1*(1), 14-21.

Phillips, R. (2003). *Stakeholder theory and organizational ethics.* San Francisco: Barrett-Koehler.

Pimentel, B. (1996, August 5). Netcom settles Scientology copyright suit. *The San Francisco Chronicle,* p. A22.

Purves, A. C. (1998). *The web of text and the web of God: An essay on the third information transformation.* New York: Guilford.

Religious Technology Center v. FACTNet, Inc., 901 F. Supp. 1519 (D. Col. 1995a).

Religious Technology Center v. FACTNet, Inc., 907 F. Supp. 1468 (D. Col. 1995b).

Religious Technology Center v. Henson, 116 F.3d 1486 (9th Cir. 1997), rev'd in part, 229 F.3d 1158 (9th Cir. 2000).

Religious Technology Center v. Lerma, 897 F.Supp. 260 (E.D.Va. 1995a).

Religious Technology Center v. Lerma, 897 F.Supp. 1353 (E.D.Va. 1995b).

Religious Technology Center v. Lerma, 1996 U.S.Dist. 15454 (E.D.Va. 1996).

Religious Technology Center v. NETCOM, 923 F.Supp. 1231 (N.D.Cal. 1995).

Religious Technology Center v. NETCOM, 1997 U.S.Dist. NEXIS 23572 (N.D.Cal. 1997).

Religious Technology Center v. Ward, 1999 U.S.App. NEXIS 19937 (9th Cir. 1999).

Religious Technology Center v. Ward, 33 Fed. Appx. 884. (9th Cir. 2002).

Religious Technology Center v. Wollersheim, 796 F.2d 1071 (9th Cir. 1996).

The Rick A. Ross Institute. (1996-2000). *Scientology.* Retrieved October 22, 2005, from http://www.rickross.com/groups/scientology.html

Roper, J. (2005). Symmetrical communication: Excellent public relations or a strategy for hegemony? *Journal of Public Relations Research, 17,* 69-86.

Rubach, M. J. (1999). *Institutional shareholder activism: The changing face of corporate ownership.* New York: Garland.

Scammell, M. (2000). The Internet and civic engagement: The age of the citizen-consumer. *Political Communication, 17,* 351-355.

Scientology granted tax exemption by the U.S. (1993, October 14). *The New York Times,* pp. A1, A18.

Scientology kills. (n.d.). Retrieved July 1, 2005, from http://www.scientologykills.org/

Scientology lies. (2005, July 6). Retrieved July 25, 2005, from http://www.scientology-lies.com/

Scientology suit takes on cyberspace: Church claims infringement of copyright. (1995, March 2). *The San Francisco Chronicle,* p. A3.

Scientology versus the Internet. (2005, July 18). Retrieved July 25, 2005, from http://en.wikipedia.org/wiki/Scientology_vs._the_Internet

Scientology wins first Internet fight: Landmark case says copyright laws apply to material in cyberspace. (1996, January 20). *The Denver* (CO) *Post,* p. A-17.

Sect wins copyright suit. (1996, January 23). *The Australian.* Retrieved October 15, 2005, from Academic Universe (Lexis-Nexis)

Simons, H. W. (2001). *Persuasion in society.* Thousand Oaks, CA: Sage.

Speech in electronic space. (1995, August 22). [Editorial]. *The Washington Post,* p. A16.

Springston, J. K. (2001). Public relations and new technology: The impact of the Internet. In R. L. Heath (Ed.), *The public relations handbook* (pp. 603-614). Thousand Oaks, CA: Sage.

Stewart, C. J., Smith, C. A., & Denton, R. E., Jr. (1994). *Persuasion and social movements* (3rd ed.). Prospect Heights, IL: Waveland Press.

Taylor, M., Kent, M. L., & White, W. J. (2001). How activist organizations are using the Internet to build relationships. *Public Relations Review, 27,* 263-284.

Thorpe, J. (1996). The open door to piracy: The truth about why some access providers have become part of the problem of Internet piracy. *Freedom, 28*(1), 4-7.

Touretzky, D. S. (1997a, January 19). *NOTs scholars home page.* Retrieved March 2, 1998, from http://www.cs.cmu.edu/~dst/NOTs/

Touretzky, D. S. (1997b, January 19). *OTIII scholarship.* Retrieved March 2, 1998, from http://www.cs.cmu.edu/~dst/NOTs/

Touretzky, D. S. (n.d.a) *Dave Touretzky's page: Who, what, where?* Retrieved July 25, 2005, from http://www-2.cs.cmu.edu/~dst/

Touretzky, D. S. (n.d.b). *The NOTs scholars home page (Scientology).* Retrieved July 25, 2005, from http://www-2.cs.cmu.edu/~dst/NOTs/

Touretzky, D. S. (n.d.c). *OTIII scholarship.* Retrieved July 25, 2005, from http://www-2.cs.cmu.edu/~dst/OTIII/

Touretzky, D. S. (n.d.d). *The secrets of Scientology.* Retrieved July 25, 2005, from http://www-2.cs.cmu.edu/~dst/Secrets/index.html

20/20 Sunday. (1998, December 20). [Transcript]. New York: ABC News. Retrieved October 22, 2005, from Academic Universe (Lexis-Nexis).

United States. Commission on Security and Cooperation in Europe (1997, September 18). *Religious intolerance in Europe today* [Hearing before the Commission on Security and Cooperation in Europe, 105th Congress, 1st session] (Serial No. CSCE 105-1-5). Retrieved October 26, 2005, from http://www.csce.gov

Wallis, R. (1976). *The road to total freedom: A sociological analysis of Scientology.* London: Heinemann Educational Books.

Wallsten, P. (1996, February 10). Out-of-town critics plan protest against Scientology. *St. Petersburg* (FL) *Times* (*Seminole Times* ed.), p. 3.

Wasserman, E. (1995, November 19). Scientologists trying to silence cyber critics; chilling effect on Internet feared. *The* (New Orleans, LA) *Times-Picayune,* p. A26.

Weaver, C. K. (2001). Dressing for battle in the global economy: Putting power, identity, and discourse into public relations theory. *Management Communication Quarterly, 15,* 279-288.

Weick, K. (1979). *The social psychology of organizing* (2nd ed.). New York: Random House.

Wiesdendanger, B. (1993). Electronic delivery and feedback systems come of age. *Public Relations Journal, 49*(1), 10-14.

Wilcox, D. L., Cameron, G. T., Ault, P. H., & Agee, W. K. (2003). *Public relations: Strategies and tactics* (7th ed.). Boston: Allyn & Bacon.

Xenu. (n.d.a). *Operation clambake: The fight against Scientology on the Net.* Retrieved February 22, 1998, from http://www.xenu.net

Xenu (n.d.b). *Thought control and Scientology.* Retrieved October 22, 2005, from http://www.xenu.net/archive/infopack/7.htm

chapter 9

Cross-media Comparisons of Employee Recruitment Messages Between 1990 and 2000

Theresa A. Russell-Loretz

Cheney and Vibbert (1987) argued that identity is *the* issue in public relations as organizations seek to differentiate themselves from competitors and build identification with specified publics. Almost two decades later, the scholarly literature on organizational identity reflects increased attention (e.g., Ashforth & Mael, 1989; Cheney & Christiansen, 2001; Christiansen & Cheney, 2000; Fombrun, 1996; Moingeon & Soenen, 2002). Yet few studies have examined the role of visual representations in the construction of an organizational identity designed to attract outsiders to become insiders—that is, employees.

This chapter focuses on the definitional power of the corporate persona vis-à-vis recruitment messages. Not only does power reside in the definitional act of framing the corporation as employer, but power also resides in the ability to determine who does and does not "fit" the definition of an ideal employee and who is and is not included in depictions of "our people." Indeed, recruitment messages are what Brummett (1994) has referred to as "sites of struggle over meaning" (p. 68) that embody issues of significance in the U.S. workforce.

For example, the remnants of turn-of-the-century Horatio Alger (e.g., 1904) stories, persistent in recruitment messages in the early 1990s (Russell-Loretz, 1995a), have defined the meaning of success to all who would accept the opportunities the United States presented to them through hard work and unquestioning subordination to the status quo. Yet throughout the 20th century, the meaning of equal opportunity has been contested by civil rights activists, feminists, and labor activists who pointed to direct and indirect means of exclusion used by corporate employers, leading to increased government regulation and oversight under the U.S. Equal Employment Opportunity Commission.

In this light, depictions of workforce diversity in recruitment messages across time and across media are historical artifacts that document the representations used in recruitment messages as corporations struggle to adapt to issues over meaning and the manner by which such meanings might be conveyed. Such texts are hegemonic in a Gramscian sense; rather than assume that social structures such as organizations necessarily dominate society, according to Mumby (1997), Gramsci used hegemony to explain the ways in which "a particular group comes to exercise intellectual and moral leadership over other groups" (p. 348). For the purposes of this chapter, then, an organization exercises its prerogative to employ recruits that "fit" within it. Power is present at the beginning of a person's employment, because the recruitment rhetoric used to appeal to him/her is definitional, outlining who the ideal employee is and inviting a recruit to identify with that definition. In the end, of course, the leadership that employers provide ultimately is dominating.

In this chapter I show the results of two studies comparing two competing strategies used to visually represent the gender and race of would-be employees. In a study of late 1980s-early 1990s corporate recruitment videos, I found a tendency to depict a range of employees who comprise various gender and ethnic categories in a "hierarchy" dominated by white males. In an exploratory study of websites available a decade later, I observed a second strategy: fewer depictions of people who, nevertheless, represented individuals of diverse gender and ethnic orientations much like a generic iconic representation. The depictions stress "unity in diversity" but illustrate what Pompper (2005) critiqued as a tendency by scholars and practitioners to "obscure" or "homogenize" differences (p. 153). Pompper's observation reminds us that this second strategy, although it avoids blatant overrepresentation of White males in the workforce, raises questions about the acceptance of differences outside of the frame of conformity, bringing us full circle to Horatio Alger's protagonist who denies himself to further the interests of the corporate employer. Consistent with a Gramscian perspective, my purpose in this chapter is to critique recruitment videos and websites with a view toward recommending and effecting needed social change (Zompetti, 1997).

Further complicating issues of power in corporate messages, as Cheney and Christiansen (2001) maintained, is the shift in media from video to the World Wide Web to convey such messages (cf. Bolter & Grusin, 1999). This shift in media has resulted in a shift in the balance of power in terms of who "controls" the message; for although a corporate author designs messages for display on the Web, individuals choose how to navigate and circumnavigate the narrative features found in video.

In the following section I provide background on the sociopolitical, economic, and technological conditions that faced corporate recruitment efforts at the debut of the 1990s and in 2000 to demonstrate the impetus for a cross-media, before-and-after snapshot of representations of diversity in recruitment messages. Next, I situate the relevant literature on recruitment messages and articulate the theory and two-stage methodology on which both studies are based. After a comparative analysis of recruitment messages, I offer critical insights for future research and practice.

BACKGROUND

The U.S. Department of Labor in 1987 predicted that demand for employees would exceed supply, prompting stiff competition for college graduates entering the job market in the 1990s (Johnston & Packer, 1987). The report stated that nontraditional job entrants (women, minorities, and immigrants) would make up 80% of the net additions to the labor force from 1987 to the end of the century (Johnston & Packer, 1987). Trade journals expressed concern for how best to fill positions and adapt to a changing workforce (Kutscher, 1990; Schauer, 1990). By the mid-1990s, diversity as a recruitment and retention issue received some attention, although mostly from a functionalist perspective on how best to manage diversity (e.g., Allen, 1995; Teboul, 1999; Wanguri, 1996). The issue of workforce diversity was depicted as significant by popular and trade press writers, who advised job seekers to scrutinize recruitment messages and other company documents to determine attitudes toward women (Dusky, 1990), whether a corporation was a desirable potential employer, and whether personal goals and values fit with organizational goals (Bolles, 1997; Crowther & Wilson, 1990).

Impending workforce diversity received attention from feminist scholars who noted the number of women entering the workforce meant a change in corporate culture. In popular culture, concern over such issues as affirmative action, racial bias, sexual harassment, and the glass ceiling resulted in numerous studies, charges of political correctness, and accounts of backlash toward women (e.g., Faludi, 1991). At the same time, workplaces increasingly relied on consultants to lead discussions about diversity as a way to gain acceptance, appreciation, and understanding of new work practices to generate greater productivity (Allen, 1995). At least one study demonstrated that college students found the presentation of diversity in recruitment literature desirable (Williams & Bauer, 1994).

Along with increased attention to diversity in the workforce during the 1990s, the technology for communicating to potential recruits changed. As more and more homes had VCRs for personal use in the 1980s, the accessibility of corporate video as a means for self-presentation became economically feasible and the medium of choice (Richardson, 1992). Corporate video was employed in a variety of settings, and dissemination of informational videos allowed applicants an alternative means to learn about a potential employer, with sound, camera pans, swipes, and moving character representations unavailable in print form: nonlinear representations that allowed viewers greater ability to either project themselves into the scene or to identify with the characters presented visually (e.g., Aarseth, 1994; Landow, 1994; Morgan, 2002).

However, in the late 1990s video was no longer new technology. Rather, most job seekers, particularly new college graduates who were the heaviest users of Web interfaces, turned to an organization's website for initial information about employers (e.g., Bucy, 2000). In fact, a website was one way for employers to distinguish the corporate "self" from others. *Fortune* described recruiting as a $17 billion-a-year industry with phenomenal growth, with 17% of *Fortune* Global 500 companies recruiting actively on the Internet in January 1998 and 45% involved in Web recruiting one year later (Useem, 1999). The *Fortune* report identified Cisco Systems as one of the largest "e-cruitment" companies: In 1999 it reportedly received 81% of resumés and hired 66 percent of its people via the Internet.

The convergence of new media, the practical challenges of recruiting an increasingly diverse workforce, and increasing curiosity about the role of organizational identity and identification on the eve of the Millennium prompted questions about recruitment messages that attract potential applicants and justify or define the employer as attractive.[1] Indeed, the texts of recruitment messages in 1990 and 2000 suggest diversity eventually became normalized as an expectation of employers. The reason: the context of hiring in 1990 was different from that in 2000, in which skilled workers were at a premium and diversity was likely addressed in other ways and not in recruitment efforts, including texts on employers' websites. A focus, then, on employers' self-presentations in recruitment messages is especially appropriate because these messages act to both define the corporate persona and work to attract outsiders to be transformed into "our people." They reveal not only what an employer's values are, but they also reveal what the employer expects the audience to value. Hence, the following research question directed the initial stage of this study: "How do employers portray an ideal employee on video?" The research question that guided a second follow-up study was, "How did portraits of the 'ideal recruit' change from messages produced in the early 1990s on video to messages produced in 2000 on the Web?"

It is one thing to identify dominant social issues at a particular point in history, but it is quite another to demonstrate how a given message illustrates a rhetor's construction of a particular audience toward an issue at a particular moment in time. For instance, the financial success of a female benefactor in a 1904 Horatio Alger story depended on her husband's hard work rather than her own, illustrating the author's depiction of a successful woman who fit the norms and ideals of her generation. Even though the story argued one's social standing could be overcome by hard work, the myth did not address issues of race or gender, in effect making such attributes invisible. Of course, at the end of the century issues of gender and race were at the forefront of discussions about equal opportunity, affirmative action, success, and the impending diversity of what Johnston and Packer (1987) called "Workforce 2000." Yet research on how these issues manifested themselves in attempts to build identification with would-be employees after the turn of the millennium remains sparse.

CORPORATE MESSAGE EFFECTIVENESS

Literature pertinent to this study comes from two angles: studies of recruitment messages and the Web as a public relations tool. In both areas, research that examines messages for depictions of a specific public is scarce, although the persuasive dimensions of these messages have been taken for granted in recruitment and attraction research.

Heath (1998) and Esrock and Leichty (1998) claimed websites enabled organizations to circumvent traditional mainstream media and offered more control over public discussion and an opportunity to forge meanings for publics. However, Cozier and Witmer (2001) challenged this, describing how computer-mediated communities forge meanings that result from others' shared experiences. In line with this view, Springston (2001) observed, "Convergence of technologies strains traditional notions of mass media" (p. 603, citing Schudson, 1992) and has shifted the balance of power from the corporate rhetor to a more receiver-centric view. From a functionalist, managerial perspective, messages have been studied for their effectiveness in attracting newcomers, as well as their accuracy, with most research focused on recruitment interviews (Jablin, 1987, 2001).

Effectiveness studies have defined success as either building a large pool of applicants or attracting qualified applicants who were the best fit for the job, premised on job satisfaction and, hence, retention (e.g., Chatman, 1989; Jablin, 1987, 2001; Rynes & Barber, 1990; Rynes & Boudreau, 1986; Wanous, 1983). Some studies (e.g., Lindquist, 1990; Lindquist & Endicott, 1986) compared message sources for effectiveness, with job fairs, college placement manual ads, executive lectures to student groups, brochures, videotapes, placement interviews, internships and cooperative work experiences, and employer-university partnership teams among the variables. Jablin (1987, 2001) reviewed studies that wondered which media helped applicants form realistic expectations about employment with a particular organization. Although the effectiveness of inducements in recruitment messages remained inconclusive (Jablin, 2001), some studies (Chatman, 1989; Wanous, 1983) have shown weak support for individuals' preferences for messages with images similar to their own.

Although this last finding might serve as an excellent justification for examinations from a rhetorical perspective, few scholars have analyzed the messages of would-be employees to unearth corporate strategies of identification. Shyles and Ross (1984) examined military recruitment brochures to determine whether messages appealed to *instrumental* values, such as job training and educational benefits resulting in personal gain, or *intrinsic* values—ends in themselves, such as commitment to or love of country. They gave a snapshot of the U.S. military's conception of values important to recruits at that time and critiqued messages from both pragmatic and ethical perspectives, asserting that messages stressing material reward were inadequate for building the unique kind of life-giving commitment demanded by military service. Indeed, comparison of appeals in recruitment campaigns directed to applicants in other industries would be worthwhile.

In another study, I (Russell-Loretz, 1995b) identified paradoxes in organizational recruitment messages as an observable impact of corporate rhetors' struggles to create ways that multiple audiences of potential employees could identify with employers. However, the study did not focus specifically on visual depictions of applicants' gender or race. Similarly, Vaughn (1997) examined the organizational identification strategies in corporate discourse in high-technology industries used to recruit individuals and socialize them to be members of the organization. Vaughn also identified innovativeness and individualism as primary values unique to high-technology organizations. However, this study also neglected to examine depictions of the ideal applicant in terms of race or gender.

In my own work (Russell-Loretz, 1995a), I discerned a value hierarchy in video recruitment messages available in the early 1990s, with organizational survival at the apex of values presented to recruits. The study described corporate employers' portrayals of organizational self, an ideal would-be employee, and the benefits of employment. These portrayals served three functions. First, these portrayals presented a self with physical, behavioral, and mental properties, and showed a desire to emulate the properties of a person, in which employees or applicants often became an organization's voice or face. At the same time, the gender and ethnic diversity of employees was featured as a desirable trait of organizational employers. Additionally, these depictions of employee diversity revealed a clear ethnic and gender hierarchy, with White males the predominant gender and ethnic group represented.

Second, the videos functioned to reaffirm the qualities of the ideal employee, closely resembling a turn-of-the-century Horatio Alger protagonist who held the virtues of loyalty, a strong work ethic, intelligence, moral fortitude, competence, and innovativeness. Third, these messages often served to define "work" as its own reward, rather than offering descriptions of tangible compensation such as salary or benefits.

Beyond the functionalist, instrumental examinations of websites as public relations tools that depict innovativeness or corporate social responsibility as a competitive advantage (Esrock & Leichty, 1999), positive associations can be built around symbols that are meaningful to addressed audiences. The next section presents a message-centered method for analyzing recruitment messages that allows study of depictions of an "ideal" recruit. Such a stance provides insights other than those that have occupied public relations scholars' studies of Web messages to date.

INTERPRETIVE GROUNDING FOR ANALYZING CORPORATE RECRUITMENT MESSAGES

Burke's concept of *identification* provided the basis for research into organizations as mutual cooperation brought about through communicative efforts. Cheney and Tompkins (1987) located the origin of Burke's use of the term "identification" in Lasswell's (1935/1965) political theory as a "psychological, sociological, and rhetorical concept" (p. 3). Based on this understanding, work by Cheney (1983), Tompkins and Cheney (1985), and Bullis and Tompkins (1989) described how members' identification imbued an organization with the power to control its image through a process that they referred to as *concertive* control, in which members act autonomously but in concert with organizational values; for this reason, the control is unobtrusive, so that the employee acts *as if* a supervisor were guiding or directing behavior. This acting in concert with organizational values occurs when the indoctrinated employee derives a job decision from what Simon (1945/1976) has termed *value and factual premises*:

> Given a complete set of value and factual premises, there is only one decision which is consistent with rationality. That is, with a given system of values, and a specified set of alternatives, there is one alternative that is preferable to the others. (p. 223)

Organizational identification is key to concertive control, Tompkins and Cheney (1985) claimed, such that employees hold organizational values as their own and reduce the chance for employees' use of alternatively held value premises for on-the-job decisions (cf. Chapter 3, this volume). They suggest concertive control may be easier to implement when managers locate applicants who identify with organizational values prior to entry, rather than relying on posthire socialization processes. Indeed, scholars and practitioners have advised as much, and employer/employee fit suggests concertive control may be at work in recruitment messages, as they depict what is customary and desirable (Jablin, 2001; McDonald & Gandz, 1992; Tompkins & Cheney, 1985; Weiss, 1989). Such identification is evident in recruitment messages that articulate organizational values and reflexively address applicants' personal values, simultaneously working to construct an employer and the audience it would invite to become part of "us."

Indeed, that there are two audiences is evident in any body of discourse that appeals to the values, attitudes, opinions, and beliefs of a particular audience (Black, 1970). For Black (1970), there is the actual, *addressed* audience and the *implied* audience indicated within the message itself. The addressed audience is detectable in ways typical of public relations research (i.e., audience analysis). The implied audience, however, is the audience the rhetor would have the audience become, how they should think about themselves in relation to the message—an ideal, as it were—suggested by the ways in which the rhetor invokes values, beliefs, and attitudes and submits them for the audience's approval. This audience can also be more obviously indicated in descriptions the rhetor makes when invoking the second person "you," as in "you want to work for a leader."

A corporate rhetor cannot hope to appeal to all the values of its applicant audience—and it necessarily should not want to do so. However, messages must conform to the values of its audience in some way, usually in general terms that will be specified later, such as a discussion of "continuing education" as a premier value during recruitment and the terms of tuition reimbursement discussed during employee orientation. Or the rhetor may appeal to a specialized audience that shares its vocabulary of values—for example, recruiters often send recent alumni to college campuses to recruit graduating seniors who have the same specialized training, rather than send a recruiter who is not trained in the field. In either case, the organizational rhetor constructs a particular audience who adheres to a specific value hierarchy. This hierarchy serves two functions: to denote which values are subordinate in case of values conflict and to project membership criteria (Perelman & Olbrechts-Tyteca , 1969). Applicants who embrace the hierarchy are extended membership; by implication, those who would challenge the preferred arrangement of values are excluded.

The two studies highlighted in this chapter focus on corporate recruitment messages produced in 1990 in video and 2000 on websites. The messages—both verbal and visual—were compared in ways that revealed similarities and differences over the 10-year span of history that lapsed. The studies are broken down into two "stages"—one for each year's worth of messages that were analyzed.

Stage 1: 1990s Recruitment Messages

The current study reflects an extension of my dissertation work (Russell-Loretz, 1995a). Because I compared recruitment messages across two points in time, the methods took place in two stages (cf. Swanson, 2004). At Stage 1, I selected a convenience sample of videos from 14 companies representing a variety of industries from over 300 recruitment videos available to job seekers through the placement center at a large midwestern university. The method used to examine these recruitment messages was "terminological algebra," introduced by Holloway (1993)[2] as a derivation of Burke's (1941/1973) cluster-agon method and Berthold's (1976) gloss of it. The method is grounded in dramatism, which assumes a speaker chooses language to name a situation in a way that reveals the motives behind what went on by examining the dynamics among the scene, act, agent, agency, purpose, and attitude toward it (Burke, 1941/1973; cf. Bostdorff, 1987). The critic determines value associations located in linguistic "equations" speakers make to explain their worlds, and then interprets meanings of terms by looking at "what goes with what" and "what is vs. what" (Burke, 1941/1973, pp. 30, 69; cf. Holloway, 1993, Chapter 3). For instance, a critic may detect that a rhetor equates "terrorism" with "cells" and with "small, undetectable infiltrators that harm surrounding areas and threaten life." The result would be a rhetor's formula for terrorism as: Terrorism = (cell = small+undetectable+harmful) = threat. Such close textual analysis also allows the critic to determine whether value associations are positive or negative (cf. Courtright, 1995).

Further, the method follows Burke's (1941/1973) admonition that a critic examine "from what through what to what" (p. 71). In this way, terminological algebra directs the researcher to follow the progress of a value association to determine transformations of a term and whether values are instrumental or terminal. For instance, when an organization asserts, "Excellent customer service allows us to grow," the terminal value is "growth," whereas "customer service" is valued because it is needed to obtain "growth." For video recruitment "terms," I substituted a visual depiction in the place of any unknown value, using narration or other audio to help me determine associations. Hence "our employees" were equated with visual descriptions of the audience. The method is not objective; the critic interprets the meanings of these descriptions.

To determine ethnic and gender representations, each time a person appeared on the monitor, his/her appearance was noted, and the individual was identified according to a gender and ethnic category.[3] At times the individual was identified and spoke on camera more than once. Each time the individual appeared, that depiction was counted. Individuals in groups up to 10 were identified and coded, but crowd scenes were not coded, and some depictions could not be categorized. Table 9.1 provides the representations of individuals in various ethnic and gender categories for 13 videos (Barton

TABLE 9.1. Video Appearances of Members of Gender/Ethnic Groups*

COMPANY	WM	WF	BM	BF	AM	AF	HM	HF
Ameritech	70	29	8	5	0	0	3	0
Fermilab	113	13	8	2	5	0	4	0
Goodyear	53	26	31	0	9	0	0	5
HL & P	41	46	18	7	5	0	0	0
Intel	75	50	1	0	0	0	0	0
Lord Corp[4]	61	23	9	0	0	0	0	0
LTV Steel	15	7	1	6	0	0	0	0
Manufacturers/ Comerica	114	86	14	22	4	5	1	0
NI Gas	36	33	7	6	0	2	0	0
Eastman	21	5	0	0	0	0	0	0
Thiokol	114	21	4	0	0	0	0	0
Wal-Mart	9	8	5	0	0	0	0	0
Weyerhaeuser	45	10	3	0	1	0	0	0

WM = White male WF = White female BM = Black male
BF = Black female AM = Asian male AF = Asian female
HM = Hispanic male HF = Hispanic female

*"Number of appearances" refers to a count of the number of times individuals within a given gender and ethnic category appear in a video. For additional information about coding determinations and exclusions, please contact the author.

Malow [n.d.] was analyzed separately and gender and ethnic representations were not counted; hence it is not represented in Table 9.1).

The method resulted in a catalogue of characteristics associated with the videos' portrayal of sought-after recruits and employees who these organizations depicted as ideal employees. To describe how "our people" put a "face" on the organizational persona and simultaneously reflect the diversity of desirable applicants, I focus next on physical properties of people represented in the videos and some scenes that heightened the focus.

Ideal Employees' Physical Properties

In these videos' depictions of a company and its prospective employees, the rhetorical line between "employee" and "company" blurred. For instance, "employee" and "company" became blurred when the employees testified about the company's worth as an employer in formal, head-and-shoulder shots as well as candid shots of employees working. Individual employees provided a face to embody the company and gave physical attributes to the organizational persona. Physical traits such as clothing, hairstyles, facial features, and skin color helped to build identification with would-be employees and suggested gender and ethnic identity, reflexively depicting which demographic groups might be considered for employment. Although these depictions may have been carefully orchestrated to meet federal mandates, portrayals of women and members of various ethnic groups demonstrated the organization's recognition that members of these groups were significant to the organization and constituted the diverse applicant pool from which it might hire.

Because these videos represented the organization's gender and ethnic diversity, the depictions themselves invite discussion, and this was especially the case for two of the videos that emphasized employees' ethnic and gender diversity. For example, Goodyear's (1990) presentation of diversity included testimony from a White female and a Black male.

> White Female: "I think the fact that Goodyear is a more traditional company is almost an asset for me as a young woman because they're realizing they haven't tapped the resources that they have and so they're going to be looking at the women harder."
>
> Black Male: "I've been in situations where people feel that, well, if there's a minority or a woman present, then it's because of some incentive program. And I don't think that's the case in what I saw at Goodyear—even in their hiring during the orientation—I looked around and I saw it was pretty much 10%, 12%—it was as if I was looking at America."

In these scenes, Goodyear advised job applicants how to view these portrayals. Rather than framing employment of underrepresented groups as tokenism or the result of mandated affirmative action, Goodyear defined its hiring practices as "representative of America" and provided further evidence of its definition of self in its invitation to men and women from Asian, Hispanic, and African American ethnic groups to join the organization. This served to enhance Goodyear's image. In contrast, videos that depicted members of only one ethnic or gender group could not lay claim to the "American melting pot" image.

In addition to Goodyear, Fermilab also explicitly claimed it valued ethnic diversity. Beyond candid shots of many employees in and around the organization, Fermilab's (1990) video featured six individuals in formal and candid scenarios. Of these, four were Caucasian males; one male, Hector Gonzalez, appeared to be of Hispanic origin; and the sixth individual was a Caucasian female, Erika Drenna, whose name and accent attested to the organization's international aegis. After the narrator discussed the organization's goals, operations, and company benefits, another voice described the type of people the organization sought.

The speaker, a Black male, appeared on camera with his name and title, "James Thompson Employment Manager" at the bottom of the screen, and said, "The laboratory pursues its scientific goals with an enlightened emphasis on equal opportunity employment. The laboratory's efforts are supported by an aggressive affirmative action program that always ensures human dignity." Within the context of its discussion of affirmative action, Thompson's ethnicity helped to symbolize Fermilab's attitude toward hiring African Americans and enhance the credibility of his statement about Fermilab's hiring practices. One equation associated with the company was: Fermilab Affirmative Action = enlightened + aggressive → human dignity; whereas, human dignity is the ultimate or terminal value. However, the association also provided an admonition about how would-be employees should view Fermilab's affirmative action policy.

In terms of the number of different ethnic groups represented, Manufacturers National Bank (1990) depicted more variety than Goodyear (1990) and Fermilab (1990), companies that explicitly drew attention to themselves as a company that "represented America" or demonstrated an "aggressive affirmative action policy." In contrast, Manufacturers National Bank, based in Detroit, MI, seemed to prefer a nonverbal statement about its search for employees from diverse gender and ethnic groups. Its demonstration of diversity included depictions of all groups listed here except Hispanic females.

Another unique feature of its ethnic representation is that Manufacturers depicted Black females as employees more often than it portrayed Black males. This feature is even more significant given that Black males appeared in all but one video (Eastman Chemical, n.d.), whereas Black females appeared in only 6 of the 13 videos. In fact, in Goodyear's (1990) video, in which the representation of all ethnic groups was heralded, a Black female was not featured nor did one appear in the background (unless in a crowd scene). Additionally, the five Hispanic female and nine Asian male appearances in Goodyear's video included appearances of the same individuals five and six times, respectively. However, Goodyear did deviate from the norm in one respect: Black males appeared more frequently than White females.

In Goodyear's (1990) video, the depictions are perhaps more complementary with regard to the distribution of the number of times White males, White females, and Black males appeared. The visual depiction of Asian and Hispanic individuals was somewhat less inclusive, because the same individuals made up the bulk of the appearances of Asian males and Hispanic females. Notably, there were no Black females, females of Asian descent, nor males of Hispanic origin depicted. Fermilab's (1990) depiction of employees was predominantly White and male and somewhat contradicted its stated "aggressive Affirmative action policy."

Interpretation of 1990 Recruitment Messages

Each corporate video provided evidence about the company's ostensible diversity or lack thereof. As a group, the videos revealed a similar collective pattern, although some videos deviated from this. Deviation from the overall pattern warrants attention because this helps differentiate an employer. For example, Table 1 reveals a common hierarchical arrangement of group appearances. Across all recruitment videos, the greatest number of appearances were Caucasian males, followed by Caucasian females, African American males, African American females, Asian males, Asian females, Hispanic males, and Hispanic females. Only one of the examined videotapes, Eastman Chemical (n.d.), depicted white employees only; 80% of employee appearances were male.

Demographic "diversity" in the workforce was (and is) an issue during the era in which the videos were created and distributed. Particularly when organizations assert they have "aggressive" affirmative action programs, they can expect scrutiny over whether the employees or recruits they depict in such messages are included in the discussion of current and potential employees. These representations of physical traits help to complete what each organization included (and excluded) in its "people equation" of ideal employees. In addition to discussion of gender and ethnicity, some employers depicted the addressed job seeker, and hence, the "ideal" recruit as "young," as might be expected. Although this investigation did not catalogue portrayals of "youth," at least one employer depicted "youth" as a valuable asset. An example of this is the video scene in which a Northern

Illinois Gas (n.d.). would-be employee declared, "I'm looking for a company that hires young, motivated people, like me." In this way, "youth" is part of the equation of "who we are looking for."

Stage 2: 2000 Recruitment Messages

To explore changes in recruitment messages in 2000, and specifically to determine whether corporate websites continued to depict an ethnic and gender hierarchy of employees and potential recruits, I selected a smaller purposive sample of six corporate websites whose videos were examined in the 1995 study, once again scrutinizing visual and verbal depictions of employees and would-be employees for articulations of the "ideal employee." The websites were examined in October and November 2000.

I began at the home page and checked for a "jobs" link. I noted the link and location (on the home page, etc.) then followed the links from there, printing pages for close textual analysis of verbal and visual depictions of employees or job hunters. I did not detail graphics or audio beyond notations of a Web interface or graphics that did not print on the pages most relevant to a job seeker. My aim was to examine discourse directed to job seekers rather than other publics, such as customers, investors, or others, who could access the site. Thus, I studied only text and visual depictions of people directed specifically to job seekers. When no information was available about the organization's diversity or its people, however, I explored the site for such information.

The approach also involved a coding difference. In the video study, each appearance of an employee was counted, so that if one female Hispanic employee appeared in several scenes, she would be counted more than once. Individuals in "candid" video shots who appeared to have specific gender and ethnic characteristics, such as an Asian male, were also counted (a group of six Asian males in a single camera shot was counted as six appearances), as were separate video scenes of the same individual. In Table 9.2, Website "number of appearances" were based on how many different page links the individual appeared on, so that each link or page was counted as a single appearance.

I also looked for "e-cruitment" tools, such as a place where one might be able to submit or build a resumé, or where an applicant might search available positions and qualifications, because these would offer insight into the ideal employee. I discuss findings next, focusing on physical traits.

Ideal Employee Depictions

Web depictions of employees were both notably fewer and smaller than video, which often featured full screen close-ups and shots of individuals. In

TABLE 9.2. Comparison of Appearances of Diversity*

COMPANY	WM	WF	BM	BF	AM	AF	HM	HF	UNKNOWN
Barton Malow									
Video	N/A								
Website	0	0	0	0	0	0	0	0	
Comerica**									
Video	114	21	14	22	4	5	1	0	4
Website	2	1	0	1	1	0	0	0	
Thiokol									
Video	114	21	4	0	0	0	0	0	13
Website	0	0	0	0	0	0	0		
Lord Corp.4									
Video	61	23	9	9	0	0	0	0	8
Website	9	4	0	1	0	0	1	0	
SBC/Ameritech									
Video	70	29	8	5	0	0	4	0	10
Website	1	1	1	2	0	0	0	2	
Intel									
Video	75	50	8	5		0	0	0	1
Website	6	3	1+	1	1	0	0	0	+family

*"Number of appearances" refers to a count of the number of times individuals within a given gender and ethnic category appear in a video. For additional information about coding determinations and exclusions, please contact the author.
**Previously Manufacturers National Bank.

contrast, webpages offered postage stamp-sized pictures of people that shared space with text, and most were head and shoulder shots. In some ways these pictures indicated a diminished level of employee "presence" in recruitment messages. As in the early 1990s videos, these organizational websites emphasized the diversity of employees, and "the opportunity to work with a diverse group of individuals" was deemed a benefit of employment. Compared to the earlier study, the gender and ethnic hierarchy seen in the videos had disappeared in organizational depictions of employees and would-be employees in 2000. In fact, in some website depictions, people had disappeared altogether. On Thiokol's (2000a, 2000b, 2000c) website, for instance, no people appeared, although photos of rockets and missiles could be accessed. On Barton Malow's (2000a) website, one individual, a woman, appeared, and this was away from the direct links to employment or benefits (2000b, 2000d, 2000e). Still, this solo representation of a female ran counter to expected depictions on a construction company website.

Intel (e.g., Intel, 2000b, 2000d, 2000e) used much of its website to address the diversity of its workforce in association with its environment. On the "our workforce" link (Intel, 2000g), the organization discussed how it "recruits and retains the best." One way, Intel (2000f) asserted, was through its "Employee Groups," which provide "networking integration, development and outreach." Intel listed these active groups: African Americans, Asians, Christians, employees from India, gay, lesbian, bisexual or transgender, Latinos, Native Americans, Muslims, and women. Similarly, SBC (Ameritech/SBC, 2000d) presented its diversity by listing the accolades it received from various organizations and publications affiliated with groups who were similar to those that Intel described.

Interpretation of 2000 Recruitment Messages

The websites depicted "the workplace" and "the people" as benefits of employment, which together constituted "the environment" as a benefit. Barton Malow's (2000c) people "build close friendships, playing softball and doing volunteer activities together." Intel (2000f) and SBC (Ameritech, 2000a, 2000b, 2000c, 2000d, 2000e) also offered volunteer opportunities and social opportunities for employees. Comerica (2000a; formerly Manufacturers National Bank) "colleagues" were depicted (in text) as having a "strong focus on customers" and a "spirit of volunteerism through community leadership and involvement." In addition, part of Comerica's vision statement emphasized its respect for people: "We are committed to delivering the highest quality financial services by . . . creating a positive environment for our colleagues, built on trust, teamwork and respect" (Comerica, 2000b).

In the websites examined here, only Intel (2000b) provided features that gave employees both a face and a voice to speak directly to recruits: On its job description page, a job seeker could link from each job position title to head shots of employees, and a click on any of these employees' faces led to a full-page (text) testimonial of the employee's experience at the company. "Sales and marketing" (Intel, 2000a) linked to seven employees identified in a right-hand frame, one of whom was pictured at the top of the frame. After clicking on her name, a full page of text allowed the employee to "answer" questions such as "What do you do at Intel?" and "What do you do when you are not at work?"

Such textual interviews with accompanying head shots were available for all seven of the sales and marketing employees identified on this link and, presumably, were available for each of the other job position links. Indeed, on the Intel "Values" section under "The Workplace: What is it like to work at Intel?" (Intel, 2000d) the site offered a subhead entitled "Our Employees Tell Our Story Best" (Intel, 2000f), a discussion that clearly demonstrates Intel values the narrative quality of employee testimony. Ironically, however, there were no candid photos of employees. One extra feature on Intel's website was the organization's reference to the egalitarian nature of Intel, where "everyone's cubicle is the same size" (Intel, 2000c). To demonstrate this, one link led to a streaming video panorama of Intel chairman Andy Grove's cubicle. Like the page from whence the link came, however, Grove and other employees were invisible.

EVALUATION OF A DECADE OF RECRUITMENT MESSAGES

Despite the limited sampling techniques used in the two stages of this study, I suggest depictions of diversity changed from 1990 to 2000 to establish a composite image of an ideal employee with which a broad array of people could identify, thereby reflecting the substance of "Workforce 2000."

Indeed, there was little to no explicit mention of diversity in recruitment webpages in 2000 when compared to recruitment messages in 1990. This observation does not necessarily mean that organizations in this study did not pay attention to the issue in 2000; however, it would suggest that the sign value of diverse representation is important, especially from a Gramscian perspective, and most likely was enacted in other textual ways, including on-site visits and other kinds of interpersonal interactions with employer representatives.The egalitarian nature of the Web is thus demonstrated not just in the empowerment of individuals navigating through the Web based on their own agenda, but it is also illustrated in Web presentations of employees and would-be employees. Notably, organizations that suggest they are interested in the diversity of "our people" tended to look more and more alike in their representations, even as there was increased attention to diversity. It is worth mentioning that, in the 2000 census, for the first time individuals could select more than one category to indicate their ethnicity to represent the true diversity of America.

Yet even with official governmental recognition of diversity, there are many ways in which corporate employers have not followed suit. First, based on the recruitment messages analyzed in this study, acknowledgement and portraits of subcultures among ethnic groups could make a difference. As Len-Rios (2002) observed, "Hispanic" or Latina/Latino subgroups are clearly distinct. None of the videos or the websites addressed these cultural distinctions, offering a more homogenized version of a particular ethnic group. Admittedly, the lack of findings in cultural differentiation is closely connected to the method, as this was not an area of specific investigation. However, one of the markers in Len-Rios' study was differences in language, and none of the five employers offered a language other than English for job seekers.

Second, the issue of same sex partner benefits merits greater attention in recruitment. Indeed, references to sexual orientations were absent in video presentations in the 1990s, one area in the discourse that reflects a change in issue status regarding gay and lesbian rights. At the dawn of the millennium, gay and lesbian support and partner benefits were presented by some employers and the discussion distinguished a company from other employers. Furthermore, an employer might distinguish itself from others with depictions of individuals with disabilities or more mature employees or job seekers; these depictions were seen only on SBC's (e.g., Ameritech, 2000a, 2000b, 2000c, 2000e, 2000f, 2000g) website, suggesting the issue had not received the critical status that "Workforce 2000" offered gender and ethnic diversity. In addition, few older workers (symbolized superficially with grey hair) were depicted, although SBC was the exception in both areas, as it listed awards it received as evidence that it is "one of the best" places to work for the "aged" and the deaf and hard of hearing (Ameritech, 2000d).

At the same time that these websites offered organizations the ability to frame the discussion of their efforts toward workforce diversity, the Web also offered individuals the opportunity to react to, identify, and frame issues within coordinated Web communities.

Indeed, it may be that Web presentations of corporate diversity were encumbered as much by cultural as technological forces, leading to some observations about the power inherent in the form of video versus Web recruitment messages. In remediation, Bolter and Grusin (1999) argued that new media forms do not replace, but rather "RE-mediate" previous media forms. In the websites examined, the self-depictions more closely resembled an assortment of brochures rather than an improvement on a visual, filmic type of medium. For instance, the tiny graphic representations of individuals were constrained as much by considerations of hardware and broadband capabilities and download time, which were much slower in 2000, as by concern with overrepresentation of individuals from one gender and ethnic group. The few iconic representations of employees, which then became hyperlinks, perhaps embodied the fascination with new technology (as seen on the Intel website [e.g., 2000e]) and the hypermediated experiments with links and streaming video that in effect called attention to the new medium (Bolter & Grusin, 1999).

Nevertheless, when corporations grant an issue such as demographic diversity definitional status, scholars and practitioners should be alert to determine if such corporate efforts are genuine. As institutions central to American society, organizations have the definitional power to proclaim who is a desirable employee and who is not. In both video and website projections, it seems the corporations in my samples were only tentatively ready to address diverse identities. Rather, companies seemed to suggest that pictures speak louder than words. This text spoke loudly about diversity and the norms of the company, but diverse voices were not heard from in 2000. It was almost as if, having addressed "diversity" visually, no additional acknowledgement of difference was required. Gone were discussions about the special attention given to women or members of specific ethnic groups. Also absent were discussions about accommodating differences. Just as recruitment messages may depict diversity, they may also define it clearly to invite participation in a broader power structure, a hegemony defined by the corporation.

One irony of this study is that, although attention was paid to the visual characteristics of employees and potential employees, most of the attributes of ideal recruits and the organizations' employees depicted in both videos and on websites were abstract or cerebral, such as the "desire to learn" or "to grow" or "to improve myself" through "non-stop challenges" or "to make a difference" within one's employment. An applicant who holds these character traits, regardless of race or gender, fits the ideal. The power of such implicit definitions of the ideal recruit seems a bit ambivalent. It is the frame for the rotating faces in which race does not seem to matter. Yet beneath the surface manifestations of diversity, there still exists an expectation of conformity in these messages, perhaps reflective of a culture that has decided not to address difference.

CONCLUSION

One advantage of the Web many have asserted is its interactive qualities, and clearly this provides some empowerment for job seekers who might at least attempt some dialogue with employers. However, the video format has its own rhetorical power, especially in the narrative format. Rhetorical form supports definitional strategies and their power. With the receiver-centric medium of the Web, where visitors can surf from link to link without following a specific pathway, no narrative progression can lead the audience from point to point (e.g., Douglass, 1994). Additionally, with no conclusion to a website in the traditional sense, the critic cannot follow the progression of a text as terminological algebra suggests, so rhetorical theory must adapt (Douglass, 1994). The iconic unifying symbol noted by Cheney (1983) seems a starting place for transformation of Burkean theory, but the dramaturgical orientation would demand, it seems to me, that *words* remain central to the concept of identification, as articulated by Burke.

One caution is that organizational representations may or may not reflect the experiences of organizational members (e.g., Cheney & Christiansen, 2001; Moingeon & Soenen, 2002). Depictions of an organizational self, as well as of the ideal recruit, may be enacted in a manner different from that attested in a recruitment video or on the Web. Thus, the definitional power of corporate recruitment images invite critique and resistance. An additional area of investigation for recruitment rhetoric, then, is to examine whether experienced identity in the workplace with regard to issues of diversity is consistent with these Web presentations (Moingeon & Soenen, 2002). In addition, a more contemporary examination of such Web presentations is certainly due. Future studies might also explore comparisons of depictions of the ideal recruit in gendered fields such as nursing, teaching, and graphic arts. Recent trends toward Blogs and online video clips also demand investigation.

This study admittedly only touches the surface of organizational portraits of ideal employees and would-be employees, yet my hope is that it offers a benchmark for future examinations to understand who is included in the equation of equal opportunity in corporate America. As Morgan (2002) wrote, "We are the first generation of hypertext readers" (p. 216); this alone should serve as an impetus for further studies to investigate how the use of cyberspace either reinforces or induces resistance to corporate hegemony. As such, the current study offers a limited "cross media comparison of rhetorical actions" to learn "how media form influences the nature of rhetorical action" (Warnick, 2005, p. 332). Further, the study addresses calls to offer interpretations and meanings that others may make of new texts and adds to discursive studies of representation in public relations (Curtin & Gaither, 2005). Finally, it attends to treatment of difference in public relations practice (Pompper, 2005), with the goal to render difference visible.

NOTES

1. During this decade the unemployment rate hit record lows, standing at an averaged annual rate of 4% in 1998 (U.S. Bureau of Labor Statistics, 2004). Indeed, Munk (1998) noted a record low unemployment rate for college grads of 1.9% and skyrocketing demand for the "gold collar" worker, asserting young knowledge workers held the balance of power, which resulted in a new phenomenon—"the bull market brat." Paradoxically, jobs were more insecure than ever as employers eliminated more positions in 1998 and 1999 than they had in any other year in the 1990s. Even so, the search for talent as the United States. approached the millennium resulted in bidding wars, signing and employee-referral bonuses, and freedom to negotiate intangible benefits.

2. The discussion of terminological algebra is abbreviated for space purposes. For a more thorough description, cf. Holloway (1993).
3. Although I agree that gender and ethnicity are socially constructed and the categories are limited by my own biases, I contend individuals do estimate race and ethnicity of visual representations of individuals with whom they are asked to identify, and that, particularly in recruitment messages, depictions of individuals who represent a particular race and/or ethnic group may be strategically used to attract applicants (cf. Avery, 2003).
4. For this study, a recruitment video (Lord Corporation, n.d.) and several webpages from the Lord Corporation (2000a, 2000b, 2000c, 2000d, 2000e, 2000f, 2000g, 2000h, 2000i, 2000j, 2000k, 2000l, 2000m) were analyzed, but no references are made within the chapter regarding specific content. The same is true of Ameritech/Illinois bell (n.d.), Intel Corporation (1990), Manufacturer's National (1990), and Thiokol (1990). Their analysis results are reflected in Tables 9.1 and 9.2.

REFERENCES

Aarseth, E. J. (1994). Nonlinearity and literary theory. In G. P. Landow (Ed.), *Hyper/text/theory* (pp. 51-86). Baltimore: Johns Hopkins University Press.

Alger, H., Jr. (1904). *Ben Barclay's courage, or, the fortunes of a store boy* (*Brave and bold,* no. 105). New York: Street & Smith.

Allen, B. J. (1995). "Diversity" and organizational communication. *Journal of Applied Communication Research, 23*, 143-155.

Ameritech/Illinois Bell. (n.d.). [Recruitment video]. Chicago: Author.

Ameritech/Southwestern Bell Corporation. (2000a). *Careers.* Retrieved Oct. 31, 2000, from http://www.sbc.com/Career/Home.html

Ameritech/ Southwestern Bell Corporation. (2000b). *Careers: Inside SBC.* Retrieved Oct. 31, 2000, from http://www.sbc.com/Career/Inside_SBC/0,2951,10,00.html

Ameritech/ Southwestern Bell Corporation. (2000c). *Careers: Inside SBC: Hot projects.* Retrieved Oct. 31, 2000, from http://www.sbc.com/Career/Inside_SBC/Hot_Projects/0,2951,8,00.html

Ameritech/Southwestern Bell Corporation. (2000d). *SBC home: Careers: Community: Commitment to diversity.* Retrieved Oct. 31, 2000, from http://www.sbc.com/Community/Employee_Investment/Diversity/02951,17,00.html

Ameritech/ Southwestern Bell Corporation. (2000e). *Careers: Management benefits.* Retrieved Oct. 31, 2000, from http://www.sbc.com/Career/Benefits/Mgmnt_Benefits/Home.html

Ameritech/ Southwestern Bell Corporation. (2000f). *Careers: Non-management benefits.* Retrieved Oct. 31, 2000, from http://www.sbc.com/Career/Benefits/Non_Mgmnt_Benefits/Home.html

Ameritech/Southwestern Bell Corporation. (2000g). *SBC home: Community: Awards & recognition.* Retrieved Oct. 31, 2000, from http://www.sbc.com/Community/0,2951.10,00.html

Ashforth, B. E., & Mael, F. (1989). Social identity theory and the organization. *Academy of Management Review, 18,* 88-115.

Avery, D. (2003). Reactions to diversity in recruitment advertising—are differences black and white? *Journal of Applied Psychology, 88,* 672-679.
Barton Malow Company (n.d.). [Video brochure]. Southfield, MI: Author.
Barton Malow Company. (2000a). *Barton Malow Company—design/construction services.* Retrieved November 4, 2000, from www.bartonmalow.com/
Barton Malow Company. (2000b). *Employment opportunities.* Retrieved November 4, 2000, from www.bartonmalow.com/Human_Resources/human_resources/employ.htm
Barton Malow Company. (2000c). *Human resources.* Retrieved October 30, 2000, from www.bartonmalow.com/human/human.htm
Barton Malow Company. (2000d). *A great place to work.* Retrieved November 4, 2000, from www.bartonmalow.com/human_resources/great.htm
Barton Malow Company. (2000e). *Student internships.* Retrieved October 30, 2000, from www.bartonmalow.com/human_resources/intern.htm
Berthold, C. A. (1976). Kenneth Burke's cluster-agon method: Its development and an application. *Central States Speech Journal, 17,* 302-309.
Black, E. (1970). The second persona. *Quarterly Journal of Speech, 56,* 109-119.
Bolles, R. N. (1987). *What color is your parachute? A practical manual for job-hunters and career changers.* Berkeley, CA: Ten Speed Press.
Bostdorff, D. M. (1987). *The contemporary presidency and the rhetoric of promoted crisis.* Unpublished doctoral dissertation, Purdue University, West Lafayette, IN.
Bolter, J. D., & Grusin, R. (1999). *Remediation: Understanding new media.* Cambridge, MA: MIT Press.
Brummett, B. (1994). *Rhetoric in popular culture.* New York: St. Martin's Press.
Bucy, E. P. (2000). Social access to the Internet. *Harvard International Journal of Press/Politics 5,* 50-61.
Bullis, C. A., & Tompkins, P. K. (1989). The forest ranger revisited: A study of control practices and identification. *Communication Monographs, 56,* 286-306.
Burke, K. (1973). *The philosophy of literary form.* Berkeley: University of California Press. (Original work published 1941)
Chatman, J. A. (1989). Improving interactional organization research: A model of person-organization fit. *Academy of Management Review, 14,* 333-349.
Cheney, G. (1983). The rhetoric of identification and the study of organizational communication. *Quarterly Journal of Speech, 69,* 143-158.
Cheney, G., & Christiansen, L. T. (2001). Identity at issue: Linkages between "internal" and "external" organizational communication. In F. M. Jablin & L. L. Putnam (Eds.), *The new handbook of organizational communication: Advances in theory, research, and methods* (pp. 231-269). Thousand Oaks, CA: Sage.
Cheney, G., & Tompkins, P. K. (1987). Coming to terms with organizational identity and commitment. *Central States Speech Journal, 38,* 1-15.
Cheney, G., & Vibbert, S. L. (1987). Corporate discourse: Public relations and issues management. In F. M. Jablin, L. L. Putnam, K. H. Roberts, & L. W. Porter (Eds.), *Handbook of organizational communication* (pp. 165-194). Newbury Park, CA: Sage.
Christiansen, L. T., & Cheney, G. (2000). Self-absorption and self-seduction in the corporate identity game. In M. Schultz, M. J. Hatch, & J. H. Larsen (Eds.), *The expressive organization: Linking identity, reputation, and corporate brand* (pp. 246-270). New York: Oxford University Press.

Comerica. (2000a). *About Comerica: Virtual career center.* Retrieved November 6, 2000, from http://www.comerica.com/comerica/main_content.html?

Comerica. (2000b). *About Comerica: Virtual career center: Career connections.* Retrieved November 6, 2000, from http://www.comerica.com/comerica/main_content.html?nav+ac/ac.vcccc_nav.html&

Courtright, J. L. (1995). "I am a Scientologist": The image management of identity. In W. N. Elwood (Ed.), *Public relations inquiry as rhetorical criticism: Studies of corporate discourse in public relations campaigns* (pp. 69-84). Westport, CT: Praeger.

Cozier, Z. R., & Witmer, D. F. (2001). The development of a structuration analysis of new publics in an electronic environment. In R. L. Heath (Ed.), *Handbook of public relations* (pp. 615-624). Thousand Oaks, CA: Sage.

Crowther, K. N. T., & Wilson, E. P. (1990/1991). How to research companies. In *The CPC Annual* (Vol. 1, pp. 20-24). Bethlehem, PA: College Placement Council.

Curtin, P. A., & Gaither, T. K. (2005). Privileging identity, difference, and power: The circuit of culture as a basis for public relations theory. *Journal of Public Relations Research, 17,* 91-115.

Douglass, J. Y. (1994). "How do I stop this thing?": Closure and indeterminacy in interactive narratives. In G. Landow (Ed.). *Hyper/text/theory* (pp. 159-188). Baltimore: Johns Hopkins University Press.

Dusky, L. (1990). How to find the companies where women succeed. *Working Woman, 15*(1), 81-88.

Eastman Chemical Company (n.d.). [Recruitment video]. Kingsport, TN: Author.

Esrock, S. L., & Leichty, G. B. (1998). Social responsibility and corporate web pages: Self-presentation or agenda-setting? *Public Relations Review, 24,* 305-319.

Esrock, S. L., & Leichty, G. B. (1999). Corporate World Wide Web pages: Serving the news media and other publics. *Journalism and Mass Communication Quarterly, 76,* 456-467.

Faludi, S. (1991). *Backlash: The undeclared war against American women.* New York: Anchor Books.

Fermilab. (1990). [Recruitment video]. Batavia, IL: Author.

Fombrun, C. J. (1996). *Reputation: Realizing value from the corporate image.* Boston: Harvard Business School Press.

Goodyear Tire & Rubber Company. (1990). [Recruitment video]. Akron, OH: Author.

Heath, R. L. (1998). New communication technologies: An issues management point of view. *Public Relations Review, 24,* 273-288.

Holloway, R. L. (1993). *In the matter of J. Robert Oppenheimer: Politics, rhetoric and self-defense.* Westport, CT: Praeger.

Intel Corporation. (1990). [Recruitment video]. Houston, TX: Author.

Intel Corporation. (2000a). *Jobs at Intel: Careers and profiles.* Retrieved November 4, 2000, from www.intel.com/jobs/careers

Intel Corporation. (2000b). *Jobs at Intel—Intel in brief.* Retrieved November 4, 2000, from http://www.intel.com/jobs/inbrief/

Intel Corporation. (2000c). *Jobs at Intel: United States: Benefits and compensation.* Retrieved November 4, 2000, from http://www.intel.com/jobs/usa/bencomp/

Intel Corporation. (2000d). *Jobs: The workplace.* Retrieved November 4, 2000, from http://www.intel.com/jobs/workplace.

Intel Corporation. (2000e). *Just for students.* Retrieved November 4, 2000, from http://www.intel.com/jobs/students/

Intel Corporation. (2000f). *The workplace: Employee rewards & development.* Retrieved November 4, 2000, from http://www.intel.com/jobs/workplace/rewards.htm

Intel Corporation. (2000g). *The workplace: The workplace of choice.* Retrieved November 4, 2000, from http://www.intel.com/jobs/workplace/choice.htm

Jablin, F. M. (1987). Organizational entry, assimilation, and exit. In F. M. Jablin, L. L. Putnam, K. H. Roberts, & L. W. Porter (Eds.), *Handbook of organizational communication* (pp. 679-740). Newbury Park, CA: Sage.

Jablin, F. M. (2001). Organizational entry, assimilation, and disengagement/exit. In F. M. Jablin & L. L. Putnam (Eds.), *The new handbook of organizational communication: Advances in theory, research, and methods* (pp. 732-818). Thousand Oaks, CA: Sage.

Johnston, W. B., & Packer, A. E. (1987). *Workforce 2000: Work and workers for the 21st century.* Indianapolis, IN: Hudson Institute.

Kutscher, R. E. (1990). Reinterpreting a *Workforce 2000* figure [Letter to the editor]. *Journal of Career Planning & Employment, 51*(1), 40.

Landow, G. P. (Ed.). (1994). *Hyper/text/theory.* Baltimore, MD: Johns Hopkins University Press.

Lasswell, H. D. (1965). *World politics and personal insecurity.* New York: The Free Press. (Original work published 1935)

Len-Rios, M. E. (2002). The Bush and Gore presidential campaign web sites: Identifying with Hispanic voters during the 2000 Iowa caucuses and New Hampshire primary. *Journalism & Mass Communication Quarterly, 79*, 887-904.

Lindquist, V. R. (1990). *The Northwestern Lindquist-Endicott report 1990, 44th annual report.* Evanston, IL: Northwestern University Press.

Lindquist, V. R., & Endicott, F. S. (1986). *Trends in the employment of college and university graduates in business and industry, 40th annual report.* Evanston, IL: Northwestern University Press.

Lord Corporation. (n.d.). [Recruitment video]. Cary, NC: Author.

Lord Corporation. (2000a). *Careers.* Retrieved October 29, 2000, from http://www.lordCorporation.com/careers.htm

Lord Corporation. (2000b). *Careers: Chemical.* Retrieved October 29, 2000, from http://www.lordCorporation.com/careers/chemical.htm

Lord Corporation. (2000c). *Careers—Chemical Products Division.* Retrieved November 4, 2000, http://www.lordCorporation.com/Careers/ChemCareer.htm

Lord Corporation. (2000d). *Careers: Corporate.* Retrieved October 29, 2000, from http://www.lordCorporation.com/careers/corporate.htm

Lord Corporation. (2000e). *Careers: Corporate Division.* Retrieved November 4, 2000, http://www.lordCorporation.com/Careers/CorporationCareer.htm

Lord Corporation. (2000f). *Careers: Mechanical.* Retrieved October 29, 2000, from http://www.lordCorporation.com/careers/mechanical.htm

Lord Corporation. (2000g). *Careers—Mechanical Products Division.* Retrieved November 4, 2000, http://www.lordCorporation.com/Careers/MechCareer.htm

Lord Corporation. (2000h). *Careers: Material.* Retrieved October 29, 2000, from http://www.lordCorporation.com/careers/material.htm

Lord Corporation. (2000i, October 2). *College recruiting.* Retrieved October 29, 2000, from http://www.lordtalent.com/splash.htm

Lord Corporation. (2000j). *College recruiting: Opportunities.* Retrieved November 4, 2000, from http://www.lordtalent.com/opportunities.htm

Lord Corporation. (2000k). *Lord: An exciting place to build a career!* Retrieved November 4, 2000, from http://www.lordtalent.com/testimonials1.htm

Lord Corporation. (2000l). [Home page]. Retrieved October 29, 2000, from http://www.lordCorporation.com

Lord Corporation. (2000m). *We've got you covered.* Retrieved November 4, 2000, from http://www.lordtalent.com/whatwe.htm

Manufacturer's National Corporation, Manufacturers Bank. (1990). [Recruitment video]. Detroit, MI: Author.

McDonald, P., & Gandz, J. (1992). Getting value from shared values. *Organizational Dynamics, 20*(3), 64-77.

Moingeon, B., & Soenen, G. (2002). The five facets of collective identities: Integrating corporate and organizational identity. In B. Moingeon & G. Soenen (Eds.), *Corporate and organizational identities: Integrating strategy, marketing, communication and organizational perspectives* (pp. 13-34). New York: Routledge.

Morgan, W. (2002). Heterotropes: Learning the rhetoric of hyperlinks. *Education, Communication & Information, 2,* 215-234.

Mumby, D. K. (1997). The problem of hegemony: Rereading Gramsci for organizational communication studies. *Western Journal of Communication, 61,* 343-375.

Munk, N. (1998). The new organization man. *Fortune, 137*(5), 62-66, 68, 72, 74.

Northern Illinois Gas (n.d.). NI Gas [Recruitment video]. Aurora, IL: Author.

Perelman, C., & Olbrechts-Tyteca, L. (1969). *The new rhetoric: A treatise on argumentation* (J. Wilkinson & P. Weaver, Trans.). Notre Dame, IN: University of Notre Dame Press.

Pompper, D. (2005). "Difference" in public relations research: A case for introducing critical race theory. *Journal of Public Relations Research, 17,* 139-169.

Richardson, A. R. (Ed.). (1992). *Corporate and organizational video.* New York: McGraw-Hill.

Russell-Loretz, T. (1995a). *Building identification in corporate recruitment videos.* Unpublished doctoral dissertation, Purdue University, West Lafayette, IN.

Russell-Loretz, T. (1995b). Janus in the looking glass: The management of organizational identity in corporate recruitment videos. In W. N. Elwood (Ed.), *Public relations inquiry as rhetorical criticism: Case studies of corporate discourse and social influence* (pp. 156-172). Westport, CT: Praeger

Rynes, S. L., & Barber, A. E. (1990). Applicant attraction strategies: An organizational perspective. *Academy of Management Review, 15,* 286-310.

Rynes, S. L., & Boudreau, J. W. (1986). College recruiting in large organizations: Practice, evaluation and research implications. *Personnel Psychology, 39,* 729-757.

Schauer, I. J. (1990). Recruitment: Innovative techniques lure quality workers to NASA. *Personnel Journal, 69*(8), 100-108.

Schudson, M. (1992). Was there ever a public sphere? If so, when? Reflections on the American case. In C. Calhoun (Ed.), *Habermas and the public sphere* (pp. 143-146). Cambridge, MA: MIT Press.

Shyles, L., & Ross, M. (1984). Recruitment rhetoric in brochures advertising the all volunteer force. *Journal of Applied Communication, 12,* 34-49.

Simon, H. A. (1976). *Administrative behavior* (3rd ed.). New York: The Free Press. (Original work published 1945)

Springston, J. K. (2001). Public relations and new media technology. In R. L. Heath (Ed.), *Handbook of public relations* (pp. 603-614). Thousand Oaks, CA: Sage.

Swanson, D. J. (2004). The framing of contemporary Christian apostasy on the World Wide Web. *Journal of Media and Religion, 3,* 1-20.

Teboul, J. B. (1999). Racial/ethnic "encounter" in the workplace: Uncertainty, information-seeking, and learning patterns among racial/ethnic majority and minority new hires. *Howard Journal of Communications, 10,* 97-121.

Thiokol. (1990). [Recruitment video]. Brigham City, UT: Author.

Thiokol. (2000a). *Main page: Employment.* Retrieved October 29, 2000, from http://www.thiokol.com/Careers/careers_find_a_job.asp

Thiokol. (2000b). *Employment opportunities.* Retrieved October 29, 2000, from http://psx.thiokol.com/psp/pserx/EMPLOYEE/HRMS/c/ROLE_APPLICANT.ER_APPLICANT_HOME.GBL?NAVSTACK=Clear

Thiokol. (2000c). *Employee benefits.* Retrieved October 29, 2000, from http://www.thiokol.com/Careers/careers_benefits.asp

Tompkins, P. K., & Cheney, G. (1985). Communication and unobtrusive control in contemporary organizations. In R. D. McPhee & P. K. Tompkins (Eds.), *Organizational communication: Traditional themes and new directions* (pp. 179-210). Beverly Hills, CA: Sage.

United States Bureau of Labor Statistics. (2004, March). *Where can I find the unemployment rate for previous years?* Retrieved July 26, 2005, from http://www.bls.gov/cps/prev_yrs.htm

Useem, J. (1999). For sale online: You. *Fortune, 140*(1), 66-70, 74, 76, 78.

Wal-Mart Stores, Inc. (1990). [Recruitment video]. Bentonville, AR: Author.

Wanguri, D. M. (1996). Diversity, perceptions of equity, and communicative openness in the workplace. *Journal of Business Communication, 33,* 443-457.

Wanous, J. P. (1983). Organizational entry: The individual's viewpoint. In R. M. Steers & L. M. Porter (Eds.), *Motivation and work behavior* (3rd ed., pp. 431-441). New York: McGraw Hill.

Warnick, B. (2005). Looking to the future: Electronic texts and the deepening interface. *Technical Communication Quarterly, 14,* 327-333.

Weiss, A. (1989). The value system. *Personnel Administrator, 34*(7), 40-41.

Weyerhaeuser (n.d.). [Recruitment video]. Federal Way, WA: Author.

Williams, M. L., & Bauer, T. N. (1994). The effect of a managing diversity policy on organizational attractiveness. *Group & Organization Management, 19,* 295-308.

Zompetti, J. P. (1997). Toward a Gramscian critical rhetoric. *Western Journal of Communication, 61,* 66-86.

Power and Public Relations Planning

chapter 10

Public Relations' Power as Based on Knowledge, Discourse, and Ethics

Peter M. Smudde

People get so used to how they think and do things, according to Michel Foucault (1969/1972), that they see those systems of thinking and doing as the ways that structure everything humans do, rather than as mere templates for thinking, speaking, and acting. This perspective means that human discourse creates and recreates human reality, including that for organizations, not the other way around. In this way, public relations, with its purview covering communication activities for a diverse range of internal and external audiences, can be seen as the key discursive actor between organizations and their publics.

Take, for example, a midsize software company based in the midwest region of the United States. (The company was real, and its specific identity has been purposely suppressed.) It had a 35-year history and seen its share of change in the technology industry, marketplace, and society. The organizing behaviors of corporate officials and their employees during those years resulted in some marked successes, a few failures, and relatively steady growth in between. The company changed its business a few times from its original line of software for mainframe computers in the late 1960s to management information systems in the 1980s to strategic planning and corporate performance-measurement software in the early 2000s—until it was fortuitously purchased by another company. Public relations was an integral part of this company throughout its years in business.

In this chapter, this anonymous company serves as an example of public relations discourse structuring what people do within their organizations. Although an historical account of the company's changes might be interesting, this chapter refrains from such an approach. Instead, it uses a simple experiential approach (because the author was the company's public relations director) to analyze selected public relations actions as the company moved into the 21st century as a way to connect the dots between Foucault's theory and public relations practice. Through this approach we can reveal implications of the power relationships that public relations facilitates between an organization and its publics. This chapter formally applies Foucault's work to public relations where it has rarely been used, and certainly on a level that would create a formative, holistic approach for both theory and practice.

For the bulk of the past century, especially over the past two decades or so, public relations has been mostly maligned for the effects of its discourse—a negative image of public relations as image mongering or spin-meistering has prevailed. What is important to remember is that public relations over many years has demonstrated high levels of influence (to varying degrees of success and, sometimes, ethics) about issues in the hearts and minds of people (cf. Cutlip, 1995; Smudde, 2004). Perhaps because of that dynamic of influence—founded on public relations' ability to measurably and ethically use language and symbols to inspire cooperation between an organization and its publics—those who malign the profession suffer from "power envy."

So the central question in this chapter is, "How can we better understand public relations' power in its discursive role within an organization and with its publics?" The answer to this question comes from an unlikely source, that of Michel Foucault and his methods of analysis. Specifically, public relations' power is message-based and influences corporate officials' behaviors in their attempts to organize resources to deal with what is going on. Because of the discursive nature of public relations, it holds a unique position in the formation of corporate destiny. Such formation is epistemic or based on the discursive practices and knowledge available at the time. We can use Foucault's "investigative strategies" to analyze the relationships between knowledge and power that are shared between organizations and their publics, evaluate the effects and effectiveness of their public relations efforts, and, most important, propose a prospective, Foucauldian approach for planning public relations action.

WHY USE FOUCAULT?

Rarely has Foucault's work been applied directly to public relations. Foucault's philosophy enjoys limited application to fields relevant to the scope of this chapter. Before the publication of this book, Foucault was used once as the sole analytical method for public relations, and it is in a case study of the HIV/AIDS issue in Thailand (Chay-Nemeth, 2001). The only other applications of Foucault to public relations are those that employ his ideas in tandem with, or to bolster aspects of, a range of other perspectives (e.g., Curtain & Gaither, 2005; Dixon, 2004; Holtzhausen, 2000, 2002; Holtzhausen & Voto, 2002; Livesey, 2002; Motion & Weaver, 2005). Foucault's philosophy has been employed in general ways, especially for management and organizational theory (Bevir, 1999; Burrell, 1988; Hardy & Phillips, 2004; Knights & Morgan, 1991; McKinlay & Starkey, 1998; Townley, 1993) and organizational discipline and culture (Barker & Cheney, 1994; Mumby & Stohl, 1991).

One possible reason why Foucault's ideas have not been used is that they may be seen as too esoteric or difficult to apply, but that depends on one's perspective and project. Nevertheless, there is a gap in the literature about using Foucault's ideas holistically and on their own for what they offer in the way of explanation, insight, and tools for both retrospective analysis of public relations and proactive public relations planning. Because of its rarity of use in public relations, I explain in this section the basics of Foucault's methods—archaeology, genealogy, and ethics—one at a time and in brief to outline this chapter's method.

Archaeology

To begin, Foucault's purpose for his work is to describe how knowledge is created through language, not to interpret that process. As he says, "One is led therefore to the project of a *pure description of discursive events*" (Foucault, 1969/1972, p. 27) to ascertain the kinds of things (e.g., rules, conventions, practices) that unify them from within. Indeed, he sees broad social implications for human discursive action:

> I am supposing that in every society the production of discourse is at once controlled, selected, organized and redistributed according to a certain number of procedures, whose role is to avert its powers and its dangers to cope with chance events, to evade its ponderous, awesome materiality. (Foucault, 1969/1972, p. 216)

Foucault provides strategies for uncovering rules and norms behind (i.e., conventions for) discourse—which can be spoken, written, or other texts—so that we better understand the social context out of which they grew and in which they are embedded.

His fundamental investigative strategy is archaeology. This method does not imply a search for historical beginnings through an "excavation" of texts. Foucault formulates a way to describe how texts are really actions (i.e., spoken, written, symbolic) that people take that reflect certain knowledge and ways of thinking in a particular period of history (Foucault, 1969/1972).

What archaeology does not define is what people specifically thought or used as points of reference in their thinking outside the discourse they created. The key to archaeology is the uncovering of rules that allowed texts to emerge through human activity in the first place. Discourse is valuable to analyze on its own—"as a monument" to knowledge—and without the need to anchor it as a sign of something else (Foucault, 1969/1972, pp. 138-139).

Texts are made up of statements. A statement "is not the same as a sentence, which is governed by grammatical rules, or a proposition, which is governed by the rules of logic; in contrast, a statement is governed by epistemological rules [or rules about knowledge-building]" (Foss, Foss, & Trapp, 2002, p. 347). Yet Foucault (1989/1996) says a statement is not so limited—it is "a set of signs" (p. 63) that can be either a sentence or a proposition. Discourse is finite and exhibits certain conditions about its existence that can be defined and analyzed.

This is the philosophy behind archaeology. It reveals the rules that allow discourse to emerge, and it identifies periods when only certain knowledge existed and allowed certain kinds of discourse to be created whereas others were not. To apply archaeology as a method for analysis, Foucault prescribed that questions be asked and answered in four categories (Foucault, 1969/1972), all of which serve to define in detail the formation of discourse:

1. Objects—How and where do individual differences among discourses emerge, according to the conventions for discursive action? Who are the arbiters of discourse conventions and discursive action? How can discourse be specified as belonging to a topic or subtopic?
2. Enunciative modalities—Who speaks, writes, or otherwise uses symbols to communicate? Where is he or she speaking/writing/symbolizing? What is the position of the discourse's subject in relation to the speaker and situation?
3. Concepts—How do statements build one from the next? How does discourse coexist with others within its subject area, those that are from another subject area, and those that are no longer accepted but

still remembered? What procedures should be followed to apply discourse from any field to the creation of discourse?

4. Strategy—What consistencies or inconsistencies are present with discourse, and why are they present? On what grounds were certain decisions made about the creation of discourse? How does discourse stand among others as authoritative in a given subject area?

The answers to these categories of questions reveal the presence among statements of any consistent patterns that yield a system of knowledge, which Foucault (1969/1972) called "discursive formations" (p. 38). When the rules for discursive formation change, they mark a new era of knowledge with "a radically different intellectual framework with which to view the world" (Foss, Foss, & Trapp, 2002, p. 348), which Foucault (1969/1972) called "epistemes" (p. 191). The fundamental purpose of discourse is the creation of knowledge, and epistemes govern the aspects of a system of knowledge. An episteme is "the total set of relations that unite, at a given period, the discursive practices that give rise to epistemological figures, sciences, and possibly formalized systems" (Foucault, 1969/1972, p. 191). Simply put, an episteme is the discourse structures that direct us in how we know what we know at a given time.

An example of an episteme from the realm of public relations would be the period of time in which the company for which I worked, with all its discourse for running the business, operated under one business model and produced a particular product line for some years. Then its discourse facilitated a switch to a new business model to produce new goods/services for the same or modified market. All discourse from the prior period in the company's history would not apply much to the new way of doing business, giving rise to the need for new discourse that echoes the company's new way of thinking and doing.

Rules of discursive practice govern epistemes, and those rules dictate what discourse can be created or uttered. A discursive practice

> is a body of anonymous, historical rules, always determined in the time and space that have defined a given period, and for a given social, economic, geographical, or linguistic area, the conditions of operation of the enunciative (i.e., ability to speak, write, or symbolize) function. (Foucault, 1969/1972, p. 117)

Extending the previous example, the company for which I worked operated within ever-enlarging epistemes, beginning with its own and progressing to that which derives from discursive practices about the market, industry, culture, economy, and beyond. These rules or conventions for discourse tell us what we should and should not do when making statements. For example,

Foucault argues that what is *not* said is as important as what *is* said. He also suggests that there are certain rules for deciding what to exclude or not, and those rules for "prohibitions interrelate, reinforce and complement each other, forming a complex web, continually subject to modification" (Foucault, 1969/1972, p. 216). The result, then, is that governing rules can and do control discursive practices, making humans the objects/product of discourse, not the subjects/creators.

Genealogy

Building off archaeology is genealogy, Foucault's (1977/1980) second investigative strategy.[1] It is a method that focuses on describing the expansive network of power relations in society—"to locate the forms of power, the channels it takes, and the discourse it permeates" (Foucault, 1976/1990, p. 11). The complementary relationship between archaeology and genealogy lies in their examination of discourse: "While archaeology involves the identification of the rules of production and transformation of discourse" (Foss, Foss, & Trapp, 2002, p. 361), genealogy "requires patience and a knowledge of details and [sic] it depends on a vast accumulation of source material" (Foucault, 1977/1980, p. 140). Genealogy's particular focus is on the relationships of power to discourse and, thus, to knowledge.

Power for Foucault is not the everyday notion of power of which people typically think. Power is a kind of unity of networked relationships instead of one-on-one relationships between people. Foucault sees power as a multiplex of relationships that work together as a group through any kind and number of human situations, which may confirm, deny, improve, or otherwise alter them. This dynamic means power is relational among humans and is therefore embodied in their institutions, from interpersonal ones to social/government ones—not that these institutions have power, but because power emanates from the system or network of human relations (Foucault, 1976/1990). We come to understand power through discourse, because "discourse transmits and produces power; it reinforces it, but also undermines and exposes it, renders it fragile and makes possible to thwart it" (Foucault, 1976/1990, p. 101). The relationship between power and knowledge is one of reinforcement, because "it is in discourse that power and knowledge are joined together" (p. 100).

To Foucault power "is not a commodity, a position, a prize, or a plot; it is the operation of the [instruments/technologies available] throughout society" (Dreyfus & Rabinow, 1983, p. 185) at a given time in a given society that results in unequal, asymmetrical relationships. Power is not restricted to, or even identical with, institutions, political or otherwise; "it is multidirectional, operating from the top down and also from the bottom up. . . . Power is productive; it is not in a position of exteriority to other types of relationships" (p. 185). Control or domination is exercised in both directions in "intentional and nonsubjective" ways because "there is no power that is exercised without a series of aims and objectives" (Foucault, 1976/1990, pp. 94-95). In short, "power is not an institution, and not a structure; neither is it a certain strength we are endowed with; it is the name that one attributes to a complex strategical situation in a particular society" (p. 93).

There are rules for undertaking a genealogical study of power, and Foucault (1977) explained what the rules are, thereby prescribing a series of steps that can be taken in any order in such a study:

1. Analyze power focused on what it can achieve through its effects at a particular level, not on stereotypical, regulated, and legitimate forms and locations of power.
2. Analyze power's direct relationship with the object of study, whether that is a person, group, or field, not the intentions or decisions about power's application, as if to point to a person or group who "has" power.
3. Analyze power in terms of the network of relationships it has among people and for its circulation among them, not as a form of repression, control, or domination over others. Remember that "individuals are the vehicles of power, not its points of application" (p. 98).
4. Analyze power from the bottom up to determine how its "mechanisms" are applied from the smallest mechanism to the largest, not to deduce power's reach from some locus into things, including broader society.

Genealogy, then, is more than a theory; it is an "analytics of power" that moves "toward a definition of the specific domain formed by relations of power, and toward a determination of the instruments that will make possible its analysis" (Foucault, 1976/1990, p. 82). To develop a theory of power, in Foucault's view, would be fruitless and superfluous because theories tend to be anchored in time to a person who created it and why that person created it. So his quest instead is to focus on power as a real thing that is "an open, more-or-less coordinated . . . cluster of relations" (Foucault, 1977, p. 199). That cluster is, then, key as a way to record and, most important, analyze what relationships there are among people that facilitate power among them.

Ethics

When we consider power relationships genealogically, we become concerned with how power affects humans for what they do and, especially, who they are and want to be. This level of analysis involves Foucault's view of ethics, the third and final investigative strategy that focuses on the self's relation to itself.[2] Ethics "concerns who human beings are said to be and the various means through which the notion of being is created" (Foss, Foss, & Trapp, 2002, p. 357). A central question for Foucault is "how individuals come to be constituted as the subject of their own experience. . . . [It is] the means by which discursive formations incite individuals to use particular means to turn themselves into subjects" (p. 358)—that is, moral subjects of their own actions. Ethics involves morals, which "consists of people's actual behaviour [sic], that is, their morally relevant actions, and of the moral code, which is imposed on them" (Davidson, 1986, p. 228). Those moral codes are rules about what is prohibited, forbidden, permitted, or required, and they explain how to value behaviors positively or negatively.

An investigation of ethics involves attention to four aspects. Because Foucault does not offer an easy summary of them, Davidson (1986) and Foss, Foss, and Trapp (2002) can be used together for such a summary as follows:

1. Ethical substance—What is it that makes us who we are (e.g., feelings, motives, needs) and has relevance in a particular situation for ethical judgement?
2. Mode of subjection—What gives us the grounds (e.g., divine law, reason, social habits) on which we can recognize certain moral obligations?
3. Self-discipline (also termed "asceticism")—What do we need to do to become better moral agents (vis-à-vis a moral code) through our actions?
4. Telos (i.e., the vision of the best person one can possibly be through ethical practices)—What is the ultimate or even perfect person that one can become (e.g., free, pure, self-reliant) through ethical behavior, and what does one need to do to realize that vision?

The results of such an ethical investigation is a subject (a person and, by extension, an organization) that lives according to moral codes and thereby is both compliant with them and equipped to attain the vision of what it (she or he) wants to be through ethical conduct. Ethics is both a creative and a critical frame for the self (Bernauer & Mahon, 1994). In this way truth has a personal relationship with one's self, because one has

> knowledge of a number of rules of acceptable conduct or of principles that are both truths and prescriptions. To take care of the self is to equip oneself with these truths: This is where ethics is linked to the game of truth. (Foucault, 1989/1996, pp. 435-436)

Note that "game" refers to "a set of procedures that lead to a certain result, which, on the basis of its principles and rules of procedure, may be considered valid or invalid, winning or losing" (Foucault, 1989/1996, p. 445).

This basic understanding of Foucault's methods establishes a foundation for analysis and application specifically targeted at investigating public relations' power. Foucault's ideas cover additional territory that is not included here. Nevertheless, the constituent elements of power include discourse, knowledge, and the self. All these aspects build on one another holistically and can be used fruitfully on public relations within an organizational context. The next section demonstrates how to apply this holistic approach to public relations in a brief description and interpretation of the software company example that began this chapter.

WHERE DO FOUCAULT AND PUBLIC RELATIONS CONVERGE?

When taken individually, Foucault's investigative strategies—archaeology, genealogy, and ethics—help us see, respectively, the formation of discourse within a given period, the relationship between power and knowledge as driven by discourse, and the relationship of one's self to itself. But when taken together, these tools build on one another and can work together as a system for analysis. As Foucault (1989/1996) said, "All my books . . . are . . . like little tool boxes. If people want to open them, use a particular sentence, idea, or analysis like a screwdriver or wrench in order to short-circuit, disqualify or break up the systems of power, including eventually the very ones from which my books have issued . . . well, all the better!" (p. 149). This approach is just what this chapter aims to do by using all three methods together on public relations.

Indeed, this chapter extends Foucault's methods by moving from traditional critique (which looks back on extant discourse) to prediction (which looks forward to planned discourse). In this way lessons from past discourse can be bridged with plans for future discursive action. Although critique is traditionally anchored in retrospective analysis, there is no reason why critical methods cannot be used prospectively to the benefit of future discourse. Criticism, then, becomes something more potent—a tool for more effective discourse rather than an exercise attaining 20/20 hindsight. This perspective is especially relevant to business because spending too much time looking in the rearview mirror means the advantage of looking down and preparing for the road ahead has been lost and the opportunities that go with it.

Here is a high-level summary on the convergence of Foucault's tools and public relations. Foucault's method of archeology allows us to view the function of public relations discourse in terms of knowledge creation for the mutual benefit of organizations and their publics. The consistent pattern of discursive occurrences at any point in an organization's history that yield knowledge would parallel Foucault's idea of *discursive formations*. Concomitantly, an organization's historical periods can be called "corporate epistemes," and they are governed in part by rules of discursive practice that public relations follows. We can examine the public relations discourse of any organization, therefore, to better reveal what is going on as its discourse creates and recreates it for itself and its publics. Foucault's method of genealogy, which complements archeology, reveals the power-knowledge and ethical relationships organizations and their publics share.

Case in Context

It is one thing to read and think about a theoretical orientation. It is completely another to live it out and see it work firsthand. That was my experience at the turn of the 21st century as I worked for a software company as its director of public relations. What I observed were discursive patterns in action that could be explained through Foucault's investigative strategies. Interestingly, it did not occur to me what I was experiencing until I was through most of a project, and when I did make that realization, I was stunned, amazed, and ever more interested in what happened and why.

Using an experiential approach (Brock, Scott, & Chesebro, 1990) I trace my experience briefly through a project in which I was involved to demonstrate an application of Foucault's methods to public relations. The purpose is to present an initial investigation about public relations that can be done fruitfully through Foucault's methods. An experiential perspective is critic-centered and thus a kind of participant observation guided by an appropriate critical method. It is meant to advance an interpretation, a reasonable insight about an event, text, or any other discursive action. The case, then, offers an authentic view of public relations that can be used and built on in various ways.

The company had recently released a new software product that was more effective and easier to use than that offered by competitors, and management wanted to secure the support of thought leaders in the market and obtain an interest among customers to buy the company's software. Those thought leaders were high-tech industry analysts who follow specific companies in particular product markets and make recommendations about buying their products, feeling comfortable with their business performance, and looking ahead for change that may come for everyone. These industry analysts are therefore unlike Wall Street analysts, who also examine companies closely but do so with the purpose of recommending the purchase, holding, or sale of stock or other securities. The kind of support industry analysts provide is discursive, both written and oral, but written discourse is the most prized. Gaining analysts' support was important because potential buyers of the company's software seek and value their opinions. Moreover, journalists covering the high-tech industry go to industry analysts as unbiased, objective, and knowledgeable sources for news stories they are writing, and those stories may well include coverage of individual companies. What analysts think and say influences the thinking and acting (especially buying actions) of others.

Discursively, the company for which I worked wanted a particular analysis firm (with which it had worked before) to prepare a report on its new flagship software product. The fact that the software company paid the firm for the analysts' work was an investment, but it wasn't a "pay for placement" matter. Most analyst firms work on "subscriptions," which means companies basically pay annually for (a) access to an analyst, who will give them sage counsel on their businesses, markets, industries, and the economy, and (b) some level of access to the analyst firm's other resources, which range from reports to research teams. Some firms work on a per-project basis, which means companies pay for what they need and the analysis firm applies its resources "objectively" to that end with a small team of analysts. Companies may also retain a firm's analysis services on a periodic basis (e.g., monthly, quarterly, annually) so that they can get what they need, when they need it, and tie it to a big-picture business relationship. The analysis firm that the software company called on was engaged in a per-project business relationship to produce a single report. In all cases, industry analysts pride themselves primarily on their knowledge and skillfulness in assessing and predicting trends, presenting balanced views of what is going on in some market or some company, and being credible voices of "objectivity" about their areas of expertise.

The report for the software company (I refer to this company henceforth as Gaucho Software) was to review the software's features, benefits, usability, capabilities, value, place in the market, and other aspects. Two top analysts from Aja Group (the name for the analysis firm that I use henceforth) were assigned to the project, and they were people with whom I dealt frequently and knew well. Top executives and experts from Gaucho Software were involved in the project as personal sources, and all of them gave the utmost attention to the accuracy and truthfulness of any information throughout the project, as did the analysts. The Gaucho officials involved included the chief executive officer, chief technology officer (who oversaw all software development), chief financial officer, senior vice president of marketing, the lead product engineer for the particular software product, and me because I was the director of public relations. Indeed, I was the point person on the project for Gaucho, setting it up, managing it, and seeing it through to fruition with Aja Group.

The project's process was simple. The analysts met with us for two days to talk about all dimensions of the software, our company, and the market. Their primary interest was the software, and other information served to fill out context. All-day meetings featured all kinds of discursive action—conversations, presentations, software demonstrations, and documentation. A full range of discourse from Gaucho Software, Aja Group, and others (including outside sources when needed) was the origin and substance of the project and its final product.

The analysts knew Gaucho Software well and could easily get up to speed on what was going on with the company. Premeeting discourse featured phone conversations and e-mail about what would take place and what the analysts planned and would need. This discourse also included some discussion about what the contractual obligations would be, and those were handled easily enough. Postmeeting discourse between the Aja Group and Gaucho Software at first focused on getting answers or material to address additional points of inquiry. Later, the postmeeting discourse focused on drafts of the analysts' report. In this latter phase of the project, the Gaucho officials responded to and suggested certain revisions on the drafts, and, interestingly, those revisions were reenactments of prior discourse. What became apparent was that the Gaucho discourse drove its management to structure its view of things and, in particular, the substance of Aja's discourse. Aja allowed Gaucho three passes at the report in draft form, as there was some level of pride of authorship and the need to preserve credibility. A final report was printed and Gaucho Software made extensive use of it in sales and communications (i.e., public relations and marketing) efforts.

Foucauldian Analysis of the Case

Because of the need to preserve the anonymity of the software company and the analysis firm, textual examples cannot be used. However, my personal account of the discursive action can reveal the kinds of dynamics relevant to a Foucauldian approach by citing selected examples.

Archaeological Investigation. This investigation is primary among the three Foucauldian methods of analysis of public relations discursive action. The first step here is defining the case's discourse object. The type of discourse sought (i.e., an analyst report) arose from the needs of companies and their customers who wanted separate, third-party, authoritative accounts of products and services available in a particular market. Such reports adhere to conventions such as impartiality, thoroughness, usability, and others. The key arbiters of what went into the report began with Aja Group analysts and then featured Gaucho Software officials; their discursive actions were affected by the expectations of target publics who would read and use the report. In this way the report's audience dictated the kind of writing conventions that should be upheld in the report, and Aja and Gaucho people enacted them selectively. The report belongs in the genre of analyst reports because of its authority from an analysis firm and, particularly, its coverage of a company that participates in the business/enterprise software segment of the high-tech industry.

The second step in this archaeological investigation of the case's discourse is enunciative modalities, or the details about the author or speaker. Ideally, the "speakers" in the report are the two Aja Group analysts who wrote the report—only one of whom was cited as its author.[3] No indication is given about those involved in the revisions, which essentially included the analysts plus the six Gaucho Software officials. Only limited indications were given about any documents from Gaucho Software, Aja Group, and other sources that were directly used in the report, which is less a matter of scholarship and more a practical matter of the effect of the wide range of discourse on the analysts' thinking about the project. Their "speech" (i.e., text) was enacted in print and shared electronically as a portable document format (PDF) file on Gaucho's website and by request from Aja Group. It was also in hardcopy and distributed via mail services. The report, then, preserves the authors' thoughts in a way that makes them accessible and usable at any time anywhere by a reader.

The third step is defining concepts. The report follows a kind of formula for content that presents an overview of the specific matters it addresses and then proceeds into detailed analyses of each topic area. The flow of statements in each topic area exhibits certain claims that are bolstered by evidence in the form of examples, quantitative and qualitative data, and graphic illustrations. Other discursive elements include pictorial representations of processes or assessments of selected topics, like product functions or company progress in a developing market. The report does not chronicle the substance of any meetings, conversations, documentation, or other discourse that was shared during the development of the report. The report exists alongside other discourse about the company, its product, and related matters, and the report may be used in tandem with other corporate discourse for various purposes. The report also stands apart from older discourse that addresses previous products, corporate performance, and other matters. This separation between the report and prior discourse is especially important given that the company no longer produced or participated in the software markets that it did in the past; however, those subjects would be addressed if, and only if, long-term, retrospective, historical accounts of the company's business were necessary—otherwise they were not addressed. The report may stand in close relation to more recent discourse about previous versions of the same product and needs to reference them in terms of what has changed. The report also would stand in relation to any other third-party discourse (e.g., news coverage) and company-created discourse (e.g., case studies, brochures, and annual reports) as a kind of supportive document. Other similar analyst reports can be compared to Aja's, (a) at least in terms of the contents' treatment of products from other companies that are in direct competition with Gaucho Software and (b) at most in terms of their upholding of the same or similar discourse conventions for analyst reports no matter what the product/service and industry.

The fourth and final step for this archaeological investigation is to define the report's strategy. The substance of the report concerns specific matters of a given software product, the company that produced it, and any customer's interest in using it for its own benefit. The report was consistent in its relatively balanced account of the specific matters it covered. There did tend to be slightly more emphasis on positive aspects of the product, company, and customer benefits/value, and at least some negative concerns or issues were mentioned and addressed with recommendations for improvement. Decisions about these content issues were based on Aja Group's analysts' assessments and Gaucho Software's officials' desires for certain textual revisions. The grounds for these decisions, from Gaucho's arena, came from several places: prior discourse about the product and the company, announced developments in the product and the company, and individual agendas for treating the subject. In this way Gaucho Software's arbiters in the discourse were participating in their corporate discursive practices and sought to advance certain statements/key messages that were consistent with what was already said or in the process of being enacted. From Aja Group's vantage point, grounds for content decisions likely were based on its analysts' participation in the discursive practices within the analyst community and, in particular, with Gaucho Software. Guided by discursive patterns, the analysts were the report's authors. The decisions for the report about Gaucho focused on matters related at least to the preservation of a balanced view, professional integrity, and an exemplary document on the firm's behalf. In the end, the report functioned well as a supportive and authoritative third-party account of Gaucho Software's flagship product, yet the reputation of Aja Group as a for-hire analysis firm resulted in limited suspicion about the true objectivity of the report.

All together, this archaeological investigation of the report reveals that it was discourse that was truly born from other discourse. Indeed, public relations and other discourse about Gaucho Software's flagship product and the company itself were responsible for both Gaucho and Aja officials' need to enact a view of things, not the other way around. The system of statements in the discourse reveals a knowledge base about the state of the product, business, market, stakeholders, industry, economy, and so on. In this way the report was the public relations' part of a "corporate episteme" about business performance management; that is, an expression of the organization's knowledge of what to do and why. The report covered selected dimensions and brought them to light in terms of a specific company's product and in the context of a public relations need to advance key messages about it. Prior corporate epistemes were market- and industry-focused on mainframe software between the late 1960s and the early 1980s and, subsequently, on management information systems from the early 1980s to the mid-1990s.

Genealogical Investigation. At this point we build on the prior investigation about the case's discursive action by showing relationships between power and knowledge, particularly between Gaucho Software and its publics and stakeholders. Remember that power goes both ways. A genealogical examination of the case begins with an analysis of power through its discursive effects. The report's focus on Gaucho Software brings much value to Gaucho because of the document's usefulness in building interest among customers who might like to buy the software. The report also brings value to Aja Group because it is an example of what the firm can do for other clients. The report balances Gaucho's, Aja's and customers' needs and expectations by presenting information in an acceptable, usable, and authoritative form.

The next step is to analyze power in direct relationship with Gaucho Software and its product. In this dimension Gaucho Software is and must be the single, most authoritative source on its own product. To not be so would be absurd and detrimental. Moreover, because Aja Group placed its stamp of approval effectively on the software and Gaucho, there is a level of further credibility and legitimacy that is conferred on the software product and its company. That is, someone else says it is good, so others (especially customers of any ilk) can believe so too. The report also spelled out the software's advantages over the competition.

The next genealogical step is an analysis of power that focuses on its network of relationships. In this case the concern is the relationship between Gaucho Software and its stakeholders. Aja Group, at the behest of and in collaboration with Gaucho Software, created a particular kind of discourse that had significant public relations value. At first there is the power relationship between Gaucho Software and Aja Group. Although the report is emblazoned with Aja Group's name and logo, its substance is largely collaborative. The analysts benefited from the wide range of discourse they used and gave Gaucho officials opportunities to recommend revisions, and they took many of them. Although the text changed markedly from the initial shared draft and Gaucho paid for the project, credit for the final product went to Aja. The analysts were, indeed, the authors of the report, as the discourse they amassed influenced how they formulated and wrote their observations, assessments, and recommendations in the report. That is really a matter of contractual agreement, and in that regard that contract has a certain degree of influence in this case because it suggests how the parties to it will behave. Because both companies agreed to the contract, we can say a cooperative arrangement existed.

The final step is to analyze the mechanisms of power from the bottom up to see how they build and work together. In this case we begin with Gaucho Software's customers (both established and potential) because they were the ultimate recipients of the report. Other stakeholders included news media and shareholders, as the company's stock was publicly traded. From a customer point of view, the report reflects information they need to make sound buying decisions about the featured Gaucho Software product. From a news-media viewpoint, the report represented a close, nearly inside, and credible source of analysis about an important software product from a top company in the market. From the shareholders' perspective, the report represented similar things and included the dimension of material information about the state of the company's business and its flagship product, thereby serving indirectly to reinforce the idea that Gaucho's stock was worth holding or buying.

Gaucho designed its software, organized support functions, produced particular communications, and did other things that customers needed. In this way, customers and other stakeholders influenced Gaucho's decisions and actions significantly, and the creation of the analyst report emerged from that milieu. Gaucho, however, had the authority to acknowledge or ignore, and apply or discard, information from its customers and beyond. To do so, however, would risk the company's reputation as being customer-centric, so such information was typically acknowledged and applied in appropriate ways. Also, even though Gaucho Software's discursive practices, including public relations and other communications, could be customer/stakeholder-driven, customers did not have responsibility for them because it was Gaucho's responsibility to act prudently in any fashion.

Overall, the genealogical investigation of the case reveals that power relationships existed among Gaucho Software, its customers and other stakeholders, and Aja Group. Indeed, the principal power relationship was between Gaucho and its customers, whether they were established or potential customers. Aja Group functioned as a facilitator of a particular discourse that fit Gaucho's purposes. The report is an example of the importance of communications between Gaucho and its customers, and they flowed more or less symmetrically. The company, however, frequently enacted other communications for strategic and opportunistic reasons that were based on customers' (even shareholders') suggestions, needs, and expectations. That means that discourse was never created only on demand when stakeholders asked for it. Gaucho Software anticipated communications needs and created discourse strategically and as occasions warranted. Power existed in a symbiotic relationship between stakeholders and Gaucho Software.

Ethical Investigation. This final area of analysis of the case focuses on the organization's self in relation to itself, which falls under Foucault's moniker of ethics. Four aspects command our attention here, and the first is ethical substance. What made Gaucho Software the company it was involved a long history of software development that began with an entrepreneurial endeavor in the late 1960s. The company grew but remained small enough over the years to react well to (and even anticipate) market shifts. The spirit of an entrepreneurial business with creative people underscored the kinds of statements in Aja Group's report about Gaucho Software's flagship product. Indeed, that idea was captured in the final report as a company strength.

The second aspect for an ethical investigation of the case is mode of subjection, or the grounds for any moral obligation. Key to Gaucho Software's pursuing the report was the need for such discourse for its stakeholders. Such discursive action was based on a combination of industry practices (especially those as exercised by competitors) and professional/corporate interests to communicate to stakeholders about Gaucho's flagship product. The software company, then, followed established practice for having the analyst report developed for its own product.

Self-discipline is the third ethical aspect about Gaucho Software's self in relation to itself. The nature of the project as one that was contractually arranged between Gaucho Software and Aja Group may not have been the best choice. The analysts were, indeed, the report's authors and had worked hard at preparing a balanced report from the discourse they amassed, even with Gaucho Software officers' suggested revisions. Questions about the report's objectivity arose, albeit rarely. After all, the project was work done for hire, as opposed to nonpaid, independent reports that may emerge from other sources, like other analysis firms or, particularly, news media.

The fourth and final aspect for ethical analysis of the case is *telos*, which concerns Gaucho Software's vision of the best company it could possibly be through moral practice. Gaucho Software's vision was to be the leader in the business performance management software market. It even went so far as to include as one of its corporate objectives the claim that it sought "to be an ethical company," which was the direct result of having to endure a financial crisis in the mid-1990s that started from improper accounting of sales in one of its overseas operations. The ultimate state of being for Gaucho Software was based on the idea of market leadership. It was a distant number two in its market in financial terms and down the list a bit on head-to-head product comparisons. Gaucho Software's extant resources at the time were getting it closer to its vision, but very slowly. The company needed to grow sales of its software products, and hopes were pinned on the flagship product to fertilize the soil for such growth.

On the whole, the ethical investigation of Gaucho Software reveals that it was a company that tried very hard to (and did) play by the rules and had difficulty getting closer to its vision because it could not penetrate the market as well as its competition. The company's colorful history made for good stories but did little for making a case for value to be gained today from its software products. The company's entrepreneurial heritage, primarily, was inspirational to employees yet anchored in a relatively successful past rather than forging practices for a brighter present and future.

Holistic Summary. Taken together, all three of Foucault's tools reveal a company that acted morally but suffered from inefficiencies in its business. It shared power relationships with its publics and stakeholders, especially customers, while possessing and applying knowledge strategically and responsibly in discourse. The company also operated within a definitive discursive formation that focused on the nature of its business at the time and relied on public relations to help perpetuate the corporate episteme—and even be there at the genesis of the next. Public relations was a valued and valuable function of particular discursive practices for the company.

Points of Consideration. This case has been illustrative, yet there are two points about it that should be considered. First, no textual examples are specifically used because of the need to preserve the anonymity of the organizations involved. Having such exacting texts would normally help in this kind of analysis, but when such texts cannot be used and the author is a primary source, the analysis can still be useful. Moreover, this study is formative, using an experiential approach to apply Foucault's investigative strategies to public relations and call for more purely Foucauldian study of larger patterns of public relations discourse.

Second, the case focuses on one public relations project and not a whole campaign or an extended period of organizational history. Because of the nature of this chapter and the limited space in which the argument can be addressed, a single project is sufficient to show how Foucault's methods work in a particular situation so that those methods may be properly and creatively applied to other situations on their own terms. After all, there's nothing so useful as generalities with grounding in the particular.

On balance, the case and the Foucauldian analysis of it reveal important dimensions retrospectively about public relations practice, especially about decision making, discourse development, and effects. Indeed, these areas can be fruitfully pursued for proactive public relations planning. Most important, Foucault gives methods for asking particular questions in three vital areas—archaeology, genealogy, and ethics—that go beyond the basic research practitioners normally would do. This understanding is the substance of this chapter's next and final section.

WHAT NEXT, PROACTIVELY SPEAKING?

One thing is certain about how Foucault's ideas have been used in the literature: It has all been retrospective applications to cases and situations that already occurred. So what do we learn in general from applying Foucault to public relations? How can his methods of archaeology, genealogy, and ethics be used in strategic public relations planning? Plus, what further applications of a Foucauldian approach to public relations could be pursued? This section briefly answers these questions to lay the groundwork for extensions of this approach in the future.

Lessons Learned about Public Relations through Foucault

Key to the application of Foucault to public relations is the bridging of his theory with practice. The goal of this investigation has been to understand how knowledge and power converge within and are applied by public relations in industry. What we gain from an application of Foucault's methods is a way to look at business processes/practices, in this case public relations, so that we might improve them. The case employed here, although focused on the development process of Aja Group's report about Gaucho Software and its flagship product, relied on the interaction of multiple discourses among the parties involved. The nature of Aja's report reflected, ultimately, the overall patterns of knowledge about Gaucho, the market in terms of customers and competitors, and value for those buying this kind of software. Notice that the discourse included not only that enacted by Gaucho, but also Aja's own and others' discourse (e.g., news reports, competitors' product information, industry, market and economic data). Because of the wide range of discourse about these dimensions, the final report enacted a new version of them. The report functioned within degrees of power over its content (primarily between Gaucho and Aja) and across layers of power among Gaucho, Aja, customers, shareholders, competitors, and so on. Indeed, the report was meant to strengthen the power relationships between Gaucho Software and its stakeholders, and did so; in a secondary way, the report served to bolster the relationship between Gaucho and Aja. The report also helped relationships between Aja Group and potential clients.

For public relations' sake, the report project solidified the department's place as a curator of corporate discourse and a key participant of corporate discursive practices. Indeed with Foucault we can even investigate how much public relations contributes to corporate discursive practices, thereby quantifying why public relations is or is not at the table with the rest of management (e.g., D'Aprix, 1997; Jensen, 1995; Shaffer, 1997).

Thus, we can see how organizations are a function of their discursive practices, which contribute to and perpetuate particular discursive formations—corporate epistemes—that guide the business. Public relations is a pivotal part of corporate epistemes, as corporate discourse drives practitioners in their work (not the other way around) on behalf of their companies. Foucault gives us a way of gauging the extent to which public relations contributes to those corporate epistemes. The intersection of knowledge and power is based on discourse and found in the ethical relationships between public relations professionals and internal and external stakeholders.

Organizations participate in discursive practices with others, ranging from stakeholder groups to society itself. A general, broad-based episteme, governed by certain discursive practices, drives the larger social milieu during a period in history. When discursive practices change, a new episteme emerges. The constituent parts of the social milieu enact the episteme through discursive practices that are particularly germane to it. The broad episteme for society would feature discursive practices about all things, but a company, for example, in a particular industry serving specific customers in a given part of the world, would enact discursive practices that help it do its business and not other practices. The broader episteme allows for specialization in groups, which explains how discursive practices in a given business are different from (yet similar to) those in other areas, like religions, politics, art, healthcare, education, and so on.

A Foucauldian analysis of public relations also reveals how texts function. Public relations texts grow out of discursive practices, which are based on the corporate episteme and the larger social episteme that exists at the time. The texts preserve the extant knowledge about and arguments for a company in all respects and serve to bridge relationships with stakeholders. The relations between an organization and its publics and stakeholders make up a power structure that goes both ways between them and fuels discursive action. The discourse enacted by both sides exhibit ethical dimensions that lie at the intersection between knowledge and power. The power relations, bounded by ethical substance, modes of subjection, self-discipline, and *telos*, reveal how public relations enables organizations and audiences to converge discursively and epistemically (in a Foucauldian sense). Stakeholders use public relations texts in ways that are consistent with the discursive practices with which they identify. If a public relations text fits their worldview, attitude, and expectations (both formal and content-related), they may act on it favorably; if not, action may be unfavorable or unlikely. Public relations discourse, then, is influential and may seek to inspire cooperation dictated by corporate discursive patterns. Audiences' willingness to assent, dissent, or exhibit passivity are the possible resulting attitudes, and supportive, opposing, or inactive actions would follow respectively.

Looking Back and Looking Forward

Retrospective learning from past examples is important. It provides details about what happened, why it happened, how successful (or not) the effort was, what could have been done better, and how can these lessons help us in the next situation. These basic issues are key to any post mortem for any project, and they should be applied in every instance of public relations action. Indeed, the Foucauldian method demonstrated in this chapter can be an effective means for discovering the strengths, weaknesses, and improvement opportunities for any public relations project, campaign, or department. For example, Aja Group's report about Gaucho Software's flagship product was strong on its argument about the software's capabilities and value plus strong in its appeal to customers, weak on addressing the product's place in the market, and in need of improvement about how the company would go about obtaining similar reports in the future from any credible source and not one that offers pay-as-you-go reports. The span of discursive action to be investigated would widen or narrow from this chapter's case. A Foucauldian approach to public relations shows that the nature of knowledge about the state of an organization and its needs is constrained by previous discourses, and that understanding helps us realize that the research and action phases of the RACE (Research, Action, Communication, and Evaluation) model are intertwined. For example, Aja Group's report about Gaucho Software's product was built on the statements of preexisting discourse about the software company, its products, the market, the industry, the economy, analysis firm reporting, and other dimensions. That field of discourse made up the research base for the project and, at the same time, inspired the actors in the project to work together and enact spoken and written discourse in particular ways that resulted in a specific document governed by particular discursive rules.

Foucault's investigative strategies would work well when looking forward to future public relations action. Using them is fundamentally a matter of perspective, of framing the problem about what to do next. Foucault's methods can be restated in the future tense, and any discursive action, power-knowledge relationships, and ethical matters can be effectively defined in advance accordingly. Foucault (1969/1972) would call such analysis a "grid" or "map" because such visualizations of relationships among discourse, knowledge, power, and the self are all interrelated and instructive about what goes with what and why. So a Foucauldian strategic public relations plan might look like a large spreadsheet or grid, or it could take the form of a traditional report format.

Whether a grid or a traditional report design is used, a plan must include a statement about what situation an organization faces and the public relations opportunity that exists. The factors of audience(s), objectives, goals, key messages, strategies, tactics, timing, costs, and measurements would be addressed when applying Foucault's three investigative strategies. Table 10.1 shows the primary areas in Foucault's methods where traditional public relations planning factors fall. In reality, all areas are covered in all three methods to some degree, but as long as there is a need to pinpoint a methodological dimension wherein an single plan factor applies primarily, the table shows it.

Notice that, as the case bears out, some factors are covered more than once, and that is valuable because the discursive, power, and self-reflective relationships become more apparent and, therefore, can be more effectively managed. The archaeological dimension of a public relations plan covers all traditional plan factors because the focus of the archaeological realm to public relations is on the formation and practices of discourse within the context of a corporate episteme. From the initial thinking about a public relations situation, through plan development, to tactical execution and success measurement, practitioners actions are guided by the discourse of their time—from within their organization and without, including the profession itself—to do what is right and effective. The genealogical dimension of the plan covers selected areas of audience, key messages, and tactics because the focus of the genealogical realm of public relations concerns power relationships primarily among those factors involved in the discursive action and the knowledge shared between an organization and its audiences. Practitioners formally document how power is an inherent part of their work as they play a role in maintaining cooperative relationships between their organizations and publics/stakeholders. The ethical dimension of the plan covers all but one public relations plan factor (i.e., audience), and that is because the ethical realm focuses primarily on the organization's self's relation to itself; all other factors apply because the organization is responsible for its public relations actions. (The public relations function is also responsible for itself.) The organization's (and the public relations function's) actions would be defined primarily in terms of its own moral code, but that code is discursively linked to the moral codes of business that would include laws, professional associations (e.g., Public Relations Society of America, American Management Association, American Institute of Certified Public Accountants, etc.), and society—which especially includes the moral influence of stakeholders.

When it comes to writing a public relations plan, a traditional or alternative format based on Table 10.1 can be used. In a traditional report format, there would be three major sections, one for each method, and four subsections for each of the questions that need answering—paying attention to the usual factors of a public relations plan as shown in Table 10.1. For a grid layout, things are more complicated but still useful. Table 10.2 is an alternative, ready-to-use plan grid or "template" that shows pragmatically how to apply Foucault's three investigative strategies illustrated in Table 10.1 directly to public relations. As Table 10.2 shows, each of the three methods would be listed in the left-most column, with each of their respective aspects and their questions listed in the next two columns. (The questions in column three of the grid are the same as those that would be answered in a traditional report format.) Along the top row would be column heads for specific public relations functions needed for a given project or campaign (e.g., media relations, community relations, investor relations, event planning, website, etc.). Other organizational areas, like advertising, product development, and so on could be added. The cells intersecting between the columns and rows would require answers to the questions listed under each method to which it applied. Note that the column widths would be much larger than those in the table to accommodate the necessary detail. Specific aspects of Table 10.1 are accounted for in Table 10.2. For example, timing, budget, and effectiveness measures are covered in the strategy dimension of archaeology and the self-discipline dimension of ethics. Only the matters of audience, key messages, and tactics are covered in genealogy.

In either a traditional report or a grid a final category would be appended that holistically summarizes things for the department, project, or campaign, especially concerning outcomes as they relate to the formation of discourse, power-knowledge dynamics, and the organization's relationship to itself. Attending to all three methods covers all interests of all publics and stakeholders, thereby providing a map for managing things and making sure things come out as anticipated. And if they do not, there would be a sense of what could be done to mitigate any anomalies.

A Foucauldian approach can be especially helpful in emergency situations, like an organizational crisis, issue, or natural disaster.[4] To the extent that these situations can be anticipated, a grid for public relations action can be prepared. Perhaps the most important thing that a Foucauldian public relations plan can do is to map power-knowledge relationships so that any discursive action can be properly and effectively focused. If a grid design were used for an emergency communications plan, it would be laid out similar to the one described earlier, but its columns would be the individual areas for handling a given emergency situation, including contact names. General grids could be prepared in advance for crises, issues, and disasters; and individual maps could supplement the general ones for particular situations that might emerge for an organization.

TABLE 10.1. Traditional Public Relations Plan Factors Applied to Foucault's Methods.

	AUDIENCE(S)	OBJECTIVES	GOALS	KEY MESSAGES	STRATEGIES	TACTICS	TIMING	COSTS	MEASURE-MENTS
Archaeology	X	X	X	X	X	X	X	X	X
Genealogy	X			X		X			
Ethics		X	X	X	X	X	X	X	X

TABLE 10.2. Template Grid for a Foucauldian Public Relations Plan.

			Media Relations	Community Relations	Investor Relations	Event Planning	Web-Site	Adver-tising	Product Development
		What is the PR opportunity, why, and what rules guide us in making it work?							
ARCHAEOLOGY	Object	Who decides what will be done and how it will be used?							
		How can we ensure our discourse upholds those rules?							
	Enunciative Modalities	Who will be the spokesperson/author?							
		What will be the specific text(s) he/she will use?							
		How is the speaker/author related to the PR opportunity?							
	Concepts	How do statements build from one to the next within our texts?							
		What is the relationship between the PR texts we create and those that already exist that relate to our opportunity?							
		How shall we apply texts from other fields to our opportunity?							
	Strategy	What consistencies and inconsistencies are present in any text we use and create? Why?							
		Why are certain decisions made about the texts we would create and would not create? What decisions are needed for timing, budget, and measurement?							
		How are our texts authoritative when compared to others like them?							

TABLE 10.2. Template Grid for a Foucauldian Public Rrelations Plan. *(continued)*

			Media Relations	Community Relations	Investor Relations	Event Planning	Web-Site	Adver-tising	Product Development
GENEALOGY	Power Effects	What can we achieve through our PR opportunity (from strategies to tactics and key messages) with our public(s)?							
	Power Relationship to Project	How does the PR opportunity allow us to apply power to our internal and external publics?							
	Power Relationship Network	What are the power relationships between the company and its external public(s)? What are the power relationships between PR and relevant areas of the business for this project?							
	Power Analysis from Public(s) View	What mechanisms exist for our public(s) to apply power to our company? What mechanisms exist for relevant business areas to apply power to PR?							

TABLE 10.2. Template Grid for a Foucauldian Public Relations Plan. *(continued)*

			Media Relations	Community Relations	Investor Relations	Event Planning	Web-Site	Adver-tising	Product Development
	Substance	What is it that makes us who we are as a company? As PR professionals?							
	Mode of Subjection	What grounds do we use to recognize moral obligations?							
ETHICS	Self discipline	How can we become better moral agents as a company and as PR professionals? How can we make the best project within the time frame, budget, and effectiveness measures?							
	Telos	What is the ideal state for our company and our PR group that can be realized through ethical behavior? How do we realize that ideal?							

Future Opportunities and Concluding Thoughts

A viable opportunity exists now to enact more Foucauldian investigations of public relations, both retrospectively and prospectively. In terms of retrospective work, scholars may employ this chapter's approach to cases of past public relations action to determine the approach's efficacy. Such work could be done in cooperation with practitioners to determine how well things worked, or not. For example, a study could be undertaken to discuss how an organization's particular public relations situation developed over time and how the relationships among the parties involved reveal the locus of public relations' power among them. In terms of prospective work, scholars and practitioners (together or separately) could apply the approach covered in this chapter, especially that for planning, to real future projects, plans, and programs (i.e., departments/organizational functions). Here, too, the purpose would be to test the planning method and template described earlier for its efficacy.

Other opportunities for future research would involve greater application of Foucault's ideas. As mentioned earlier in this chapter, not all aspects of his methods were used, and it is likely that the things that were not employed can be just as valuable or more so in additional investigations of public relations. For example, a focused study on organizational ethics (in Foucault's sense of the term) and public relations would more definitively locate the intersection of power and knowledge in the discursive practices of modern organizations. Foucault's method can also be used to understand the interrelationships among organization, stakeholders, media/media coverage, and past messages that are the pith and marrow of public relations research as well as planning. The important objective of this chapter has been to fill a gap in the literature that has not used Foucault exclusively and methodically to investigate public relations, especially as a way to plan public relations action.

Foucault (1977) once said, "It seems to me that the formation of discourses and the genealogy of knowledge need to be analysed [sic], not in terms of types of consciousness, modes of perception and forms of ideology, but in terms of tactics and strategies of power" (p. 77). Analysis works both ways: retrospectively on past discursive action and prospectively for future discursive action. Public relations clearly plays a critical role in the formation of discourse and corporate epistemes; the understanding of power-knowledge relationships among organizations, publics, and discourse; and the realization of organizations' selves in relation to themselves. Taken together, these three realms account well for public relations action and can serve as a management approach for success.

NOTES

1. Foucault turned away from his investigative strategy of archaeology and toward genealogy because he felt that the latter strategy gave him greater flexibility in investigating "the mutual relations between systems of truth and modalities of power" (Davidson, 1986, p. 224; cf. Dreyfus & Rabinow, 1983, p. 79-103) rather than investigating the individual rules for discursive production and transformation (Foss, Foss, & Trapp, 2002). Interestingly, rhetoric scholars still find archaeology a useful tool for analysis (e.g., Brock, Scott, & Chesebro, 1990; Foss, Foss, & Trapp, 2002) because, in large part, it allows critics to focus on microscopic matters of discourse and then balance that with the macroscopic issues of discourse, knowledge, and power possible through genealogy.
2. Ethics is the least developed of Foucault's investigative strategies; it is introduced in *The History of Human Sexuality: An Introduction* (Foucault, 1976/1990) and addressed in published interviews (cf. Foucault, 1989/1996). Further development of Foucault's ethics has been carried on by scholars after his untimely death in 1984, including a relatively new volume of his writings on the subject (Foucault, 1994).
3. The reason that only one of the two analysts was cited as the report's author was that, although both analysts were veterans, the one cited was fairly new on Aja Group staff and the decision was made at their firm that he would be the sole author to help boost his visibility. This decision has interesting implications, but I do not pursue them in this chapter so that I can maintain focus on my core argument. I continue to use the term "authors" when talking about the duo of analysts who wrote the report.
4. A comparison of the public relations plan I laid out here to plans recommended in the crisis and issue management literature would be interesting. Such a comparison, however, would require more depth and, perhaps, empirical testing than can be accommodated here.

REFERENCES

Barker, J. R., & Cheney, G. (1994). The concept and the practices of discipline in contemporary organizational life. *Communication Monographs, 61*, 19-43.

Bernauer, J. W., & Mahon, M. (1994). The ethics of Michel Foucault. In G. Gutting (Ed.), *The Cambridge companion to Foucault* (pp. 141-158). New York: Cambridge University Press.

Bevir, M. (1999). Foucault, power, and institutions. *Political Studies, 47*, 345-359.

Brock, B. L., Scott, R. L., & Chesebro, J. W. (1990). *Methods of rhetorical criticism: A twentieth-century approach*. Detroit: Wayne State University Press.

Burrell, G. (1988). Modernism, post modernism and organizational analysis 2: The contribution of Michel Foucault. *Organization Studies, 9*, 221-235.

Chay-Nemeth, C. (2001). Revisiting publics: A critical archaeology of publics in the Thai HIV/AIDS issue. *Journal of Public Relations Research, 13*, 127-161.

Curtain, P. A. & Gaither, T. K. (2005). Privileging identity, difference, and power: The circuit of culture as a basis for public relations theory. *Journal of Public Relations Research, 17*, 91-115.

Cutlip, S. M. (1995). *Public relations history: From the 17th century to the 20th century, the antecedents*. Hillside, NJ: Erlbaum.

D'Aprix, R. (1997). Partner or perish: A new vision for staff professionals. *Strategic Communication Management, 1*(3), 12 15.

Davidson, A. I. (1986). Archaeology, genealogy, ethics. In D. C. Hoy (Ed.), *Foucault: A critical reader* (pp. 221-233). Oxford, England: Basil Blackwell.

Dixon, M. A. (2004). Silencing the lambs: The Catholic Church's response to the 2002 sexual abuse scandal. *Journal of Communication and Religion, 27*, 63-86.

Dreyfus, H. L., & Rabinow, P. (1983). *Michel Foucault: Beyond structuralism and hermeneutics* (2nd ed.). Chicago: University of Chicago Press.

Foss, S. K., Foss, K. A., & Trapp, R. (2002). *Contemporary perspectives on rhetoric* (3rd ed.). Prospect Heights, IL: Waveland Press.

Foucault, M. (1972). *The archaeology of knowledge and the discourse on language* (A. M. S. Smith, Trans.). New York: Pantheon Books. (Original work published 1969)

Foucault, M. (1977). *Power/knowledge: Selected interviews and other writings, 1972-1977* (C. Gordon, Ed.). New York: Pantheon Books.

Foucault, M. (1980). *Language, counter-memory, practice: Selected essays and interviews by Michel Foucault* (D. F. Bouchard, Ed.). Ithaca, NY: Cornell University Press. (Original work published 1977)

Foucault, M. (1990). *The history of sexuality: An introduction* (Vol. 1) (R. Hurley, Trans.). New York: Vintage Books. (Original work published 1976)

Foucault, M. (1994). *Michel Foucault: Ethics: Subjectivity and truth* (Vol. 1) (P. Rabinow, Ed., R. Hurley, Trans.). New York: The New Press.

Foucault, M. (1996). *Foucault live: Collected interviews, 1961-1984* (S. Lotringer, Ed., L. Hochroth & J. Johnston, Trans.). New York: Semiotext(e). (Original work published 1989)

Hardy, C., & Phillips, N. (2004). Discourse and power. In D. Grant, C. Hardy, C. Oswick, & L. Putnam (Eds.), *The Sage handbook of organizational discourse* (pp. 299-316). Thousand Oaks, CA: Sage.

Holtzhausen, D. R. (2000). Postmodern values in public relations. *Journal of Public Relations Research, 12*, 93-114.

Holtzhausen, D. R. (2002). Towards a postmodern research agenda for public relations. *Public Relations Review, 28*, 251-264.

Holtzhausen, D. R., & Voto, R. (2002). Resistance from the margins: The postmodern public relations practitioner as organizational activist. *Journal of Public Relations Research, 14*, 57-84.

Jensen, B. (1995). Are we necessary? The case for dismantling corporate communication. *Communication World, 12*(7), 14-18, 30.

Knights, D., & Morgan, G. (1991). Corporate strategy, organizations, and subjectivity: A critique. *Organization Studies, 12*, 251-273.

Livesey, S. M., (2002). Global warming wars: Rhetorical and discourse analytic approaches to ExxonMobil's corporate public relations. *Journal of Business Communication, 39*, 117-148.

McKinlay, A., & Starkey, K. (Eds.). (1998). *Foucault, management and organization theory: From panopticon to technologies of self*. Thousand Oaks, CA: Sage.

Motion, J., & Weaver, C. K. (2005). A discourse perspective for critical public relations research: Life Sciences Network and the battle for truth. *Journal of Public Relations Research, 17*, 49-67.

Mumby, D. K., & Stohl, C. (1991). Power and discourse in organization studies: Absence and the dialectic of control. *Discourse and Society, 2*, 313-332.

Shaffer, J. (1997, May). Reinventing communication: A road to improving organizational performance. *Internal Communication Focus*, pp. 2-7.

Smudde, P. M. (2004). Implications on the practice and study of Kenneth Burke's "public relations counsel with a heart." *Communication Quarterly, 52*, 420-432.

Townley, B. (1993). Foucault, power/knowledge, and its relevance for human resource management. *Academy of Management Review, 18*, 518-545.

chapter 11

Science News as Public Relations Power for Universities

Katherine E. Rowan

Teresa Mannix

Timothy Gibson

Troy A. Bogino

William G. Malone

Universities, in particular public universities, play a crucial role in democratic societies. The ideal of "the university," although never quite realized in practice, is nonetheless a powerful one. The University of Washington's (2001) mission statement effectively captures the important role played by universities. The university is an independent institution dedicated to "the preservation, advancement, and dissemination of knowledge." Knowledge is preserved in university "libraries and collections, its courses, and the scholarship of its faculty." Knowledge is advanced through "many forms of research, inquiry and discussion, [which is] disseminated through the classroom and the laboratory, scholarly exchanges, creative practice, international education, and public service."

It is this last function of the university—the dissemination of knowledge—that is the subject of this chapter. For knowledge to play a role in the formation of scientific, industrial, or social policy, it must be disseminated.

To have relevance, new research must enter at some point into wider public discussion. As many scholars have learned, simply publishing one's work in a peer reviewed journal—and watching it sit unread on a dusty shelf—is most likely an insufficient and ineffective medium for contributing to wider social, political, and scientific debates.

In this regard, one important—but sometimes overlooked—mechanism for disseminating knowledge and creating a public discussion about research is through the university public relations office. Decisions made by public relations staff play a key role in determining the kinds of research that find their way to wider audiences. University public relations officers are in this way important guardians of the public trust that universities will act as an independent forum for the production and distribution of knowledge, a forum sheltered from the influence of status, money, and power.

But how do university public relations professionals go about the daily business of disseminating new knowledge to wider publics? What criteria do they draw on to decide "worthy" from "unworthy" knowledge? In what ways, if at all, are their decisions subject to the influence of financial and social power, both inside and outside the university? This study is an attempt to investigate these questions and the larger role of social power in the dissemination of research knowledge.

GROUNDING IN THE "PUBLIC SPHERE"

In exploring these questions, we draw on the work of Habermas (1962/1989), particularly his concepts of "public sphere" and the "ideal speech situation." As Peters (1993) explained, Habermas' concept of public sphere actually condenses two distinct senses of public—"the public" as an aggregate of individuals that excludes no one a priori and "public" as publicity or openness (as opposed to "private" or "privacy"). In this sense, the public sphere refers to those moments when sovereign citizens gather together to discuss and intervene within matters of common concern—the affairs of state, the regulation of community life, the workings of key nodes of social power. The public's ability to do so, of course, rests on institutions dedicated to communicating the affairs of the state and other social institutions. The crucial roles of dissemination and public relations thus lie at the heart of public sphere theory and its view of democratic practice.

Importantly, for Habermas (1962/1989) the public sphere is conceived as a forum that is, in spatial and social terms, set aside from both the private sphere (the realm of family and the marketplace) and the state (the seat of political authority). The public sphere thus acts as a gathering place for otherwise private citizens where they can collectively observe, discuss, and influence governments and other institutions of social power. For Habermas, it is the independence of the public sphere—its institutional separation from both the economic power of the marketplace and the political power of the state—that allows it to act as an open forum for civic discussion and debate where public opinion can be formed on the basis of critical reason, independent of influence of economic or political interests.

Drawing on Habermas, it is our view that university public relations professionals should understand their role as cocreators—along with researchers, institutional funding sources, journalists, and the wider public itself—of a particular "public sphere" (i.e., of a particular public conversation about the production, evaluation, and dissemination of knowledge). In this conversation the focus of debate is not merely "What should we do?" in terms of social or economic policy, but it is more fundamentally, "What is truth?" For example, are genetically modified organisms harmful to the planet's ecology? Is the process of climate change spurred on by human energy consumption? Will a certain drug help those suffering depression?

The answers to these kinds of questions depend, according to public sphere theory, on a rational-critical-ethical debate. As Habermas would argue, this debate should be open to all and its outcome should be determined by the force of the best evidence and argument rather than the force of social status or economic power. A situation in which the "force of the better argument" is the dominant force, trumping all other forces such as the desire for social status and money—this is what Habermas (1962/1989, 1998) means by the "ideal speech situation" (Burleson & Kline, 1979; Ritzer, 1996).

RESEARCH ABOUT UNIVERSITY PUBLIC RELATIONS

Poised as they are on the boundary between the university and the wider public, university communicators play a crucial role in nurturing this open, critical, public discussion about scholarly research. Their decisions to publicize or not to publicize particular forms of knowledge help determine the form and shape of the public discussion of scholarly ideas. For this reason it is important to scrutinize the professional practice of university public relations staff, including especially the criteria used to determine what research findings are fit for public consumption and how independent such decisions are from the influence of internal and external sources of power.

This chapter describes how research findings become part of university public relations. It also investigates the extent to which university public relations practice is subject to pressures from university administrators, external funding sources (from both industry and the state), and outside interest groups. Finally, after exploring the professional norms and practices of university public relations staff through two empirical studies, our conclusion explores how Habermas' notion of "ideal speech"—the regulative norms that he suggests are embedded in ordinary discourse and should inform the conduct of dialogue within any democratic public sphere—can help public relations professionals work within the social power relations between their institutions and their constituents to create the conditions for an open, critical, and public discussion about university research.

Before presenting our own findings, we discuss (a) the reasons why many organizations pay for and publicize research, (b) traditional standards used to decide what research to showcase to wide audiences, and (c) how such decisions may be inappropriately influenced. Once this background information is provided, we present data from two studies and then discuss ways in which Habermas' concept of "ideal speech" can function as a regulative ideal for university public relations experts. Regulative ideals are conditions that Habermas says humans can never fully achieve, but by striving for them, they come closer to their enactment (Burleson & Kline, 1979; Habermas, 1962/1989).

Why Organizations Want to Conduct and Share Research with the Public

As noted earlier, most universities view the production and distribution of research as one of their core missions. The production of knowledge, however, comes with a price. Accordingly, most universities try hard to secure funding for research but also to maintain independence from inappropriate influence or power exerted by funding groups. Unfortunately, maintaining a reputation for careful, independent research is challenging. In the last 25 years, state funding for public universities in the United States has dropped at least 10% across the nation whereas costs for running universities have risen (Lee & Clery, 2004). The drop has occurred because supporting public higher education is a discretionary cost for the states, and expenses in some mandatory areas, such as Medicaid and prisons, have risen. The decrease in state support has meant that universities have had to become creative in thinking about ways to raise funds.

The benefit of this creativity is that universities are finding new ways to be entrepreneurial and save taxpayer money. The risk is that when research universities are focused on raising funds, they may become too concerned about increasing revenues and not sufficiently concerned about the quality and independence of the research they generate. It is possible their criteria for showcasing scholarly work may be tainted by the desire to please some potential donor.

In the United States, the federal government is by far the largest funding source for university research. According to Machen and Shackelford (2003), federal funding to universities for research totaled $19.2 billion in 2001, an amount that constituted 59% of all such funding. The other two major contributors were state and local governments, which contributed 7% of all dollars, and private industry, which also contributed approximately 7%. Indeed, leaders in academe have actively sought other sources of revenue to run higher education institutions over the last 10 years because they felt they had "no alternative but to seek new revenue elsewhere" as state governments provided state institutions with less funding but gave them more autonomy (Newman, Couturier, & Scurry, 2004, p. 41). These figures mean that 66% of the research and development dollars universities receive comes from U.S. taxpayers or other sources, including private ones.

However, in some fields the ratio of private to government funding has changed dramatically in the last several decades. For example, according to the National Center for Public Policy and Higher Education, "Private spending for food and agricultural research tripled between 1960 and the 1990s, while federal and state support declined. By the 1990s, support for such studies had dropped to less than two percent of the annual federal research budget" (Irving, 1999, p. 8). This funding landscape means that federal research dollars given to particular kinds of universities, such as land-grant universities, which focus on agricultural and engineering research, have been declining in some fields.

The Mission of Land-Grant Universities

Certain universities in the United States are specifically chartered to engage in activities that support agricultural and engineering activities. These are called "land-grant" universities, and there is at least one in every state except Rhode Island. Land-grant universities were created when President Abraham Lincoln signed the first Morrill Act in 1862. Zimdahl's (2003) analysis of 49 land-grant university mission statements showed that, although worded differently, all describe their mission as being one of education, research, and service. Specific phrases used in the mission statements of these agricultural, engineering, and natural resource programs say that they will provide learning and education, serve the needs of people, serve societal goals, and provide research on the environment and natural resources, drawing from science to do so.

Despite these common phrases, mission statements are interpreted differently. Some administrators believe that all universities must seek alliances and partnerships with groups that can provide funding. For example, David Ward (2002), president of the American Council on Education, the major coordinating body for all United States higher education institutions, wrote,

"As institutions promote their individuality and autonomy, they will also need to enter into a wide array of partnerships and strategic alliances to maximize effectiveness and quality." Ward's view translates for many university administrators into a focus on securing increased funding through aggressive marketing of academic programs, increases in tuition, and encouragement of faculty research that will bring in grant dollars. In this view, strategic partnerships with government or corporate groups that will yield funds for the university are desirable.

A contrasting view is offered by Carey (2000), who argued that it is the essence of the university tradition to defend itself against the encroachment of power. By this he means that universities have historically played an important role as independent institutions dedicated to the production and dissemination of knowledge. In the past, institutional practices were established that blunted the ability of powerful interests (e.g., the state, industry, the church) from shaping the direction of scientific and humanistic research and discourse. These institutional practices include the faculty tenure system, academic freedom policies, and the tradition of "arms length" relationships between the legislature and the day-to-day operations of the institution. Although criticized as the "ivory tower," the university has played an important role in nurturing a dialogue that strives to resemble Habermas' ideal speech situation. Carey (2000) wanted to see this tradition of independence preserved in light of recent encroachments from industry, particularly from efforts to appropriate universities' reputations for independence while at the same time using funding to shape the kinds of knowledge produced within the university.

WHAT CONDITIONS FOSTER THE BEST COMMUNICATION OF THE BEST RESEARCH?

University communicators face a wide variety of opportunities to announce news of research findings from anywhere in their institutions. Deciding what to do and how is a critical step in making the most of the news for both the university and the scholars who did the work. University communicators tend to use two sets of criteria to help them decide how to publicize research: traditional criteria and implicit, or "gray area," criteria.

Traditional Criteria

University communicators use at least four explicit, traditional criteria for deciding how to share research news. These criteria or values assess research quality, understandability, newsworthiness, and availability. One cannot share research news if there is no research being conducted or if those doing research are not cooperative.

Quality. First, university communicators cannot be expert in all topics studied at their universities. To assess the quality of a professor's research, they learn whether this work has survived a process known as scholarly, peer, or blind review. Peer review involves colleagues with appropriate expertise reading and judging manuscripts to decide if they are worthy of publication. As Frey, Botan, and Kreps (2000) explained, "Today, most scholarly journals use a blind-review process, whereby reviewers are not told the name or institutional affiliation of the person(s) who submitted the manuscript. The goal is to judge the work on its merits, not on the reputation or the institutional affiliation of the researchers" (p. 54).

Understandability. Second, research findings must be understandable to the university communicators promoting them, journalists reading their press releases, and to the public. Dunwoody (1986) found that, surprisingly, social scientific research is more likely to be written about in the mass media than is news from the natural and physical sciences. In part, this is because social scientific research findings are more likely to be understood and their relevance to readers appreciated by editors of wide-circulation outlets more than research in fields such as mathematics or physics. Unfortunately, it also means that there is little mass media coverage of the substantial research dollars being spent in fields such as physics and engineering.

Newsworthiness. Third, research must be newsworthy to be considered important enough to share with a larger audience. Determining what counts as news is one domain in which university public relations or media relations officers may wield influence over what university research the public learns about and what it does not. According to traditional criteria for determining newsworthiness, reporters and editors ask themselves whether a wide audience would find some set of research findings novel (new, distinctive), salient (i.e., having an effect on the intended audience), timely (recent), proximate (local), prominent (concerning prominent people), interesting, or conflict-ridden. Criteria like these are widely taught and used by many mass media outlets to select news stories for TV news programs, Internet news sites, newspapers, and magazines (e.g., Fedler, Bender, Davenport, & Drager, 2001). Information that meets some of these criteria is considered more likely to be of interest to a wide audience than information that does not.

Availability. Some researchers are very proactive in sending information about their research to university communicators for distribution to the mass media. Other faculty are more shy or less cooperative. Not surprisingly, those who communicate—and communicate well—are more likely to get publicity and, possibly, funding for their work.

Implicit Criteria and "Gray Area" Concerns

Beyond these widely shared criteria, there are several on which there is far less agreement. Three "gray area concerns" are: (a) whether the news itself poses a risk versus a benefit to the university, (b) the status of the research itself as emergent science or mainstream within a certain scientific community, and (c) conflicts of interest—whether public universities should be communicating research that could earn the researchers, as individuals, money. It is in these less widely agreed on matters that inappropriate exertions of power are more likely to occur.

Risk versus benefit to the university. Should university communicators ask prior to releasing news whether their communications would benefit or harm the university's ability to generate funds? Several years ago, the University of Vermont produced a guide to vegetarian eating as a way of helping its students, some of whom were vegetarian. In this case, the guide was not a product of basic research, but a service to a key stakeholder group: students who were vegetarian and needed to eat healthily. Communicators at the university thought the guide was important and widely useful, so they publicized its availability. Unfortunately, not everyone appreciated their efforts. The New England Dairy and Food Council criticized this move. It questioned why a land-grant university, chartered to promote state agriculture, was producing a document that seemed to work against the profitability of dairy farmers (University of Vermont employee, personal communication, May 1, 2000). This example illustrates the sort of scenario that university communicators might consider if they were to use the criterion of "risk versus benefit to the university" as a basis for deciding whether to disseminate news.

Emergent or mainstream science. Also unclear is the matter of whether research findings must be widely supported in an appropriate scientific community before they are shared with lay audiences. Dunwoody (1999) said that both professional communicators and the public need to understand the difference between emergent and consensus or mainstream science. *Emergent science* is a phrase she used to describe single, peer-reviewed studies that scientists view as competent but which have not yet stood the test of time. *Consensus science*, on the other hand, refers to a body of work that many in a particular field have replicated or begun to use as part of their own working knowledge. Trachtman (1989) offered a similar distinction between science information from a single study or two and science "knowledge"; he sees science knowledge as the science found in textbooks or what Kuhn (1970) called "paradigmatic" science.

Conflict of interest. One final criterion that university communicators may consider is whether those conducting the research will benefit financially if their findings are widely publicized and praised. Should university communicators use public funding to publicize research that might make private individuals wealthy? One survey found that scientists acknowledge a potential link between getting their names in the newspaper and getting research funds (Dunwoody & Ryan, 1985). Of course, one cannot do many kinds of research without funding. If research findings are useful, perhaps those who produced them should benefit financially. Explicit standards would help university communicators manage these questions.

Finally, and most disturbing, is the opposite situation in which industry seems to have used illegitimate force to prevent research news with direct impact on public health from being known. The pharmaceutical industry has violated federal law by failing to publicly disclose clinical trials when there was disappointing news concerning drug effectiveness (Vedantam, 2004). More widely recognized is the tobacco industry's deliberate concealment of cigarette smoking's health effects (cf. Chapter 4, this volume).

These last three criteria for selecting news to share with media and other stakeholder groups suggest contexts in which appropriate or inappropriate exercise of power is most likely to play a role in what research news the public does or does not get from universities. Consequently, we asked the following research questions:

RQ_1: What factors affect the likelihood that the public will read or hear about "emergent" scientific research that seems to benefit some stakeholders and harm others?

RQ_2: With whom do university communicators work?

RQ_3: What criteria do university communicators consider before releasing research findings to media or showcasing findings in news releases and other outlets?

RQ_4: What obstacles do university communicators face when releasing science news to mass media?

RQ_5: How do university communicators manage situations where research has been privately funded?

To explore the first research question, we used a case study. In Study 1 we took a microlevel or "narrow field of view" look at the ways in which audiences at four science communication conferences said they would handle public dissemination of a single scientific study conducted by scientists whose research is viewed as "emergent." The four research questions remaining were attempts to learn whether the results of the case study were anomalous or widespread, so in Study 2 we took a more macrolevel or "wide angle field of view" by conducting in-depth interviews with 12 writers and administrators at the nation's top 50 universities in terms of federal dollars given for research. The Human Subjects Review committee at the first author's university approved the study methods used here.

STUDY 1

The idea for Study 1 arose when the first author led several workshop and conference sessions with university communicators and science writers on the topic of risk communication (Rowan, 2000a, 2000b, 2000c, 2000d, 2001). To tailor these sessions to participants' needs, she sent an e-mailed survey to participants in two of the workshops, asking for descriptions of their communication challenges.

Method

Context and participants. The sampling method used was that of census: Each known conference participant was sent a survey. To the e-mailed questionnaire there were 23 responses from 70 possible respondents. Respondents included scientists in fields such as genetics and horticulture, university administrators, agricultural school deans, science writers, U. S. Department of Agriculture Cooperative Extension officials, and media relations officers working for agricultural schools. Responses dealt with an array of issues.

Concerns about role conflict in connection with communicating biotechnology research were prominent among the responses.[1] Consequently, the first author decided to focus the workshop content on participants' values associated with communicating agricultural biotechnology research news.

Assessment of responses to the e-mailed survey. Comments about challenges involved in communicating agricultural biotechnology research were categorized in three groups: those who (a) were uncertain about their roles, (b) were in favor of biotechnology, or (c) cast themselves as facilitators responsible for creating forums for discussion of agricultural biotechnology research and issues.

First, some science writers at land-grant institutions said they were uncertain about the roles they should play in communicating agricultural biotechnology. One individual said he felt uncomfortable being perceived as a "cheerleader" for GMOs or genetically modified organisms. On the other hand, he worried about inadvertently providing fuel for anti-GMO activists when writing about possible environmental harms that bioengineered crops could cause native plants. A university administrator asked, "Is it feasible to think that land-grant communicators can be objective in the GMO debate when much of the GMO research at the university is in partnership with industry?" Another wondered, "What do we mean when we say, 'Extension [i.e., university extension agents] provides unbiased, research-based information?'"

A second group of respondents said universities should promote the benefits of biotechnology. One person wrote, "We have already identified the growing opposition to technologies to increase the productive capacities of plants and animals and industrial processes." Another described her university's experiences with vandalism at agricultural biotechnology laboratories (cf. Spangler, 2001). The perspective of these survey respondents is presented in a University of Georgia research magazine in which two scientists wrote, "The future of our food supply may well be dependent upon who is most vocal and most convincing [about biotechnology]: protestors or scientists" (Parrott & Paterson, 2000, p. 38). A third group rejected the view that they had to be either objective about, or partisan concerning, biotechnology. These individuals said land-grant institutions have an obligation to create forums for careful consideration of any important scientific research. Among those wanting universities to be forums for discussion, there was uncertainty about how to manage such discussions. One person asked, "How do you avoid this 'us vs. them' mentality in communicating about GMOs?"

Using a single news release to elicit participants' values. A portion of each workshop and conference session was focused on discussion of a single, thought-provoking news release. This release reported results of a study funded by the U. S. Department of Agriculture. The study was published in the *Proceedings of the National Academy of Science*, a peer-reviewed and prestigious journal. The study found that releasing a transgenic fish into the wild could cause extinction in native populations (see Appendix A for the release).

In his news release about this research, Purdue University writer Chris Sigurdson presented Muir and Howard's (1999) findings in a clear and entertaining way. The text discusses mating in the animal world and likens some dimensions of animal sexuality to sexual attraction among humans. Further, the release explains that humans' notions about improving plants and animals may not always lead to good environmental outcomes. As it notes, humans are interested in enhancing animal features such as size, and enhancing species size or growth does not always enhance species' viability.

Results of Study 1

> RQ_1: What factors affect the likelihood that the public will read or hear about "emergent" scientific research that seems to benefit some stakeholders and harm others?

Audience members at the workshops and conferences had differing reactions to this release. These reactions can be categorized as (a) reluctance to disseminate this release because of fear of losing biotechnology funding, (b) reluctance to disseminate the release because of doubts about the quality of its science, or (c) praise for the release and the opportunity to discuss interesting research.

Reluctance to release because of fear of jeopardizing funding. At the Orlando, Florida, "Risk Communication Superworkshop," sponsored by the Agricultural Communicators in Education and the U.S. Department of Agriculture, one science writer said in one-on-one conversation with the first author that her dean would "never allow this story to be written." She explained that the dean was under pressure from scientists and corporations to promote research on biotechnology. Her perception was that the dean felt publicizing research on potential harms of agricultural biotechnology would be inconsistent with these promotional goals.

Reluctance to showcase this research because of doubts about research quality. Some scientists and science writers questioned the claims made by study authors Muir and Howard (1999). They doubted that the authors had supported their claim that introduction of a transgenic fish could lead to species extinction. Some audience members at the American Association for the Advancement of Science (AAAS) meeting session said the study conclusion rested on too many assumptions. They wondered whether results obtained in the confines of an aquarium in one study were sufficient grounds to support the study's conclusion. Essentially, they were saying that Muir and Howard's work was "emergent," not "consensus," science, and its accuracy and importance were still a matter of debate.

Enthusiasm for disseminating this release. Others supported dissemination of the release and the goal of publicizing research on both risks and benefits of agricultural biotechnology through mass media outlets. At the AAAS meeting, Susanna Hornig Priest, a science communication professor now at the University of South Carolina, said:

> People should distinguish between the short-term risk, that there's going to be a brouhaha in the public about the fish, and the long-term

> risk of eroding this trust that is crucial between the university and the public that mostly pays the bills of that university. . . .
>
> I think publicizing research about risks of biotechnology is the most pro-science, if not the most pro-biotech thing, longer term, that we can do. We are making an assumption that publicizing research that suggests a risk is anti-science or anti-biotechnology. I think from a communications point of view, that is absolutely wrong. That's the way to destroy this trust we are talking about. (Borchelt & Triese 2001; cf. Priest, 2000, 2001)

Sigurdson (2000), the author of the release, said that he viewed Muir and Howard's (1999) work as a good example of "science policing science," a statement Muir made in the release. That is, in Sigurdson's and Muir and Howard's view, scientists have an obligation to study biotechnology and call attention to both benefits and risks. Sigurdson recalled a comment by Paul Raeburn, former president of the National Association of Science Writers, who had talked about this release at the Orlando conference. Raeburn said that if the media think an institution "sat on" a legitimate story, that perception moves the story from page 20 to page 1. Failing to write a national news release about nationally funded research that unearths a surprising finding is dangerous to university credibility. Such a failure, Raeburn and Sigurdson said, could easily change the story from one about interesting research to a story about institutional efforts to "cover up" findings of interest to the public but detrimental to some funding group (C. Sigurdson, personal communication, May 11, 2000).

Interpretation. This narrowly focused look at one news release about one scientific study suggests that in some cases there may be legitimate and illegitimate reasons why federally funded research findings are not widely publicized. Specifically, the legitimate concerns had to do with whether the research was well conducted. To answer this question, one needs to see this single study in the context of dozens of other similar studies. That is, this study about transgenic fish and hazards associated with them needs to become, after dozens of years of research, less a product of "emergent" science and more a product of "consensus" science (i.e., if its findings are replicated).

The illegitimate reasons for not sharing this research have to do with fear that showcasing this research might cost a university private or even federal funding. Purposefully downplaying interesting research findings because they might upset a potential donor seems an obvious example of the illegitimate use of power. If this sort of decision making occurs, it is illegitimate because it focuses on the short-term goals of financial success for a single university division at the expense of the long-term goal of creating "an ideal speech situation" (Habermas, 1962/1989)—in which the university functions as a forum for open and careful consideration of intriguing findings by all interested publics.

To find out whether the "case of the transgenic fish" was anomalous or symptomatic of public relations practices and values at many universities, we conducted Study 2.

STUDY 2

In Study 2, we were interested in knowing how decisions about showcasing research are made at universities in general. Because universities receiving large federal research grants are the ones with the greatest responsibility to show they are using public funds well, we decided to interview university communication officers and administrators at the nation's Top-50 research universities as determined by Lombardi et al. (2003; cf. Bennof, 2003).

Method

The Lombardi Program ranks private and public universities according to criteria such as the amount of federal dollars obtained annually and the universities' endowment assets. The list includes private and public universities. Among the private universities included are Johns Hopkins, Harvard, Massachusetts Institute of Technology, Yale, Princeton, Stanford, and Emory. Among the public universities are the Universities of Michigan, Wisconsin, Washington, Illinois, and Minnesota, as well as the University of California, Berkeley, the University of North Carolina, Chapel Hill, and Texas A & M.

Participants and interview procedures. A list of senior individuals in media relations at the Lombardi Top-50 universities was developed. These individuals were contacted by e-mail and invited to participate in 40-minute telephone interviews with one of the investigators. Those individuals who did not respond were e-mailed again after 1 week. A research team comprised of graduate students interviewed 12 participants in 1 month. Each interviewee was asked to give him or herself a code name so that anonymity would be protected. Interviews lasted 40 minutes or longer and were conducted by telephone. Interviewers took extensive notes during the phone conversation and then transcribed their notes. Questions probed interviewees' backgrounds, individuals to whom they reported at work, professional memberships, relations with media, challenging situations, and crisis preparedness. Interview transcripts were read and re-read until recurring themes and illustrative statements were identified. This chapter reports answers to a subset of the questions posed.

The interview subjects were either directors or vice presidents of university media relations/communications departments or science writers. Each participant held a bachelor's degree, and seven of them had earned a master's degree. Their degrees were in a range of fields, some in communication, some in other humanities, and at least one in the natural sciences. Their length of time in their current position ranged from 2.5 years to 29, with most having worked in their current positions for about 5 years. The 12 interviewees all had some form of communication or media relations background prior to assuming their current positions in university communications. For example, "Dogwood" had worked in media relations for a medical institution. "Dale" had been the communication director for the mayor of a large midwest city, and "Library" had worked as a local business reporter.

Results of Study 2

Because power cannot be exerted if a stakeholder group is not consulted or represented in some way, we wondered with whom these individuals worked.

> RQ_2: With whom do university communicators work?

Several interview questions elicited information about the work environment for university communicators. Responses showed that these individuals are interacting with staff members in their communication offices, senior university administrators, and journalists. Seven respondents reported directly to a vice president, two reported to the university president, two reported to a program director, and one to a managing editor.

Most respondents discussed their ready access to high university officials and their rapport with journalists when asked why they were effective at their work. For example, Dogwood said:

> The most important part of my job in many ways is serving as a trusted go-between between reporters and administrators who, naturally, are frequently quite suspicious of each other. I view my job as being someone who helps bridge the gap and interpret and translate the institution for the public through the media.

Similarly, Alexander said, "I have tremendous access. We have an officers' meeting twice a week, and we can meet with the president whenever we want." Jamie's access seemed to be at a lower administrative level than Dogwood and Alexander's; however, she said,

> I seldom deal directly with the president, [but] my boss and his boss have ready access. The senior vice president is literally 50 feet away from the president. That's critically important, having the top communications individual involved early is important.

Another respondent noted that "not being overwhelmed by PhDs" helped him to be effective at his work, a comment that suggests he interacts with administrators and research scientists.

Another question that shed light on participants' interaction patterns dealt with perceptions of media as allies, adversaries, or somewhere in-between. Many felt that the media fell between ally and adversary. Library said, "You can't control them, but you have to use them." Jamie added, "I have to respect their independence. If they write a good story and I agree, it's natural [to be allies]. Sometimes they take an adversarial role."

Others answered that journalists were always allies. Mark said, "If a researcher needs funding, the media helps to obtain money from investment firms through the publicity. This line of thinking is pretty standard across the board." However, Mickey said:

> All of the above. We often think of the media as being an ally when we have a good story that they want to write on. They are adversaries when they don't put in what we want. The reality is that they have to do their job and as professionals it is important for us to give them both sides of the story.

RQ_3: What criteria do university communicators consider before releasing research findings to the mass media or showcasing these findings in news releases and other outlets?

A number of the respondents said that scientific research has to be peer reviewed, published in scholarly journals, or presented at national conferences before it can be released by their offices. Alexander, the media relations leader of his organization, said, "We have to make sure research is peer reviewed and/or published. All research is on a continuum—some research is not going to get published. It's challenging to massage egos." Several also talked about the review process for a news release before it is sent out. Usually, the key players involved (i.e., researchers, department chairs, supervisors) check the content for accurateness before the draft is final. Matt, a news officer, added, "We also have to take into consideration political reasons and make people higher up happy like administrators, donors, and chairs of departments." Mickey summarized the thoughts of many saying, "First of all, is it newsworthy? Second, who cares?"

Participants also discussed instances that caused them to be either more or less cautious about talking to journalists. According to Boris, he has learned to be more skeptical of the promises of research:

> We had one case where, before HIV had been identified, a researcher claimed to have discovered the problem causing AIDS and called the media. He had not done peer review. I published something saying we disowned him, etc. It falls under the venue of fairness. I'm more skeptical of people's claims than anyone on the outside. It's about building trust.

Similarly, Alex told a story about

> a genetically engineered mouse that was smarter than a regular mouse. It got a lot of play. I might have been more circumspect about explaining what a "smart mouse" is, more technically focused. A lot goes into being smart.

She said that the story made people think that researchers were closer to finding solutions to memory problems than was really the case. Dogwood said that experience in media relations has made him more comfortable with sharing research news:

> Not that I am less cautious, but I feel more comfortable in erring on the side of openness. Part of that comfort is understanding that there is a very high level of integrity in the people that I represent and just trusting them to tell me the whole story that I need to know.

RQ_4: What obstacles do university communicators face when releasing science news to mass media?

In responding to this question, some respondents emphasized their institutions' preference for openness in sharing research findings; others discussed internal politics as a source of power that squelched the release of news.

Several of the interviewees explained that disagreements were not about *whether* or not to publicize something, but rather *how* to do so. Dale said:

> There is no disagreement about the substance of a potential release. If we were doing research in an area that is controversial, we would not disagree about releasing that. We are a public institution, so we approach

> all of our information as public information. We are a conduit and liaison for how the university contributes to the state and region. We are transparent in how we do media relations.

In contrast, Yosemite has a problem spot in her organization:

> We lock horns with the [name omitted] committee. They have put the kaput on the news. It has to do with internal politics. One time there was a problem when a faculty member came to me and I wrote the release before talking to the division chair.

Jamie had an example of disagreement within his staff. "There was research that involved monkeys," he said.

> Some staff didn't want to portray the monkeys in the research setting. I thought it was okay to show a picture of the monkey, just not in the research area. The question was whether or not to show a photo at all. In that case, I decided it would be appropriate to show a picture of the researcher with the monkey. Others didn't like showing the animal. There were a very few objections from animal rights groups.

When asked about the biggest challenges they face in sharing research findings with wide audiences, interviewees said the most difficult part is relaying a complex idea to general audiences and encouraging editors to be interested in research. As Jamie said, "We must explain it clearly so that we don't use too much detail where we can lose the reader, or the media." He added that research that does not meet this standard is only published in scientific journals. "The overriding challenge is to convey the excitement of fundamental theoretical research," said Alex. "We just had one in quantum physics. [They found that the] quantum behavior of molecules can be controlled in a way previously not thought possible. The challenge is trying to describe something that has to do with quantum physics." Alexander said, "Our specialist on obesity is quoted like 10 times a day. Other science is really hard to get an outlet."

RQ_5: How do university communicators manage situations where research has been privately funded?

Responses to this question showed that this issue is a real one for universities, and criteria are emerging for its management. Library said that at his institution there are discussions about allowing commercial entities to use the name of the university. "We've asked for a policy definition; what's appropriate and what's not." For example, he said that university scientists are pressured by corporations to allow them to use the name of the university, so in their advertising they can say, "Big University says to take vitamin X." He continued, "Now as corporations downsize research and development, they look more at universities. Pharmaceutical companies are the worst—a lot of debate and negotiating. I see it as a growing issue. There's credibility and objectivity at risk."

Some respondents said universities have policies in place to prevent any conflict of interest in situations in which a private organization has paid university faculty to do research. Alexander says, "We're really conservative. Protocol is very rigid. I know that we have full control." Jamie added, "When we do corporate agreements, the wording says that the corporation has no say over what we publicize. In the funding of research, we are careful to maintain independence. . . . We refuse to connect our name with their marketing efforts." Although agreements may ensure that private companies do not control the message, private organizations still can have the right to review releases before they are distributed. As Alex said,

> [Private or corporate funding for research] can have some effect. It's just another group of people who want to review things. I don't think there's a change in how I report the story. I just have to show a draft to people.

DISCUSSION

The public relations power of universities may come in part from whether universities function as independent forums for discussion of important research. Across Studies 1 and 2, university communicators varied in their understanding of this power.

In Study 1 and Study 2, some respondents seemed to see themselves as news reporters who happened to work at universities. These respondents frequently invoked three criteria for assessing research news—peer review as a criterion for judging quality, newsworthiness, and understandability. It seemed that invoking explicit criteria such as "Is the work peer reviewed?" and "Is the work newsworthy?" helped them to select "stories" for dissemination that were likely to have wide appeal. These communicators had regard for the interests of the public, but they may not have a clear sense of the university as a distinct entity purposefully independent from outside powers so that its knowledge production work can benefit all. In contrast, others saw the sharing of all research findings as their role. As Dale said, "We are a public institution, so we approach all of our information as public information." For Dale, safeguarding the public's right to publicly funded research findings was important.

Unlike Dale, and the university communicators who saw themselves principally as journalists, there were other communicators who may put specialized interests ahead of the public good or may feel forced to do so. These individuals might be viewed as "institutional cheerleaders." For example, there was the communicator who confided that her dean would never allow her to disseminate findings that reflected negatively on agricultural biotechnology research. It is impossible to know whether her dean truly has this view, or whether this communicator's perceptions are needlessly preventing important research from being disseminated. Similarly, some communicators may be forced into the institutional cheerleader role if they either choose or feel forced to cover research news generated more to massage faculty egos than because the work being reported is truly important. In an era in which there are more and more industry-government-university partnerships, and in which universities need the funding from such partnerships to survive, it is understandable that many university public relations professionals would mainly want to make their bosses and key funding sources happy.

In contrast to those university communicators who saw themselves as journalists who happened to work at universities or those who were institutional cheerleaders, there was a third group who might be called champions of universities as open, public spheres in Habermas' (1962/1989) sense of that phrase. These individuals saw themselves as creating university communications that were separate from undue influence, but focused on providing new understanding of the world's very real problems. That is, these individuals seemed to articulate Habermas' sense of the legitimate power that universities should be enacting.

For example, Sigurdson's news release cast the transgenic fish story *not* as a story solely about biotechnology's possible harm to native fish populations but more broadly and more boldly as "science policing science." Sigurdson drew this notion from Muir and Howard (1999). In this case, both the university public relations professional, Sigurdson, and the scientists studying transgenic fish, were trying to present new understandings that they believed they had an obligation to share (although those findings may still turn out to be unsupported). Priest also articulated this vision in her comment that "publicizing research about risks of biotechnology is the most pro-science, if not the most pro-biotech thing, longer term, that we can do." In another context, "Library" indicated that he was aware of how much university independence and credibility could be threatened if universities gave their names to advertisers wishing endorsements such as "Big University says to take vitamin X." In these cases, individuals had a commitment to maintaining the openness and integrity of universities and science communication.

Of these three initial characterizations of university communicators—as journalists, institutional cheerleaders, or champions of the university as public sphere—it is the third role that would be most conducive to helping universities tap their fullest and most legitimate power. According to Habermas (1962/1989), although it is never fully achievable, human beings can begin to create the ideal speech situation by generating communication that is maximally understandable, truthful, sincere, and just. In future research, it would be interesting to learn what public relations professionals believe are the principal obstacles to achieving maximum understandability, truthfulness, sincerity, and justice in dissemination of university research news.

It would also be interesting to talk with university public relations officers about steps to increase universities' capacities to fulfill the conditions of the ideal speech situation. For example, to enact the conditions of ideal speech, a university news release about important new scientific findings might list websites where thought-provoking findings are presented that differ from those of a home institution's own scholars. This step might seem to work against a university in the short run, but eventually it should have the opposite effect of earning trust and respect (for more discussion and examples, cf. Rowan, 1999).

Still another vehicle for enhancing the justice of university science news would be to create advisory councils comprised of community members, retired faculty, students, alumni, and current faculty in philosophy, ethics, social science, and communication, particularly those who study science communication and public relations. These advisory councils could meet with university communicators on a periodic basis to listen to their challenges. Advisory councils might aid university communicators in managing situations in which scientists and university communicators find themselves at odds. Advisory councils could lend perspective in such situations and help articulate policies for the management of situations in which financial arrangements interfere with a university's interest in sharing research findings with the public.

Advisory councils might also function as the embodiments of "the public." In many of the comments made in Study 2, there seemed to be more discussion of what administrators or journalists thought than about what the public thought. There is no single entity that can represent "the public," but an advisory council might include individuals who can comment on the perspectives of principal stakeholders or key publics (McComas, 2003).

University public relations professionals do important and difficult work. To date, public relations scholars know relatively little about them. Scholars should learn more about the ways in which the issues discussed in this chapter are explored at conferences of, for example, the National Association of Science Writers, the Council for the Advancement and Support of Education, and the Public Relations Society of America, groups to which many university public relations professionals belong. The studies reported here did not include large numbers of participants. Consequently, it is also be important to follow up this chapter with studies that have a larger sample size.

CONCLUSION

This study found that, among several dozen university communicators, some values are widely used in distinguishing the needs of special interests from those of the larger public good. Additionally, there are also "gray areas" in which university communicators are uncertain of the values they should endorse and the roles they should enact. University communicators varied in the extent to which they appreciated their potential to help universities be independent, respected forums at which the best research is showcased and discussed. Some university public relations professionals understood and valued this role and how they functioned within the social power relations with university constituents. Others did not seem to see it or were equally aware of the obstacles they faced in creating such forums. In future research, public relations students, scholars, and professionals need to think about ways in which the role of universities in helping societies probe, debate, and find truth can be fully achieved and appreciated.

NOTE

1. *Biotechnology* is a broad term that refers to any intervention by humans to alter a plant or animal's genetic makeup. Making wine and cheese are traditional forms of biotechnology. More controversial and less traditional are endeavors known as *genetic engineering* that create genetic modified organisms (GMOs). Genetic engineering involves inserting, removing, or altering a specific gene in a plant's or animal's genetic makeup to bring forth traits in that plant or animal that humans view as desirable. A well known genetically modified plant is Monsanto's Bt corn, a plant that has a gene that makes it distasteful to certain insects (U.S. Department of Agriculture, n.d.).

REFERENCES

Bennof, R. (2003). Federal academic science and engineering obligations increased 10 percent in FY 2000. *InfoBrief: Science Resource Statistics*. Arlington, VA: National Science Foundation. Retrieved April 10, 2004, from www.nsf.gov/sbe/srs

Borchelt, R. E., & Triese, D. (2001, February 25). *Communicating the future: A research agenda for understanding public communication of science and technology* [Tape of session including participant comments]. Panel presented at the annual meeting of the American Association for the Advancement of Science, San Francisco.

Burleson, B. R., & Kline, S. L. (1979). Habermas' theory of communication: A critical explication. *Quarterly Journal of Speech, 65*, 412-428.

Carey, J. W. (2000). *The Carroll C. Arnold distinguished lecture: The engaged discipline.* Washington, DC: National Communication Association.

Dunwoody, S. (1986). The scientist as source. In S. M. Friedman, S. Dunwoody, & C. L. Rogers (Eds.), *Scientists and journalists: Reporting science as news* (pp. 3-16). New York: The Free Press.

Dunwoody, S. (1999). Scientists, journalists, and the meaning of uncertainty. In S. M. Friedman, S. Dunwoody, & C. L. Rogers (Eds.), *Communicating uncertainty: Media coverage of new and controversial science* (pp. 59-80). Mahwah, NJ: Erlbaum.

Dunwoody, S., & Ryan, M. (1985). Public information persons as mediators between scientists and journalists. *Journalism Quarterly, 60*, 647-656.

Fedler, F., Bender, J., Davenport, L. D., & Drager, M. W. (2001). *Reporting for the media* (7th ed.). Fort Worth, TX: College Publishers.

Frey, L. R., Botan, C. H., & Kreps, G. L. (2000). *Investigating communication: An introduction to research methods* (2nd ed.). Needham Heights, MA: Allyn & Bacon.

Habermas, J. (1989). *The structural transformation of the public sphere: An enquiry into a category of bourgeois thought* (T. Burger, Trans.). Cambridge, MA: MIT Press. (Original work published 1962)

Habermas, J. (1998). *On the pragmatics of communication.* Cambridge, MA: MIT Press.

Irving, C. (1999). UC Berkeley's experiment in research funding: Controversial $25 million agreement with Novartis raises academic freedom questions. *National CrossTalk, 7*(4). Retrieved August 9, 2001, from http://www.highereducation.org/crosstalk/ct1099/news1099-berkeley.shtml

Lee, J., & Clery, S. (2004). Key trends in higher education. *American Academic, 1*(1). Retrieved April 5, 2005, from http://www.aft.org/pubs-reports/american_academic/issues/june04/Lee.qxp.pdf

Kuhn, T. S. (1970). *The structure of scientific revolutions* (2nd ed.). Chicago: University of Chicago Press.

Lombardi, J. V., Capaldi, E. D., Reeves, K. R., Craig, D. D., Gater, D. S., & Rivers, D. (2003, November). *The top American research universities.* Gainesville, FL: The Center. Retrieved April 10, 2004, from www.thecenter.edu

Machen, M. M., & Schackelford, B. (2003, August). Academic R&D spending maintains growth from all major sources in 2001. *InfoBrief: Science Resource Statistics* (NSF Publication No. NSF 03-327). Arlington, VA: National Science Foundation. Retrieved April 5, 2005, from http://www.nsf.gov/pubsys/ods/getpub.cfm?nsf03327

McComas, K. A. (2003). Trivial pursuits: Participant views of public meetings. *Journal of Public Relations Research, 15*, 91-116.

Muir, W. M., & Howard, R. D. (1999). Possible ecological risks of transgenic organism release when transgenes affect mating success: Sexual selection and the Trojan gene hypothesis. *Proceedings of the National Academy of Sciences, 96*, 13853-13856.

Newman, F., Couturier, L., & Scurry, J. (2004). *The future of higher education: Rhetoric, reality, and the risks of the market.* San Francisco: Wiley & Sons.

Parrott, W. A., & Paterson, A. H. (2000). The GMO controversy and the ivory tower: It's time again for "activist scientists." *University of Georgia Research Reporter, 30*(4), 37-38.

Peters, J. D. (1993). Distrust of representation: Habermas on the public sphere. *Media, Culture, and Society, 15*, 541-571.

Priest, S. H. (2000). U. S. opinion divided over biotechnology? *Nature Biotechnology, 18*, 939-942.

Priest, S. H. (2001). *A grain of truth: The media, the public, and biotechnology*. New York: Rowman and Littlefield.

Ritzer, G. (1996). *Sociological theory* (4th ed.). New York: McGraw-Hill.

Rowan, K. E. (1999). Effective explanation of uncertain and complex science. In S. M. Friedman, S. Dunwoody, & C. L. Rogers (Eds.), *Communicating uncertainty: Media coverage of new and controversial science* (pp. 179-200). Mahwah, NJ: Erlbaum.

Rowan, K. E. (2000a, January 13). *Making lemonade: Earning trust, explaining complex issues, and squeezing the best from situations gone sour*. Presentation at the "Making Lemonade" workshop sponsored by Colle-McVoy and the American Agricultural Editors Association, Inver Grove Heights, MN.

Rowan, K. E. (2000b, May 10). *Whose side are you on? Risk communication concepts and principles for scientists, extension communicators, and university administrators*. Presentation for the Risk Communication Superworkshop sponsored by Agricultural Communicators in Education and the U. S. Department of Agriculture, Orlando, FL.

Rowan, K. E. (2000c, July 24). *Communicating agricultural biotechnology: Research-supported guidelines*. Presentation for the annual meeting of Agricultural Communicators in Education, Washington, DC.

Rowan, K. E. (2000d, November 30-December 1). *Science and risk: How can Extension work in an atmosphere of risk, perceived risk, and controversy?* Presentation for the University of Wisconsin Extension Biotechnology in Agriculture Conference, Madison, WI.

Rowan, K. E. (2001, February 25). *Whose side are you on? Perceptions of effective science news coverage among scientists, journalists, and public affairs officers*. Paper presented at the annual meeting of the American Association for the Advancement of Science, San Francisco.

Sigurdson, C. (2000, July). *Bigger is not always better* [Press release]. Purdue University, West Lafayette, IN. Retrieved April 10, 2001, from http://www.ansc.purdue.edu

Spangler, H. (2001). Firebombing won't stop these biotech scientists. *Prairie Farmer*. Retrieved March 15, 2003, from http://www.farmprogress.com/frmp/articleDetail/0,8055,2868+40,000.html

Trachtman, L. E. (1989). What does public understanding of science really mean? *Bulletin of Science, Technology, and Society, 9*, 369-373.

U. S. Department of Agriculture (n.d.). *Frequently asked questions about biotechnology*. Available at www.usda.gov/agencies/biotech.faq.html

University of Washington. (2001). *PART I: Institutional objectives and roles: Chapter 1: Role and mission of the university.* Retrieved October 12, 2005, from http://www.washington.edu/faculty/facsenate/handbook/04-01-01.html

Vedantam, S. (2004, July 6). Drug makers prefer silence on test data. *The Washington Post*, pp. A1, A4.

Ward, D. (2002). *Connection to the future: Strategic plan 2002-2005.* American Council on Education. Retrieved April 5, 2005, from www.acenet.edu/plan/challenges.cfm

Zimdahl, R. L. (2003). The mission of land grant colleges of agriculture. *American Journal of Alternative Agriculture*, *18*, 103-115.

APPENDIX A. PRESS RELEASE DISTRIBUTED BY PURDUE UNIVERSITY'S SCHOOL OF AGRICULTURE, (SIGURDSON, 2000)

Bigger not always better

·By Chris Sigurdson

Call it "Biotechnology--with your eyes open." Well aware of the promising potential of biotechnology for modified crops with novel uses, Purdue Agriculture scientists also are charged with investigating the possible risks. Animal scientist Bill Muir has found one.

Muir, a geneticist who works with populations of animals, and his colleague, Purdue biologist Rick Howard, found that releasing a transgenic fish into the wild could damage native populations, even to the point of extinction.

A transgenic organism is one that contains genes from another species. The Purdue research is part of an effort by Purdue and the U.S. Department of Agriculture to assess the risks and benefits of biotechnology and its products, such as genetically modified fish. The study was published in the *Proceedings of the National Academy of Science*.

The researchers used medaka, a minute Japanese fish, to examine what would happen if genetically modified male medakas were introduced into a population of unmodified fish. The research was conducted in banks of aquariums in a laboratory setting, and the results were modeled for farm-raised fish of economic importance, such as salmon or tilapia.

The results warn that transgenic salmon and tilapia could present a significant threat to native wildlife. "Transgenic fish are typically larger than the native stock, and that can confer an advantage in attracting mates," Muir says. "If, as in our experiments, the genetic change also reduces the offspring's ability to survive, a transgenic animal could bring a wild population to extinction in 40 generations." Extinction results from a phenomenon that Muir and Howard call the "Trojan gene hypothesis." By basing their mate selection on size rather than fitness, female fish choose the larger, genetically modified but genetically inferior males, thus inviting the hidden risk of extinction.

The study demonstrates scientists policing science, Muir says. "I hope people understand that scientists are investigating the risks of biotechnology as well as the benefits, so decisions can be made with as much information as possible. It's important to understand the risks so they can be addressed."

The dominance of sexual preference over Charles Darwin's classic theory of survival of the fittest is not unknown to wildlife specialists and geneticists. Muir likes to use the example of the male bird of paradise with its long swells of gloriously colored plumage as an example. "The male bird of paradise with the longest, thickest tail attracts the most females. Subsequent offspring also exhibit the long tail and also compete well for females. Unfortunately, the birds with the biggest tails also have the biggest problem escaping predators who appreciate large birds pinned in place by their plumage. Obviously, the bird with the most sex appeal is the also the worst choice as a fit mate. Not unlike high school, some might say."

The researchers' next goal is to replicate the study with larger fish of economic importance in a larger environment. They're looking for an indoor swimming pool where they can raise tilapia and check the results of the medaka study.

A Prospective Look at Power

chapter 12

Problems as Opportunities—The Power and Promise of Public Relations

Peter M. Smudde

Jeffrey L. Courtright

Throughout this book the contributors have demonstrated that the dynamics of power often pose problems for public relations practitioners, yet the problems need not always predict negative outcomes for organizations. In public relations, power is both rhetorical and organizational. The power of public relations is rhetorical, as it relies on the skillfulness of people, as corporate symbolic actors, to inspire cooperation between an organization and its publics. It is also organizational, as its symbolic action is infused with the role and prominence of an organization as it addresses matters in context for itself and its publics. Taken together, the power of public relations as rhetorical and organizational means it is also social because it concerns the welfare, thoughts, and feelings of people locally and globally.

A problem often can present opportunities and challenges for public relations to optimize, even if it rises to the level of a crisis, for example. In the opening chapter, we historically situate understandings and misconceptions of the practice's power and review literature relevant to the power dynamics of public relations practice. This book moves beyond this literature, which tends to focus on either how public relations campaigns create power or the power of female practitioners within the practice itself. Instead, the chapters in this volume illustrate the creation and perpetuation of power for good or ill and from a variety of perspectives. Our cases have ranged from traditional rhetoric in German's chapter on Hillary Rodham Clinton, to new applications of critical theorists such as Courtright's use of the work of Michel de Certeau to track the power relationships between the Church of Scientology and its critics on the Internet, to Russell-Loretz's grounding in the work of Antonio Gramsci to investigate the devaluation of diversity in corporate recruitment efforts.

Certainly some of the cases suggest a tendency for public relations to be a tool by which to deflect criticism via questionable means. The most obvious of these are O'Connor's study of Philip Morris and Taylor and Kent's examination of the Malaysian government and its handling of the Chinese language issue. Yet the framing of public relations as problematic is not necessarily tragic (cf. Burke, 1937/1984); that is, a problem need not result in domination by an organization or a negative view of public relations. A more appropriate way to frame public relations is comic (cf. Burke, 1937/1984) and focused on opportunities in humanistic ways. On one level, this orientation corrects for misunderstandings about the influence of public relations in civil interactions and stereotypes of public relations as "spin doctoring" or "mere rhetoric." Edwards' chapter on Avon's sponsorship of the cancer walks and Brand's study of Merrill Lynch illustrate public relations practices done for the right reasons, with differing results in corporate power.

A HUMANISTIC FRAME FOR PUBLIC RELATIONS' POWER

The matter of public relations' power, then, is seen optimistically as much more of a humanistic enterprise of socially dynamic and necessary symbolic action that is meant to inspire cooperation between an organization and its publics. Communications professionals "are in the business of producing symbols. They, much more than others in the organization, tell various publics 'what the organization is.' They share identity, manage issues, and powerfully 'locate' the organization in the world of public discourse"

(Cheney & Dionsopoulos, 1989, p. 139). Organizations function within a larger context of social, political, economic, technological, and cultural environments. Because of their roles in these contexts, they communicate with internal and external publics in many ways. Yet, "despite all other measures of what a company is or should be, what really counts is the meaning internal and external people enact on behalf of or in response to it" (Heath, 1994, p. 118).

Public relations officials make sense of what's gone on for an organization in terms of the present, past, and anticipated future. Their work involves "the measured and ethical use of language and symbols to inspire cooperation between an organization and its publics" (Smudde, 2001, p. 36). Practitioners do not merely report on social situations; they focus on connecting the dots between specific situations and the larger context. The ways they do this are meant to inspire people to analyze their situations critically, spark creative ways to address situations symbolically, and identify with what is going on in human situations. Public relations officials would likely place themselves in a position where they can empower people with humanistic attitudes, motives, and symbols of authority to act for the good of society.

Public relations "problems" can be viewed as literal dramas. They each have a definitive scene, specific action, particular people playing certain roles, special means for the people to do their action, real purposes behind the management of things, and attitudes that frame actors' actions. So communications professionals do not just retell the story of an issue or crisis in context; they create discourse that emphasizes the dramatic dimensions inherent in it and invite the involvement of the publics with the organization in communication about it. That involvement is cooperative and ethical. It fosters constructive dialogue about the good, the bad, and everything in between—all of which should ultimately help target publics to identify with the organization and its messages (Smudde, 2001).

Public relations professionals "attempt—admittedly with varying degrees of success—to *control* the ways internal and external environments discuss such key concepts as values, issues, images, and identities" (Cheney & Vibbert, 1987, p. 173; emphasis added). Such discussion is possible through the structuring of people's thinking about the dramas enacted in public relations discourse. A tragic view of control would result in public relations' power over publics. We advocate a more comic, humanistic approach—that we be public relations counsels with a heart, to borrow Burke's (1937/1984) phrase (cf. Smudde, 2004b). The notion of "control" reflects public relations professionals' quest to establish identification with their organizations' publics and stakeholders. In other words, their quest is to ethically inspire cooperation between an organization and its publics.

THE FUTURE STUDY OF PUBLIC RELATIONS' POWER

At the end of the first case study book ever to apply rhetorical criticism to public relations phenomena, Kathleen German (1995) issued a call for the application of critical theory to the field. At the time, just a handful of studies were extant (e.g., Moffitt, 1992; Walker, 1994). Since then, many articles have used critical theory as a grounding for such studies. The present volume adds to this list with chapters grounded in the work of Pierre Bourdieu (O'Connor, chap. 4), Michel de Certeau (Courtright, chap. 8) Michel Foucault (Jerome et al., chap. 5; Smudde, chap. 10), Antonio Gramsci (Russell-Loretz, chap. 9), and Jürgen Habermas (Rowan et al., chap. 11). Allusion also has been made in *Power and Public Relations* to the American philosopher and critic, Kenneth Burke, whose theory of symbolic action certainly raises questions of power (Appel, 1993). Although Burke's concepts have been applied in the public relations literature, especially in analyses of crisis rhetoric (e.g., Courtright & Hearit, 2002; Hearit, 1997), the issue of power has not arisen to our knowledge.

We strongly suggest that more study of power and its various aspects be undertaken in the future, beginning with these theoretical groundings and building on others. Although O'Connor (chap. 4, this volume) and Ihlen (2002, 2004, 2005) have explored Bourdieu's theory of capital, we suspect that more can be gleaned from his writings on symbolic capital and power to better understand the dynamics of public relations practice (cf. Moingeon & Ramanantsoa, 1997). Although Gramsci has been applied in other subfields of communication (e.g., organizational communication; cf. Mumby, 1997; political communication; cf. Murphy, 1992), earlier application of his work to public relations (Sholar, 1994) suggests that more can be mined. Similarly, organizational communication scholars have applied Anthony Giddens' theory of structuration for many years (e.g., McPhee, 1989), yet only recently has the theory been applied to public relations (Durham, 2005). Giddens' work holds great promise for the field. The field also might capitalize on Mickey's (1997) application of the work of Jean Baudrillard to public relations phenomena.

In contrast, concepts from the writings of Michel Foucault and Jürgen Habermas are far from newcomers to the public relations literature. The latter particularly has been applied to public relations ethics (e.g., Burkart, 2004; Leeper, 1996; Salter, 2005), so Jacobson and Storey's (2004) and Rowan et al.'s (chap. 11, this volume) studies presage continued application of Habermas to the issue of power. Similarly, Foucault figures prominently in the public relations literature, beginning with Holtzhausen's (2000; Holtzhausen & Voto, 2002) call for practitioners to become "activists" within the organization and Chay-Nemeth's (2001) application of Foucault's investigative strategies (cf. Smudde, chap. 10, this volume). Most recently, Foucault was central to articles in two special issues of the *Journal of Public Relations Research* (Curtin & Gaither, 2005; Motion & Weaver, 2005), one featuring work on macro- and micropolitics (cf. Jerome et al., chap. 5, this volume).

IMMEDIATE NEXT STEPS

More than anything this volume is meant to view a dimension of public relations that all too often has been assumed to be easily understood and, thereby, neglected in the literature. Such an "armchair perspective" of power, as Courtright calls it in Chapter 8, stifles knowledge growth and practice improvement. Power is truly a multifaceted topic with much to give, as the contributors in this book have shown. Indeed, power poses opportunities to the profession that can be more effectively investigated, understood, and acted on in ethical and effective ways.

Where do we go from here? Obviously first steps include pursuing the kind of future studies outlined previously. Such work addresses the basic activities of knowledge building that is important in any field. It builds on the *epistemological* foundations of public relations—how knowledge about the subject is defined and built through study of it. Such work must also bridge theory with practice. Investigations about the practice of public relations subsumes an *ontological* view—what it means to be a field of study and an arena of professional practice. The epistemological base for public relations upholds an ontological dimension, and the latter contributes to the former. The ontological work published about public relations helps to define the field and what is practiced in it. In this way, the ontological dimension to public relations gives us opportunities to explore more deeply and systematically the day-to-day "stuff" of public relations' value to individuals, organizations, communities, society, the field itself, and other relevant fields of study.

This volume addresses the epistemological and ontological dimensions to power and public relations. Practitioners, scholars, and students, then, have a more holistic view of public relations' power than has ever been available. The contributors to this volume have modeled approaches that give us additional philosophical and pragmatic footing on which to make sense of patterns in the research, discover gaps in the literature, and reveal some telling things about the methods, theories, and perspectives in which the field is addressed, studied, and practiced (cf. Smudde, 2004a). More important, the chapters here give us useful and usable methods for tending to public relations' power. The challenge is to improve public relations practice and outcomes through this greater understanding of power. The job will not be easy, but it should be more fruitful than it has been because we now have a guide. And the conversation about power and public relations will continue and become ever more revealing.

REFERENCES

Appel, E. C. (1993). Implications and importance of the negative in Burke's philosophy of language. *Communication Quarterly, 41,* 51-65.

Burkart, R. (2004). Intermezzo: Consensus-oriented public relations (COPR): A concept for planning and evaluating public relations. In B. van Ruler & D. Verãiã (Eds.), *Public relations and communication management in Europe: A nation-by-nation introduction to public relations theory and practice* (pp. 459-465). Berlin: Mouton de Gruyter.

Burke, K. (1984). *Attitudes toward history* (3rd ed.). Berkeley: University of California Press.

Chay-Nemeth, C. (2001). Revisiting publics: A critical archaeology of publics in the Thai HIV/AIDS issue. *Journal of Public Relations Research, 13,* 127-161.

Cheney, G., & Dionisopoulos, G. N. (1989). Public relations? No, relations with publics: A rhetorical-organizational approach to contemporary corporate communication. In C. H. Botan & V. Hazleton, Jr. (Eds.), *Public relations theory* (pp. 135-157). Hillsdale, NJ: Erlbaum.

Cheney, G., & Vibbert, S. L. (1987). Corporate discourse: Public relations and issue management. In F. M. Jablin, L. L. Putnam, K. H. Roberts, & L. W. Porter (Eds.), *Handbook of organizational communications: An interdisciplinary perspective* (pp. 165-194). Newbury Park, CA: Sage.

Courtright, J. L., & Hearit, K. M. (2002). "The good organization speaking well": A paradigm case for institutional reputation management. *Public Relations Review, 28,* 347-360.

Curtin, P. A., & Gaither, T. K. (2005). Privileging identity, difference, and power: The circuit of culture as a basis for public relations theory. *Journal of Public Relations Research, 17,* 91-115.

Durham, F. (2005). Public relations as structuration: A prescriptive critique of the StarLink global food contamination case. *Journal of Public Relations Research, 17,* 29-47.

German, K. M. (1995). Critical theory in public relations inquiry: Future directions for analysis in a public relations context. In W. N. Elwood (Ed.), *Public relations inquiry as rhetorical criticism: Studies of corporate discourse in public relations campaigns* (pp. 279-294). Westport, CT: Praeger.

Hearit, K. M. (1997). On the use of transcendence as an apologia strategy: The case of Johnson Controls and its fetal protection policy. *Public Relations Review, 23,* 217-231.

Heath, R. L. (1994). *Management of corporate communication: From interpersonal contacts to external affairs.* Hillsdale, NJ: Erlbaum.

Holtzhausen, D. R. (2000). Postmodern values in public relations. *Journal of Public Relations Research, 12,* 93-114.

Holtzhausen, D. R., & Voto, R. (2002). Resistance from the margins: The postmodern public relations practitioner as organizational activist. *Journal of Public Relations Research, 14,* 57-84.

Ihlen, Ø. (2002). Rhetoric and resources: Notes for a new approach to public relations and issues management. *Journal of Public Affairs, 2,* 259-269.

Ihlen, Ø. (2004). Norwegian hydroelectric power: Testing a heuristic for analyzing symbolic strategies and resources. *Public Relations Review, 30,* 217-223.

Ihlen, Ø. (2005). The power of social capital: Adapting Bourdieu to the study of public relations. *Public Relations Review, 31,* 492-496.

Jacobson, T. L., & Storey, J. D. (2004). Development communication and participation: Applying Habermas to a case study of population programs in Nepal. *Communication Theory, 14,* 99-121.

Leeper, R. V. (1996). Moral objectivity, Jürgen Habermas's discourse ethics, and public relations. *Public Relations Review, 22,* 133-150.

McPhee, R. D. (1989). Organizational communication: A structurational exemplar. In B. Dervin, L. Grossberg, B. J. O'Keefe, & E. Wartella (Eds.), *Rethinking communication* (Vol. 2, pp. 199-212). Newbury Park, CA: Sage.

Mickey, T. J. (1997). A postmodern view of public relations: Sign and reality. *Public Relations Review, 23,* 271-284.

Moffitt, M. A. (1992). Bringing critical theory and ethical considerations to definitions of a "public." *Public Relations Review, 18,* 17-29.

Moingeon, B., & Ramanantsoa, B. (1997). Understanding corporate identity: The French school of thought. *European Journal of Marketing, 31,* 383-395.

Motion, J., & Weaver, C. K. (2005). A discourse perspective for critical public relations research: Life Sciences Network and the battle for truth. *Journal of Public Relations Research, 17,* 49-67.

Mumby, D. K. (1997). The problem of hegemony: Rereading Gramsci for organizational communication studies. *Western Journal of Communication, 61,* 343-375.

Murphy, J. M. (1992). Domesticating dissent: The Kennedys and the freedom rides. *Communication Monographs, 59,* 61-78.

Salter, L. (2005). The communicative structures of journalism and public relations. *Journalism, 6,* 90-106.

Sholar, S. E. (1994). Habermas, Marx and Gramsci: Investigating the public sphere in organizational communication and public relations courses. *Journal of Communication Inquiry, 18,* 77-92.

Smudde, P. M. (2001). Issue or crisis: A rose by any other name.... *Public Relations Quarterly, 46*(4), 34-36.

Smudde, P. M. (2004a). Concerning the epistemology and ontology of public relations literature. *Review of Communication, 4*(3-4), 163-175.

Smudde, P. M. (2004b). Implications on the practice and study of Kenneth Burke's "public relations counsel with a heart." *Communication Quarterly, 52,* 420-432.

Walker, G. F. (1994). Communicating public relations research. *Journal of Public Relations Research, 6,* 141-161.

Contributors

Troy A. Bogino (BA, George Mason University, 2003) is a master's student and graduate teaching assistant at George Mason University. He is studying health, risk, and crisis communication.

Jeffrey D. Brand (PhD, Indiana University, 1995) is associate professor and chair of the Department of Communication at Millikin University in Decatur, Illinois. He teaches courses in public relations, media law, and argumentation. His research interests focus on corporate reputation management, social movements, and religious and environmental discourse. His research has appeared in *Journal of Applied Communication Research*; *Argumentation and Advocacy*; *Journal of Communication and Religion*; *Race, Gender & Class*; *North Dakota Journal of Speech and Theatre*; and the *National Forensic Journal*. He is the recipient of the 2000 Central States Communication Association Journal Manuscript Award and was the 2000 Scholar of the Year for the North Dakota Speech and Theatre Association.

Jeffrey L. Courtright (PhD, Purdue University, 1991) is associate professor of communication at Illinois State University. He teaches courses primarily in public relations, with specialties in community relations and religious rhetoric. His research interests focus on corporate reputation and the production and perception of organizational image, particularly when it applies to nonprofit and/or religious organizations. His work has appeared in *Communication Studies*, *Public Relations Review*, *Journal of Mass Media*

Ethics, and *Journal of Communication and Religion* (he also has served on the editorial board for the last decade). He has contributed chapters to *Public Relations Inquiry as Rhetorical Criticism: Case Studies in Corporate Discourse and Social Influence* (Praeger, 1995) as well as *Power in the Blood: A Handbook on AIDS, Politics, and Communication* (Erlbaum, 1999). His most recent collaborations with Keith Michael Hearit also include a chapter in *Responding to Crisis: A Rhetorical Approach to Crisis Communication* (Erlbaum, 2004). He is currently the Ethics Officer for the Central Illinois chapter of PRSA.

Heidi Hatfield-Edwards (PhD, University of Georgia, 2002) is assistant professor in the Department of Humanities and Communication at the Florida Institute of Technology, where she teaches public relations and other coursework. She previously taught public relations at Pennsylvania State University. She has nine years' experience in communication, working in television, radio and print media, and public relations and marketing. At the University of Georgia she taught public relations communication and worked as a research assistant for the George Foster Peabody Awards. She has a BA from the University of Florida and an MA from the University of Wisconsin-Madison. She is a member of the Association for Education in Journalism and Mass Communication, the International Communication Association, and the National Communication Association.

Joe S. Epley (APR and PRSA College of Fellows) has nearly 40 years of experience in public relations, beginning in 1968 when, after a 10-year career as a television journalist in Asheville and Charlotte, North Carolina, he began Epley Associates in Charlotte. He grew the business over three decades to be a major independent public relations firm in the southern United States. During that time, he has helped advance the profession locally, nationally, and internationally. He is a founding partner and a past chairman of the WORLDCOM Public Relations Group, the world's largest network of independent public relations firms with offices in more than 100 cities around the globe. He also is a charter member of the Council of Public Relation Firms and served on its board of directors for three years. A global leader in the Public Relations Society of America (PRSA), he has been chairman of the Counselors Academy, national president of PRSA, president of the PRSA Foundation, and chair of the prestigious PRSA College of Fellows. He has lectured about public relations and issues management in several countries, including at the U.S. Defense Information School, the British Public Relations Institute, and the Russian Foreign Ministry's University for International Relations in Moscow. He was instrumental in introducing the first formal course of study in western-style public relations in the Soviet Union and organizing the Russian Public Relations

Association. His wide range of community and industry service accomplishments earned him election to the University of North Carolina's Public Relations Hall of Fame in 1991 and the Defense Information School's Hall of Fame in 1993. He was awarded the Charlotte Public Relations Society's Infinity Award in 1981 for Outstanding Contributions to the Profession.

Kathleen M. German (PhD, University of Iowa, 1976) is professor in the Department of Communication at Miami University in Oxford, Ohio. She is primarily interested in rhetorical criticism and public address. Although she has taught courses ranging from interpersonal communication to conflict management to intercultural communication, her primary focus is teaching rhetorical theory and criticism. She has published over 25 refereed articles and 10 book chapters and is co-author of the most widely used public speaking textbook in the United States. She has presented over 50 papers at international, national, and regional conferences. She has worked with intercultural communication in the Czech Republic, Japan, and Nigeria. Her current research interests include filmic narration in World War II documentaries and discursive formations in social issues such as AIDS. Her dissertation developed an original theory of crisis-language use in the legitimation rituals of eulogies for heads of state.

Timothy A. Gibson (PhD, Simon Fraser University, 2001) is assistant professor in the Department of Communication at George Mason University. He has authored a number of publications on local media, political discourse, and urban development, most notably the book, *Securing the Spectacular City: The Politics of Revitalization and Homelessness in Downtown Seattle* (Lexington Books, 2003) and articles in the *Journal of Communication Inquiry* and *Critical Studies in Media Communication.*

Angela M. Jerome (PhD, University of Kansas, 2002) is assistant professor of communication at Western Kentucky University, where she teaches courses in organizational communication, organizational rhetoric, and communication theory. After receiving a BA in corporate and organizational communication and an MA in communication at Western Kentucky University, she completed a PhD with an emphasis in rhetoric and organizational communication. She then taught four years at Illinois State University. Her research interests are mainly in the area of crisis response. She has a co-authored an article in *Communication Theory* entitled, "On Organizational Apologia: A Reconceptualization." She also has completed image-repair studies concerning Texas A&M's Bonfire collapse, NASCAR driver Tony Stewart, and Arthur Andersen, among others, that have been presented at regional and national conferences.

Michael L. Kent (PhD, Purdue University, 1997) is assistant professor in the School of Communication at Western Michigan University, where he teaches undergraduate and graduate courses in communication and public relations. Michael conducts research on public relations, new technology, dialogue, and international communication. His research has appeared in *Public Relations Review, Public Relations Quarterly, Critical Studies in Media Communication, Communication Studies, Gazette*, and several other journals and books. Before coming to Western Michigan, he worked for five years as the graduate advisor in the Department of Communication Studies at Montclair State University and taught for a year at SUNY Fredonia College in upstate New York. He taught in Spring 2006 at the University of Latvia as a Fulbright Award recipient.

Joseph A. Knudsen (MA, Illinois State University, 2004) is an instructor in the Department of Speech and Theater at Wilbur Wright College in Chicago. He was an account executive with Ruder-Finn Chicago upon graduation. During his undergraduate career at Ball State University, he primarily pursued the study of interpersonal communication while focusing on minority communication through his work in sociology. He was the recipient of the Donald P. Knott Scholarship and a finalist for the Outstanding Communication Senior Award while at Ball State. He also was a leader on the university's speech team, receiving national recognition as one of the top orators in the country in 2002.

Teresa Mannix (BA, George Mason University, 2001) is assistant director of news and information services at the University of Mary Washington, from which she earned her baccalaureate degree journalism. She is currently a master's student at George Mason University, focusing on public relations. She also has worked for two daily newspapers in the Washington, DC, area and at a public relations office for a division of the U.S. Navy. She is president of the Fredericksburg Public Relations Society. She is also a member of the College Communicators Association of Virginia and the District of Columbia, and the Virginia Press Women.

William G. Malone (BA, George Mason University, 2004) is an editorial assistant who lives in Alexandria, Virginia. He works for *Clinical Laboratory News*, a news magazine published by the Washington, DC-based American Association for Clinical Chemistry. He writes about the industry of in-vitro diagnostics and the activities of the U. S. Food and Drug Administration.

Mary Anne Moffitt (PhD, University of Illinois, 1990) is associate professor at Illinois State University. She teaches undergraduate and graduate courses in public relations management, campaign communication, and campaign message design. At the undergraduate level, she also teaches courses in gender and religion and culture. At the graduate level she teaches seminars in public relations, critical approaches to message analysis and design, and qualitative research methods. Her research interests are in public relations campaign strategy, public relations campaign message design, and corporate images as received in audiences as they relate to organizations. She has published articles in *Communication Theory*, *Journal of Public Relations Research*, *Public Relations Review*, and *Women's Studies in Communication*, as well as the book *Campaign Strategies and Message Design* (Praeger, 1999); she also has co-edited a communication theory textbook, *Communication Theories for Everyday Life* (Allyn & Bacon, 2004).

Amy O'Connor (PhD, Purdue University, 2004) is assistant professor of communication at North Dakota State University. O'Connor's dissertation ("In the Boardroom of Good and Evil: An Assessment of the Persuasive Premises of Values Advocacy Campaigns") was completed during a two-year Purdue University Research Foundation grant. Her research interests include corporate advocacy, crisis communication, and family and work issues. Her work also has appeared in *Public Relations Review*.

Katherine E. Rowan (PhD, Purdue University, 1985) is professor and associate chair of the Communication Department at George Mason University in Fairfax, Virginia. Her research concerns the public relations challenges of earning trust and explaining science through the mass media. She teaches public relations, mass media writing, and risk communication courses and has published extensively on these topics. She has given presentations on science, risk, and crisis communication for organizations such as the Southeast Louisiana Hurricane Evacuation Task Forces, the National Library of Medicine, the College Communicators Association of Virginia, Agricultural Communicators in Education, the U. S. Environmental Protection Agency, the U. S. Department of Agriculture, and the National Academy of Science.

Theresa A. Russell-Loretz (PhD, Purdue University, 1992) is assistant professor of communication at Millersville University. Her teaching includes public relations courses in writing and research and campaigns; public speaking, and rhetoric. Her research interests include recruitment communication, service learning, school public relations, and feminist perspectives on public relations. Her earlier work on employment recruitment videos appeared in *Public Relations Inquiry as Rhetorical Criticism: Case Studies in Corporate Discourse and Social Influence* (Praeger, 1995). She was recently chair of the Public Relations Division of the National Communication Association.

Peter M. Smudde (PhD, Wayne State University, 2000) is assistant professor and coordinator of the public relations program at the University of Wisconsin–Whitewater. He moved to higher education full time in 2002, which marked a career change after 16 years in industry. His industry experience includes planning, writing, editing, and evaluating a full range of public relations, marketing, executive, and technical discourse for companies of various sizes and in many industries. He has held an executive-level position in corporate communications and worked in corporate, agency, and entrepreneurial enterprises, ranging from General Motors Corporation to successful family-owned companies. He has served 50 clients and operated his own consulting practice since 1998. He was adjunct faculty at the University of Michigan Business School, where he taught business communication courses in the MBA program, and at Wayne State University, where he taught the capstone, graduate public relations course. His research has appeared in *Public Relations Quarterly*, *Communication Quarterly*, *Communication Teacher*, *Review of Communication*, *Visible Language*, *Technology Century*, and *Technical Communication*. He has won many awards for his industry work, including awards from the Public Relations Society of America, the International Association for Business Communication, and the Society for Technical Communication. In 2005 Pete received a Wisconsin Teaching Fellowship from the University of Wisconsin System for a project developing a unique approach to teaching and learning in public relations courses.

Maureen Taylor (PhD, Purdue University, 1996) is associate professor in the Department of Communication at Western Michigan University. She taught previously at Rutgers University. She has published over 30 articles and chapters on topics that include public relations, communication in nation-building and civil-society campaigns, international public relations, and the ways in which new communication technologies build organization-public relationships. Maureen has traveled extensively around the world and has conducted public relations research in Malaysia, Taiwan, Bosnia, and Croatia.

Author Index

Subject Index

HM1221 .P67 2007

Power and public
relations
c2007.

2008 01 29

0 1341 1049886 9

Printed in the United States
200544BV00016B/43-48/A

9 781572 736818